JOHANNES CARDINAL WILLEBRANDS

Church and Jewish People

New Considerations

PAULIST PRESS
New York/Mahwah, New Jersey

Library of Congress Cataloging-in-Publication Data

Willebrands, J. G. M.
    Church and jewish people: new considerations
    Johannes Willebrands.
      p. cm.
    Includes bibliographical references and index.
    ISBN 0-8091-0456-3
    1. Catholic Church — Relations — Judaism. 2. Judaism — Relations — Catholic Church. 3. Christianity and antisemitism. 4. Judaism (Christian theology) I. Title.
    BM535.W496 1992
    261.2′6—dc20   91-46374
                                        CIP

Published by Paulist Press
997 Macarthur Boulevard
Mahwah, New Jersey 07430

Printed and bound in the
United States of America

Contents

III. THE POPE AND THE JEWS

IV. THEMATIC ESSAYS

V. THE SHOAH—AUSCHWITZ

VI. VARIOUS ADDRESSES

APPENDICES

I. OFFICIAL CATHOLIC TEXTS ON JEWS AND JUDAISM FROM VATICAN COUNCIL II

Second Vatican Council:

II. THE COMMISSION FOR RELIGIOUS RELATIONS WITH THE JEWS

In memory of Father
Cornelis Adriaan Rijk

Preface

I

The publication of the present selection of Cardinal Willebrands' addresses and articles on the church and the Jewish people is a most important contribution to the knowledge of the development of Catholic-Jewish relations since Vatican II. Nobody can speak with greater authority on the subject. Nobody among the living has had a greater influence on the development of those relations during the last three decades. As secretary of the Secretariat for Promoting Christian Unity, which was originally entrusted with this task, and since 1974 as president of the Holy See's Commission for Religious Relations with the Jews, he has had until recently the major responsibility for directing and promoting this work. In pursuing this mission he has not only faithfully followed in the footsteps of his great predecessor Cardinal Bea of blessed memory, who played such a decisive role in this field during Vatican II, but has introduced into it numerous new ideas, regarding both substance and organization. He symbolizes today, more than anyone else, the spirit of *Nostra aetate* and the new Catholic theology on Jews and Judaism it inaugurated.

II

Moreover, the Jewish partners in the International Catholic-Jewish Liaison Committee have learned to see in Cardinal Willebrands not only a great wise man whose deep faith and high intellectual qualities they have often admired, but also a real friend, a warm human being who has a deep respect for their convictions, who would listen to them, who could understand their sensitivities and who was always ready to look for constructive solutions when serious problems arose. They are grateful for the spirit of openness and frankness which has characterised our relationship and which has to a great extent helped overcome tensions and crises whenever they occurred.

It is surely not an accident that Cardinal Willebrands is of Dutch origin. There is no doubt that the Dutch tradition and his Dutch upbringing have had a decisive influence on his formation.

The Dutch people have for centuries given an example of tolerance and respect for religious minorities. Is it necessary to remind the reader in the year in which we commemorate the 500th anniversary of the expulsion of the Jews from Spain how many Spanish and Portuguese Jews found asylum on Dutch soil? During the terrible period of the Shoah the Dutch people showed in a remarkably courageous way its solidarity with the persecuted Jews. After World War II the Dutch were perhaps the only people in Europe who showed deep regret and shame about the destruction of their Jewish citizens to whom they had been very much attached and who had constituted a very lively and creative part of the population.

I shall never forget—nor will my colleagues—the session of the International Catholic-Jewish Liaison Committee in Amsterdam in which Cardinal Willebrands spoke movingly of his own personal experience during those frightful days when, as a chaplain in the center of Amsterdam, he had closely watched the tragedy. He recalled vividly some of the bonds forged with Jews whom he had tried to help—often in vain.

One of my colleagues, Jordan Pearlson, has recently reminded us, in an article of this session, that Cardinal Willebrands spoke of "how religious sanctification of prejudice lent a special ferocity to hostility and how in the limited years left to him he would work to eliminate once and for all any trace of that sanctification."

Such experiences easily explain the very high esteem and affection in which the Cardinal is held by his Jewish partners in the dialogue.

III

I have referred to the new Catholic theology on Jews and Judaism inaugurated by Vatican II. It has been formulated in a series of texts, notably the Declaration on the Relationship of the Church to non-Christian Religions of October 28, 1965, *Nostra aetate,* which defines in its most important chapter, No. 4, the relations of the Catholic Church with the Jewish people.

The adoption of this declaration was truly a revolutionary development, as is demonstrated by the fact that of all the documents promulgated by the Second Vatican Council, it is the only one which contains no reference whatsoever to any of the church's teachings—patristic, conciliar or pontifical.

This was followed by other important texts, notably the two statements by the Holy See's Commission for Religious Relations with the Jews, presided over by Cardinal Willebrands, known as the "Guidelines" of 1974 and the "Notes for Preaching and Catechesis" of 1985. In addition, there exist a great number of important statements by the pope, by international, national and local church bodies which complete and develop those basic statements.

Two major principles stand out as decisive landmarks in the new approach: the recognition of the Jewish people as a living and creative reality and the affirmation that to understand the Jews, Christians must strive to learn by what essential traits the Jews define themselves.

The new texts stress the spiritual bond between the church and and the Jewish people

They underline the Judaic roots of Christianity, starting with the Jewish origin of Jesus himself, the Virgin Mary and of all the apostles.

They do away with old teachings in which the Jewish people were depicted as a people of deicides, a rejected and cursed people.

They proclaim that God does not repent of the gifts he makes and that consequently the "old" covenant with Israel has not been abolished.

They recognize that the history of Judaism did not end with the destruction of Jerusalem, but developed a religious tradition of its own, rich in religious values.

They state that the permanence of Israel is a historic fact and a sign to be interpreted within God's design. It allowed Israel to carry to the whole world a witness of its fidelity to the one God while preserving the memory of the land of their forefathers at the heart of their hope.

They condemn antisemitism at any time and by anyone.

They proclaim the necessity to present an objective image of Jews and Judaism free from prejudice and offense.

They admit that a false religious vision of the Jewish people was in part responsible for misjudgments and persecutions during the course of history.

They envisage mutual understanding and respect and fraternal dialogue in our future relationship.

Each of these statements is of very great importance and has to be read against the classical attitude of Christian theology toward the Jews. It seems to me, however, that the last principle is perhaps the most important: mutual understanding and respect. That is indeed the message of society in our time. No longer simple tolerance—that was the watchword of eighteenth-century enlightenment.

All this has stimulated a new and serious theological reflection such as has not been seen for decades. Outstanding theologians, whose numbers are steadily growing and include many new and young voices, have made important contributions to the new doctrine, and an ecumenical cross-fertilization of ideas related to a new Christian concept of Jews and Judaism has come about and continues to produce stimulating effects.

But we have not only witnessed the beginning of a new theology. We have also institutionalised our relations with the central bodies of the Christian churches. We have set up a representative Jewish group for this purpose, the International Jewish Committee on Interreligious Consultations (IJCIC), and we have established an International Catholic-Jewish Liaison Committee which meets regularly and at which we discuss common concerns. The jointly published book, *Fifteen Years of Catholic-Jewish Dialogue 1970–1985,* describes some of these important encounters.

IV

In his lectures and articles Cardinal Willebrands tries to give a vigorous description of the evolution that has taken place in the Catholic-Jewish relationship since Vatican II. *Nostra aetate* is the central piece on which the new teaching is built.

He recalls the overwhelming vote by which the declaration

was adopted by the council: "It is important to note that the Church through her bishops was *united* on the question of how to relate to the Jews and Judaism, not torn apart by it. This has been, and remains, the solid guarantee of the changed, renewed attitude toward the Jews and Judaism in the Catholic Church. It is like a house built on a rock (cf. Mt 7:24 ff.)—nothing ever can tear it down."

And in another context he speaks of "the fundamental achievement" *Nostra aetate* "meant for the Catholic Church" and "that what happened since *Nostra aetate* is proof enough of the firmness of our resolve and the coherence of our decision." "Jewish-Christian relations are there to stay grounded as they are not on any transient phenomenon of any kind . . . , but on a re-newed consciousness of the 'mystery' of the Church."

He knows about and recognizes the asymmetry between the Catholic Church and the Jewish people as partners in the dialogue and the necessity to address the consequences of this situation in our relationship.

But he knows also that "Jewish-Christian relations are an *un-ending affair,* as are love and brotherhood, but also (regrettably) hate and enmity. The main point is to change the fundamental orientation from hate to love, from enmity to brotherhood. It is a question of people. . . . Still more it is a question of *hearts.*"

He does not avoid the most delicate problems that the new teaching raises. Again and again he deals with the question of anti-semitism and states with great simplicity: "Antisemitism is simply anti-Christian."

He even raises with courage and frankness the question: "Are the New Testament and Christianity antisemitic?" And while ve-hemently affirming that basically Christianity is antithetical to any antisemitic sentiment, he admits that some texts of the New Testa-ment "have had a long-lasting negative effect on the Christian view of Jews and Judaism. In fact, it must be admitted that they had 'antisemitic' consequences." "For centuries an image of Jews and Judaism has been projected which was inspired mostly, if not exclu-sively, by such negative references." "Some and perhaps many interpretations of Christianity throughout the ages have been un-just and prejudiced against Judaism. Sometimes such misguided interpretations have been translated into practice, legal or otherwise, seriously discriminating, attacking, oppressing, and even violently mishandling Jews, to the point of physical suppression. This has obviously nourished, in the Greco-Roman world, a form of antisemitism coming from pre-Christian sources. . . . But it has also quickly developed into a form of antisemitism of its own." And to conclude: "The Christian body of belief and practice is one thing. Historical and cultural realizations of that body of belief and practice is quite another."

He stresses repeatedly the dire "need for proper knowledge of things Jewish in the Catholic academic community" "to discover and appreciate our Jewish roots" and the necessity for the study of antisemitism "in the history of the Church."

In another address he says: "We have to make every effort of cleansing Catholic thought of any residue of religious anti-Judaism or antisemitism because we have seen the abyss of horror into which hatred for the Jewish people exploded in our midst in Europe. This task has to be assumed by education, theology, catechesis, social action, the legal field and many more."

He stresses that "special veneration is due to . . . the places in which the crime of frightful genocide was perpetrated against the Jewish people." "After the Shoah, above all, we cannot and must not keep silent or remain inert when we come face to face with violence, be it open or occult, physical or spiritual, against persons, groups, nations, for reasons of race, religion or nationality."

And we should not forget that it was Cardinal Willebrands who by his statement of September, 1989 paved the way for the solution of the unhappy conflict concerning the convent at Auschwitz.

He was one of the first to condemn the infamous resolution of the United Nations equating Zionism with racism.

With regard to Israel, we find the first positive statement by a Vatican agency in the "Notes on the correct way to present the Jews and Judaism in preaching and catechesis" published under his signature.

Moreover, he quotes repeatedly the words of Pope John Paul II in his Apostolic letter of April 20, 1984: "After the tragic extermination of the Shoah, the Jewish people began a new period in their history. They have a right to a homeland, as does any civil nation, according to international law. . . . For the Jewish people who live in the State of Israel and who preserve in that land such precious testimonies to their history and their faith, we must ask for the desired security and the due tranquility that is the prerogative of every nation and condition of life and of progress for every society."

And he calls for "a solid theology concerning the Jewish people that in some respects has not yet been elaborated with sufficient maturity and organization."

V

The texts reproduced in this volume address themselves both to Catholics and to Jews.

To Catholics, because of the new vision of the church on the Jews, the new Catholic theology on Jews and Judaism is still confined, in many regions, to an intellectual elite, to a restricted number of people in the leadership of our communities while this new teaching should in fact be made to be known in much wider circles.

At the same time these texts should stimulate new theological reflections on the subject. Cardinal Willebrands has said on numerous occasions that we are still at the beginning of our dialogue. Pope John Paul II himself said in his famous speech in the Rome Synagogue "that the path undertaken is still at the beginning" and "therefore a considerable amount of time will still be needed, notwithstanding the great efforts already made on both sides, to remove all forms of prejudice . . . and to present to ourselves and to others the true face of the Jews and Judaism, as likewise of Christians and Christianity. . . ."

There are theological questions to which no definite answers have yet been given. What follows for the faith of the individual Christian from the affirmation that the "old" covenant with Israel is still valid? And the most important but very complex question: "What is the relationship between the Hebrew Bible and the New Testament?" still awaits a theological response that takes into account the different positions held by Jews and Christians on the subject and respects the autonomy and integrity of both.

A number of Christian scholars have also rightly stressed that for the time being, most of the new theology has been developed in connection with the exegesis of scriptural texts. They have pleaded for a more radical review of Christian approaches and have emphasized, in particular, the necessity of treating the relationship to Judaism as a central theme in systematic theology. In other words, it has to become an essential subject in *all* parts of church dogmatics if the traditional anti-Judaism is to be overcome.

But the texts address themselves also to the Jews. They are the living account of the systematic and sincere effort of one of the leading figures of the Catholic Church to live up to the call of Vatican II, of the "firmness of resolve" to build and develop on its basis a new relationship with the Jews and in doing so to listen carefully to the Jewish partners. After centuries of "teaching of contempt," of tensions, confrontations, there is still a great deal of skepticism in our ranks about accepting the new theology of the Catholic Church as a really new beginning in our relationship. There still prevails in large circles mistrust, suspicion and resistance or indifference, and very few understand that we are engaged in a long process that will take several generations to be fulfilled. Cardinal Willebrands once said: "It has taken us two thousand years to arrive at *Nostra aetate.* It cannot be expected that everything will be undone, magically, in twenty years."

I feel sure that the publication of the texts will contribute in no small way to overcome the mistrust and suspicion in our ranks and will convince many of the sincerity and perseverance of all who take part in the effort.

This volume shows that much has been achieved in the last few decades. It also shows that much remains to be done. May the voice, the vision and the wisdom of Cardinal Willebrands guide this work also in the future.

Gerhart M. Riegner
Geneva, 1st January 1992

Introduction

The relationship between Jews and Christians has been a serious and painful problem for both communities since the very beginning of Christianity, even at the time of Jesus. On one hand, Jesus affirmed to the Samaritan woman that "salvation is from the Jews." But he went on to say that "the hour is coming and is now here, when true worshipers will worship the Father in spirit and truth" (Jn 4:22–23). In other words, the great tradition handed down through the Torah, the prophets, in the Psalms, indeed in the entire Hebrew Bible, will be fulfilled: "The Lord will arise upon you [Jerusalem], and his glory will appear over you. Nations shall come to your light . . ." (Is 60:2–3). St. Paul, who had preached his faith as a Pharisee and rabbi, feels this tension with "great sorrow and increasing anguish in my heart" (Rom 9:2). He develops his theological vision on this matter in his letter to the Romans, chapters 9 to 11. It was precisely this teaching that was so clearly developed and expressed in the Second Vatican Council's declaration *Nostra aetate*.

Misunderstandings and hostility between Jews and Christians developed very early. Anti-Judaism, however, is a phenomenon of varied origins which pre-dates Christianity. Feeding on racism and various ideologies, it is not by any means limited to the Christian world. But certain forms of antisemitism were inspired by wrong interpretations of the Christian faith in which the love that the prophets, St. Paul, and Jesus himself had for the Jews is absent. The Second Vatican Council solemnly proclaimed the authentic Christian teaching on this question, "sounding the depths of the mystery which is the church remembering the spiritual ties which link the

1

people of the new covenant to the stock of Abraham," acknowledging "that in God's plan of salvation the beginning of her faith and election is to be found in the patriarchs, Moses, and the prophets."

How often the words of the Shema, "Hear, O Israel: the Lord is our God, the Lord alone. You shall love the Lord your God with all your heart and with all your soul and with all your might" (Dt 6:4), resounded in the Nazi extermination camps when the Jews on their way to the gas chambers sang this confession of faith and love, which constitutes them as people of God.

The declaration of the Catholic Church, assembled at the Second Vatican Council, which acknowledges the spiritual ties which link her to the people of the Sinaitic covenant, affords the basis for true repentance, *teshuvah.* "Remembering her common heritage with the Jews, and moved by the gospel's spiritual love and by no political considerations, she deplores the hatred, persecution, and displays of antisemitism directed against the Jews at any time and by anyone" (*Nostra aetate*, 4) including those acts in which she shares responsibility through the actions of her members. But these considerations on repentance not only express remorse, asking for God's acquittal of sin. They also demand a new way of thinking, a *metanoia,* a new concept of our relations with the Jewish people, a concept more faithful to the teaching of the gospel. The council asks purification in order to gain a new heart and a new spirit. This concerns not only the individual person: the act of the council was a communal act which must bear fruit in all the members of the church. As Rabbi Soloveitchik says, "Evildoing is the product of a certain atmosphere . . . [of] the path of sin," and "Through repentance of purification man is reborn and he gains a new heart, a renewed spirit, another outlook on life and different horizons" (Joseph Soloveitchik, *On Repentance,* Mahwah, NJ: Paulist Press, 1984, pp. 55–59).

The council's teaching stands in direct continuity with the words of St. Paul:

> They are Israelites, and to them belong the adoption, the glory, the covenants, the giving of the law, the worship, and the promises; to them belong the patriarchs, and from them, according to the flesh, comes the messiah, who is over all, God blessed forever. Amen (Rom 9:4–5).

Even though the Jews have never acknowledged Jesus as the holy anointed one and savior of all humanity, "as regards election they are beloved for the sake of their ancestors, for the gifts and the calling of God are irrevocable" (Rom 11:28–29). This authentic primitive Christian vision was restored by the council, which, based on the principles of our faith, called upon us to change our attitudes regarding the Jews, moving toward a full reconciliation as children of the same heavenly Father.

It was precisely for this reason that responsibility for religious relations with the Jews was entrusted by Pope Paul VI to the Secretariat for Promoting Christian Unity as a distinct office, becoming an autonomous commission linked to the Secretariat in 1974.

As president of this commission from its inception until 1989, I guided and promoted its work with the generous assistance of its secretaries: Fr. Cornelis Rijk, Fr. Pierre-Marie de Contenson, OP, Msgr. Jorge Mejía, and Fr. Pier Francesco Fumagalli. All of them have given the best of themselves with great dedication and competence.

The present publication includes a number of articles and addresses given on various occasions to promote new relationships with the Jews. The collection is not published so much for the sake of scholarly research, but rather for the purpose of furnishing an overview of my reflections on the developments that took place after Vatican II, gathered together here at the request of many Catholic and Jewish friends.

Some of the writings in this book appear for the first time in any language. Others are translations of works already available in other languages, and still others are reprinted here.

The material found here is divided into six categories: (1) reflections on the occasion of anniversaries of *Nostra aetate* (1975–1985), (2) Augustin Cardinal Bea and his promotion of relations with the Jews, (3) the popes and the Jews, (4) thematic essays (1977–1990), (5) the *Shoah* and Auschwitz, and (6) various addresses (1970–1991). At the end a bibliography of my other writings on Jewish-Christian relations is provided, along with a succinct general bibliography on this topic. This will make it possible to evaluate the material in its broader context, and to pursue further research in the area of Catholic teaching on Jews and Judaism.

For the sake of providing a more complete picture of the situation, I thought it would be useful to add an appendix which includes the most important conciliar documents: *Lumen gentium* n. 16, *Nostra aetate,* and *Dei verbum* nn. 14–16. And since the over twenty-five year history of warm relations between Jews and Christians has been marked by other important events, including very recent ones, I thought it good to add at least the two documents published in 1974 and 1985 by the Holy See's Commission for Religious Relations with the Jews, and the texts of the two most recent and very important encounters which took place in 1990 in Prague and with Pope John Paul II in Rome.

It is my deepest hope that, listening obediently to the word of God, by means of dialogue and cooperation according to the tradition of both Israel and the church, the two peoples of the covenant will more and more be able to walk side by side as friends, brothers and sisters "in the faith of Abraham," toward the fullness of redemption. May they work together for peace in justice and charity for the benefit of all people, all the nations and all creation, for the glory of God our Father.

I.

On the Anniversaries of *Nostra aetate* (1975–1985)

Ten Years in the New Spirit
of the Vatican Council*

We are assembled here today in deep friendship to commemorate the tenth anniversary of the council declaration *Nostra aetate.* I am particularly happy to participate in this meeting because, together with the late Cardinal Bea, I lived through its many vicissitudes and directly experienced all the ups and downs, both public and private, of the discussion concerning it. I witnessed the stages of the successive ballots which led the council to draw up the project of the decree "De Judaeis." This project was distributed to the central preparatory commission in June 1962 and resulted in the promulgation of the *Declaration on the Relation of the Church to Non-Christian Religions,* section four of which treated of "The Jewish Religion." I feel that, at this center, it would be superfluous to recount the details of this complicated story. I shall simply recall the fact that, at the final ballot, the text received the placet of over ninety-six percent of the voters. Let us recall Pope Paul's homily to the council on the day of the promulgation of the decree, October 28, 1965, a little over ten years ago. It ended with this paragraph (which was, in fact, the penultimate):

> The universal community of priests, religious and faithful should rejoice at this promulgation as at a new manifestation of that love for which Christ did in fact ordain the hierarchical ministry. May this manifestation of the enhanced beauty of the face of the Catholic Church be considered by the followers of the other religions, above all by those united with us by the fatherhood of Abraham, especially the Jewish people, today no

* Rome, 1975; see Bibliography, n. 1.

7

longer the object of reprobation and suspicion but of respect, love and hope.

You will notice that in this solemn pronouncement referring to the declaration *Nostra aetate* as a whole, the holy father, after mentioning descent from Abraham, specified "maxime Hebraei." He thus deliberately stresses the very special links that unite Jews and Christians, looking not so much to common historical points of reference as to faith and knowledge of the God who revealed himself to Abraham. He thus suggests the perceptiveness and depth with which the relations of Catholics with Jews should be considered and lived. Within the larger framework of spiritual brotherhood in Abraham we have a special affinity which nothing can diminish.

Though well understood, it must nevertheless be said that this unique affinity should not cause us to forget and hence to neglect the Muslims nor the followers of other religions. One of the great biblical teachings which our modern mentality, pervaded by a somewhat simplistic egalitarianism, often finds difficult to accept is that in the divine plan of salvation each person has his own special place and his own special role. On this plane, priorities and preferences, far from being expressions of an arbitrary injustice, are on the contrary concrete applications of a transcendent justice. In fact, this priority and this election are the means chosen by the Almighty, who is supremely faithful but also supremely free, to offer through human mediation the means of salvation to the whole of humanity. If these means are to be adequately adapted to man's nature they must necessarily be individualized and localized in space and time. This sense of the concreteness of human things, and hence of God's plan, is one of the fruits which we Christians can gather from our friendly and perceptive relations with the Jews, relations which the declaration *Nostra aetate* specifically urges us to develop and to initiate, because so far very little has been done in this field. In some countries, especially those with the largest Jewish population in a national context that is, at least culturally, mainly Christian (I have in mind, for example, the United States of America, Canada, Argentina, Brazil and France), not only the spontaneously formed Jewish-Christian groups, but also the authorities of the Catholic Church and of the local Jewish communities have already contributed to the development of these relations and to the creation of a new atmosphere which will enable them to be greatly expanded in the near future.

A real dialogue has been started in those countries which we have done no more than mention, always in the way most appropriate to the locality; this is also true of other countries such as Spain. It is to be hoped that this dialogue, together with other forms of collaboration considered opportune by both parties, should continue to develop. Such development is particularly important in the fields of Jewish-Christian relations and of ecumenism properly so-called, because relations at the local level will succeed in changing mentalities and will finally make possible the real, concrete initiation of a new global relationship between the church and Judaism.

However, openings for action at the international level are not for that reason less important. Vertical or worldwide relations necessarily stimulate local communities and confront them with demands to which they should respond. On the other hand, they have their own importance and necessity insofar as they involve the whole church, affecting both Christians and the large Jewish organizations concerned with religious tradition, whose sphere of influence goes beyond local interest and the different currents that can be detected within Judaism.

You all know that for many years there has existed within the Secretariat for Christian Unity an office specializing in relations with Judaism. Professor Rijk, now director of SIDIC, guided it from the beginning with zeal and competence, and I would like to take this occasion of expressing to him once again, publicly, my sincere gratitude. A year ago this office was promoted to the status of "Commission for Religious Relations with the Jews," thus realizing a project elaborated several years ago. This change is in itself a progress, a step forward, in the sense that, although such an administrative change is a token, it also affords new possibilities of dialogue and of initiative within the Catholic Church.

It is for us to exploit these new possibilities so as to make the teaching of *Nostra aetate* pass into the sensitivity, into the spirit, into the actions of Christians. In accordance with this implementation of *Nostra aetate,* we should mention on occasions such as our celebration today the publication of *Guidelines and Suggestions for Implementing the Conciliar Declaration Nostra Aetate (No. 4)* which appeared at the beginning of 1975.

By offering further possibilities of development, the publication of this document—like the creation of the new commission—imposes on all Christians in their relations with the Jews an added responsibility, a new duty. In the introduction to *Guidelines and Suggestions* the aim is expressed thus: "On the practical level in particular, Christians must therefore strive to acquire a better knowledge of the basic components of the religious tradition of Judaism: they must strive to learn by what essential traits the Jews define themselves in the light of their own religious experience." We must weigh well the meaning of these words.

I do not wish, nor am I able, to enter into details today. By stressing the fact that the declaration is addressed to Catholics, I want to ask all Catholics—not only those engaged in dialogue with Jews—to realize the seriousness of the suggestions proposed and to make their own the general orientation given in this document. If this is done, positive and important results can be expected. To return to the words of the introduction already quoted: they speak of "the religious tradition of Judaism" and of the "Selbstverstandnis" of the Jews, always in "the light of their own religious experience." You are well aware that our commission was formed for religious relations with the Jews. The specific mention of the religious aspect is sometimes seen as a restriction on the responsibility of this commission, even as a restriction which renders almost impossible the free development of dialogue.

The Jews understand themselves primarily as a people; yet the question immediately arises: Why, in what sense a people? What factors have determined the origin and the formation of this people? Could it be that the Jewish religion itself created the people? We Christians also understand ourselves as a people, and for us also our peoplehood is shaped by our religion. Yet it is clear that we are not a people in the sense of being a definite nation. If at this point we stress a difference between the Jewish people and the Christian people, it remains nevertheless true that it is the religious element that determines our understanding of ourselves as a people.

Here the fact that the document *Guidelines and Suggestions* does not speak of the state of Israel can also be understood. We recognize all the problems connected with the existence of the state of Israel. The state as such is a political fact. From the Jewish point of view, the bond uniting all Jews, individually and collectively, to the state of Israel is often stressed. The political problem in itself is not within the competence of our commission, so it should have no place in the document. The religious aspect which, for many Jews, exists also in the link between the people and the state, or, more precisely, the territory of a state, has not been discussed in depth by Catholics and Jews. This religious aspect of the "Selbstverständnis" of the Jews, and also of the Christian conception and interpretation, would be, on the other hand, more a religious and, to a certain extent, a theological problem. Touching this specific aspect, Jewish-Christian dialogue does not exclude discussion even on this point. However, we leave consideration of the political element involved here to those who consider themselves responsible in the political field.

In this sense Cardinal König has said: "We need to keep in mind that the *Guidelines* is not a political but a religious document." Speaking of the state of Israel he continues: "It deals with a problem much discussed also among our Jewish interlocutors; it is therefore obvious that the Catholic Church is less well-equipped to take up a position."

Another point that has caused surprise and a certain difficulty is the co-existence in the document of the affirmation of the dialogue, and of the duty of Christians to testify to their faith. The difficulty experienced by some in understanding that these two statements are compatible shows how urgent is the need for dialogue.

If, when two persons meet, one reveals himself to the other just as he is, opening his heart, explaining himself, by the very fact that he does this he witnesses to himself and to his convictions. Such openness demands trust and, dare I say, a sense of brotherhood, because one has to be sure of being listened to and of being accepted with the same trust that has inspired the self-communication. This communication can also be called witness. And it is precisely in this sense of communication of oneself and of one's principles that the document *Guidelines and Suggestions* intends the word "witness" to be understood when it says: "[Catholics] must take care to live and spread their Christian faith while maintaining the strictest respect for religious liberty in line with the teaching of the Second Vatican Council."

Certainly, dialogue between Catholics and Jews is weighed

down by history, and we are grateful that it is now possible to engage in it with trust and mutual respect. For it is without doubt the declaration of the Second Vatican Council that has opened up this possibility. The new document for the application of the council declaration gives many concrete suggestions for the development of this dialogue. Moreover, in 1970 the Secretariat for Christian Unity published a declaration on the subject, *Reflections and Suggestions for Ecumenical Dialogue.* The problem of honesty or of the relationship between dialogue and witness is not new. It is intrinsic to ecumenical relations of all kinds and is present in a very special way in dialogue between Jews and Catholics.

I have spoken of the weight of history. If a certain proselytism has, during the centuries, caused spiritual harm to all confessions, it has certainly damaged those who were guilty of it. In the relations between Jews and Christians we hope that errors and negligences will be diminished. This imposes renunciation of a certain way of witnessing which would indeed be none other than a caricature of true witness and, in fact, its negation.

In conclusion I would like to express the wish that a true dialogue based on religion and on real collaboration may enrich us both, Jews and Christians alike, as we work in different ways for the realization of the eschatological hope, the final establishment of the kingdom of the Most High. This very hope is a common and essential element of faith and confers on our dialogue its own consistency and personality.

A last word. I have just said that the council declaration *Nostra aetate* has, during the ten years of its existence, already inspired certain concrete realizations at both local and international levels. Among these we must mention the SIDIC center which has invited us here today. We hope that, in collaboration with the Commission for Religious Relations with the Jews, it will bear much fruit in the future.

In fact, this evening's meeting celebrates also the tenth anniversary of the foundation of SIDIC, the international service of Jewish-Christian documentation. Considering to what extent relations between Christians and Jews have suffered in the past from lack of knowledge and information, the SIDIC center has already played an important role. I know that a fruitful exchange of information between SIDIC and the commission has already begun. I rejoice at this and hope that in the future this collaboration will, in reciprocal independence, develop still more.

However, SIDIC is not only a center or a service of information and documentation. It is also a meeting place whose unofficial character should facilitate encounter in an atmosphere of freedom and seriousness. I want to stress these points because SIDIC is thus serving the cause which the Second Vatican Council had so much at heart. May the Lord bless its work.

"We Are Spiritually Semites": Fifteen Years after *Nostra aetate**

The celebration of an anniversary of a religious event does not only mean commemoration in the ordinary and usual sense of that word. We are gathered here this evening, thanks to an invitation from SIDIC in Rome, for the fifteenth anniversary of the solemn promulgation by Vatican Council II of the Declaration *Nostra aetate* on the relationship of the church to non-Christian religions. The section speaking of relations with Judaism is certainly the most developed and the richest in content, standing out in the general text of the Declaration because of its theological importance. We will not here recall it to mind simply as an historical occurrence and so only reaffirm its having had existence at a moment in the past. In its true meaning, to commemorate goes much further than that. According to the theological and liturgical sense of anamnesis, it causes the fact to which the commemoration refers to live again in the present, and projects its existence into the future. The event thus takes on fresh dimensions in every commemoration and goes on living in the present; it is enriched by the experience gained over the years since its beginning, and reveals hidden but valid potentialities for the future. So memory is not bound to the past, but should inform the present, and commit the future.

LINK BETWEEN TEXT AND LIFE

How does the Declaration *Nostra aetate* present itself to us with its paragraph 4 when seen in this light, fifteen years after it was

---

* Rome, 1980; see Bibliography, n. 5.

promulgated? First of all we have to say that it does not come to us as a bare text, however valid and significant it may be, but still just one of many such published by ecclesiastical organs in recent or past times. A council text is never simply a bare text to Catholic Christians (nor, for that matter, to other Christians). In a certain way it is a work of the Holy Spirit. It therefore possesses a potentiality of its own which enables it to live and act within the church. There is no need even for it to be a "perfect" text. There are very few perfect texts in the history of the church. But it is precisely that inherent potentiality that enables comparison between text and life, constantly deeper understanding of it and the bringing of new historical situations to bear upon it, helping us to read the texts that we are commemorating in a fresh way, yet always in continuity with their fundamental meaning.

How could we fail to recall at this moment the personality of him whom I venerated and loved as master and father—Cardinal Bea? He convinced the council fathers, and through them the whole church, of the spiritual relationships that link Christians and Jews. Cardinal Bea spoke with patience and wisdom, but also with love rooted in faith and ripened by biblical research into the relations between Jews and Christians. He taught and inspired fresh and deeper understanding of the identity and religious truth of the Jewish people.

The fourth paragraph of *Nostra aetate* thus presents itself to us, as we commemorate it today, as having been singularly enriched by the experience of the intervening years. We read it today in the light of *Guidelines and Suggestions* for its implementation, published in 1975. That text was deliberately rendered simple and generic: it is a text cadre as they say in French, a framework. It suggests in fact to Catholics ways and means of applying *Nostra aetate* to the various contexts of the church's pastoral life: liturgy, education, action. The council text enters in this fashion into the concrete reality of the cells through which the church's life runs. The text certainly comes out looking renewed and up to date, concerned with the present.

STATEMENTS AFTER NOSTRA AETATE

The same may and ought to be said of comments and references to our text coming from popes and various episcopates over the years. The text itself inspires and quickens and gives the main line, but their comments and references exert influence in their turn upon the text and allow us to undertake a "reexamination" of it. This is not the place for listing all those documents: they have been brought together into two or three important collections. Yet it is always useful to recall some of them precisely because of their value as interpretations and topical applications of *Nostra aetate*. We would recall two among papal texts in this field: Paul VI's discourse to participants in the fifth meeting of the International Liaison Committee between the Catholic Church and Judaism, January 10, 1975, and John Paul II's speech to representatives of world Jewry on March 12 last year. I must add the Holy Father's speeches to Jewish communities in various countries that he has recently visited: Mexico, the United States, France, Brazil. Among texts issued by episcopal conferences, we all know those of the bishops of the United States, the French episcopate, the German episcopate, the conference of Latin American episcopates at Puebla in Mexico, the synods of the archdiocese of Santiago, Chile, and so on.

It is not only a matter of texts. Life itself, that is, the progress of the dialogue with Judaism which was called for by the council, sets the texts within the context of lived reality. This context absolutely cannot be disregarded in a commemoration like ours today. It is not possible, however, to report on everything that has happened in this field since the dialogue with Judaism is developing more or less everywhere at all levels. We would just now mention the series of annual meetings of what is called the International Liaison Committee between the holy see and world Jewry. These began in 1971, the latest having been held at Regensburg in Bavaria last October. Other gatherings of the same committee have been held at Rome and Jerusalem (1976) and Toledo–Madrid (1978), all places of significance for our common history in both its bright and its sad aspects. There should be no need to say that these meetings are certainly not mere academic exercises, purely theoretical affairs. On the contrary, there is inquiry into questions pertaining to each side's identity, questions that have divided us for almost two thousand years. There is, for example, the very complex question of the church's universal mission and the distinction between that mission and so-called proselytism which does not respect human dignity and liberty. A certain amount of time is always devoted at such meetings to communication effected by both sides and problems and difficulties as still exist and reappear in our relationships. It is still right, however, to emphasize once again that such encounters on the international level are but one aspect or element, although the most evident one, of a broad texture of gatherings, meetings, dialogues and interchanges of all kinds. They occur at all levels and by now it is impossible to keep track of them all. Thanks to SIDIC, which is our host this evening, and thanks to other initiatives, the two communities meet in Rome as well; they talk and are beginning a dialogue. This dialogue has its special features and demands which, as we said, will not fail to be reflected upon those other texts.

We cannot be totally unaware of the fact that Jews in Italy, particularly those in Rome, are those who always were and are closest to the apostolic see. This undoubtedly sets up a special relationship.

This life is developing and spreading like a river, like the one mentioned toward the end of the book of Ezekiel (cf. Ez 47:1–12), restoring and cleansing the land that it traverses. It is in this context that certain acts take on a quite particular value with regard to our commemoration. Let us think for a moment here of certain acts on the Catholic side, acts of the holy see itself. The Commission for Religious Relations with Judaism was set up through the work of Paul VI on a date that almost coincided with the ninth anniversary of *Nostra aetate* (October 22, 1974). That act certainly had more than practical relevance only; it had theological and pastoral relevance above all, and we have not yet exhausted all its possible consequences. Acts of that kind have come from the Jewish side also. Catholics will never be able to forget the feelings of fraternity and understanding participation that were shown on the Jewish side in the autumn of 1978 on the occasion of the deaths and elections of two popes in the brief period of two months. Written testimonies of such fraternity and participation in sorrow fill numerous pages of the Acta Apostolicae Sedis, the official organ of the holy see, and of our own Information Service. But what was expressed in writing was only a reflection of that fraternal and heartfelt attitude. It in its turn marks out a precedent, and shows a path to be followed by Catholics. It is impossible to trace out the course taken, as we remarked, by such acts on both sides.

If then we consider the text of paragraph 4 of *Nostra aetate* in this context, what elements appear as being most important, most topical, most urgent for great reflection and more decisive application? In the brief time here available I would propose some elements which spring to my mind.

First of all, fresh light is shed upon the initial statement in paragraph 4 which says that the church searches into her own mystery and so discovers the link uniting her with the people born of Abraham. This means that relations between the Catholic Church and Judaism are not as it were extrinsic ones, overlaying the reality of the church herself, but on the contrary they flow from the consciousness that the church has of herself. In fact she has her roots in Judaism, not only in that of the Old Testament, but also in that which is intertestamental, from which matrix rabbinical Judaism also comes. Contemporary Judaism, here worthily represented, declares itself the heir of the latter. Well, this theological foundation of dialogue and relationships has been brought to light more clearly by the texts and deeds of the last fifteen years on one and the other side. To give one example, I would refer to the expression adopted by the holy father, John Paul II, in his speech of March 12, 1979 to representatives of the Jewish communities. The pope said that the two religions are linked at the very level of their own religious identities. This is an affirmation of prime importance and it will need going into more deeply. From the pastoral point of view, that is from the point of view of the Catholic Church's daily ministry, this means that having a relationship with Judaism and with Jews is almost an imperative of her distinctive reality.

SPIRITUALLY WE ARE ALL SEMITES

We have likewise seen more clearly than ever how every form of antisemitism, of discrimination, whether violent or attenuated, is absolutely incompatible with the requirements of the Christian faith and ethic. We might say that, for a Christian, being antisemitic is a *contradictio in adiecto,* as the scholastic formula has it. This expression might be rendered as follows: it is at the same time a negation of what it affirms.

It may happen that the religious element sharpens opposed feelings in a dispute of any kind involving Christians and Jews, whereas it ought to facilitate understanding and rapprochement on the human level.

We would recall here that almost fifty years ago, on September 6, 1938, Pius XI told a group of Belgian pilgrims that we Christians are spiritually Semites. That statement of principle has never lapsed. Indeed, the experience of this period of fifteen years has served to make it more valid and true. Paradoxically, attempts at ideological justification of antisemitism only set that declaration of the pope in even brighter light. For one thing, they call forth a reaction on the part of church leaders, as we saw on the occasion of the recent occurrences in Paris. I would here once more decidedly condemn those occurrences. But it is not a question of reactions only. There is also question of a patient labor of formation and education. This begins with catechesis, continues with religious instruction, and culminates in the sermon of the Sunday liturgical celebration. The way to be covered is long and difficult; prejudices are met with on it, but also new and old theological and exegetical problems that are not always easy to resolve. We know that Jewish communities in many parts of the world try to find ways of presenting Christianity in a more objective light, one corresponding to the deep reality of the faith. We appreciate such efforts, we follow their development with interest, and we rejoice greatly at results already achieved.

LEARN HOW JEWS DEFINE THEMSELVES

Recent years have let us rediscover in an even livelier fashion the importance for the Jewish consciousness of certain elements or facts that tend to define it according to its proper identity. Among these a very special value is given to the monstrous experience of persecution and extermination during the Nazi period which is usually called the holocaust.

Contemporary Judaism defines itself in some way on the basis of that experience. It tries to see in it the certainly psychological but also theological reason for its vital need for security and a guarantee of being able to subsist. This explains, at least in part, the constant association of religious and political factors (the latter at national and state levels) which is so characteristic of present-day Judaism.

For their part, Christians try to understand this special attitude. But also, in accordance with our tradition, they seek to distinguish between what flows from the religious reality and what has the value of legitimate requests in the political order. These latter are always subject to the contingencies of changeable circumstances. It also seems to me that the experience of recent years has caused us to give greater value to the urgency and present worth of the testimony afforded in the contemporary world by monotheistic faith and by conduct deriving therefrom. This means the proclamation of a fatherhood and a providence that is common to all mankind which makes all brothers and children of God, all sharers in the same inviolable dignity which extends as well to the fundamental communities within which human life is carried on.

And here mention must be made of the family amongst other things. The General Assembly of the Synod of Bishops that has just concluded concerned itself at length with the family. So many common values unite us with Judaism in this field. The values of justice and peace find their proper place in this context. There is much talk of them today, but in order to be truly respected and fruitful they must find their original inspiration again, that is, the revelation made to the fathers and, according to our Christian faith, brought to completion by Jesus. Jews and Christians can and ought to collaborate for the good of man himself who, according to our common faith, was created in God's image (cf. Gen 1:26).

Our commemoration, our remembrance and actualization of the past can in this way help us to interpret the present and show us the way to follow for the future—a threatening future yet full of hope.

May the Lord grant us, Jews and Christians together, the gift of living up to the requirements of this renewed call of which the present anniversary reminds us.

Nostra aetate: A Catholic Retrospective*

It is with great pleasure that I have accepted the invitation of the three well-known institutions sponsoring this colloquium, called together to commemorate the twentieth anniversary of the conciliar Declaration *Nostra aetate,* No. 4, promulgated (as we all know) on October 28, 1965. It is indeed significant that the president of the holy see's Commission for Religious Relations with the Jews should participate in this celebration and has been asked to be the first speaker tonight. I am grateful, therefore, for the occasion thus offered to me to say a few words on *Nostra aetate,* No. 4, twenty years after its promulgation.

The first point I want to make is a very simple one, although extremely significant. It is a statement of fact. All the information we receive in our Commission for Religious Relations with the Jews indicates that throughout this year 1985 there have been or will be a lot of similar or comparable celebrations of this twentieth anniversary.

To quote only the more important: the International Liaison Committee, composed of representatives of the International Jewish Committee on Interreligious Consultations (better known by the acronym IJCIC) and of our Commission, will meet in this same city of Rome, in late October, precisely on the date of the anniversary, to celebrate the event with one of its regular meetings, the twelfth of the series. I look forward to this occasion which will in some ways be the official commemoration of this event, on the part of the two bodies set up, one by the Catholic Church and the other by a large, highly representative body of world Judaism, for the sake of dialogue—more precisely, for the sake of implementing *Nostra aetate.*

* Rome, 1985; see Bibliography, n. 11.

We are well aware also of the program prepared, and in part implemented, by some major Jewish organizations linked with IJCIC, to bring the celebration to local congregations, Jewish and Catholic (or, as the case may be, Anglican, Lutheran, Methodist, Presbyterian and so forth). This is happening mainly in the United States, where these organizations have their headquarters. Those organizations are the American Jewish Committee and the Anti-Defamation League of B'nai B'rith, one of the sponsoring bodies of this colloquium.

I would like to say now, as a second point in this address, that I see a great significance and promising implication that we are meeting in a Catholic faculty of theology, which is also one of the sponsoring bodies of this colloquium.

This is again a sign of the times. I think it is only honest to say that twenty years ago a colloquium of this kind, hosted by a Catholic theological faculty, would have been impossible. True, there were courses on Judaism and Judaica offered in some places of higher learning, in Rome and elsewhere. And I feel I should give credit to the Angelicum (as it was then called, and still is, in day-to-day speech) that in years well before *Nostra aetate* not only was biblical Hebrew taught here (by a fellow countryman of mine, Fr. Duncker), but also Mishnaic Hebrew, and "the sayings of the fathers" (Pirke Aboth) were read and explained here in the original language. (Msgr. Mejía tells me that it was here that he learned his Hebrew and received his first introduction to post-biblical Jewish literature.) And the Angelicum was not perhaps such a rarity on this account.

THE WORK OF CARDINAL BEA

Things such as these should not be passed over in silence or be forgotten, simply because of the progress we have made since. On the contrary, such "prolegomena" (as one could call these facts) go a long way to explain why there were, and are, people in the church who could carry *Nostra aetate* successfully through to its promulgation by the council and to commit themselves since to its proper implementation in the daily life of the church.

And, of course, this leads me to think of Cardinal Bea who introduced so many students to the love and appreciation of things

Jewish, when he was teaching at the Pontifical Biblical Institute nearby, and thereafter was chosen providentially to steer the way for *Nostra aetate* through several council and extra-conciliar debates, and to preside over the first decisive steps in its life in the church.

Yes, at this level at least, the past was not that negative. Otherwise it would be hard to explain how such an overwhelming majority of bishops recognized in *Nostra aetate,* No. 4, their own faith and the faith of the Catholic Church when voting in favor of the document in the final session, on October 28, 1965. So did the pope. So did the popes that followed and the bishops ordained since, as—I hope—we shall see in the Extraordinary Assembly of the Synod of Bishops meeting in Rome from November 25 onward.

When I mentioned the Catholic theological faculty hosting this meeting, I had two things in mind which I would like to share with you in a very simple way.

The first is again a statement of fact. Nowadays many of the pontifical universities in Rome have a chair of Judaism, or some courses on this subject. Sometimes the teacher is a Jew, as in the Lateran University. In other cases, as recently in the Urbaniana, a congress on a very typically Christian subject—To bring Christ to humankind—turned to our office, not only because they wished the ecumenical dimension or context of that theme to be present, but also because they wanted some kind of presentation about the theological aspects of Jewish-Christian relations and the questions posed by them.

Such a development, I believe, is also a consequence of *Nostra aetate* and should be underlined today in this context. Quite obviously, it is not limited simply to the Roman universities. The Catholic theological faculty of Lucerne in Switzerland has had, for some years now, an "Institut für christlich-jüdische Forschung," committed to theological dialogue with Jewish scholars and forming students in the austere discipline of reading and interpreting primary Jewish sources.

This is an occasion too for mentioning and praising the remarkable work being done, for many years now, in the Institute for Judeo-Christian Studies in Seton Hall University, in South Orange, New Jersey. The Institute is associated with Msgr. John M. Oes-

terreicher, one of the pioneers in the field of Jewish-Christian relations and the theological investigation of both Jewish and Christian
sources in matters that link one to the other.

More recently still, a Jewish-Christian college is being planned
in Selly Oak, Birmingham, where several major Christian denominations will be represented. This is not the occasion for a complete
list. I am not seeking to give you a catalogue, but to draw your
attention to what I am convinced is a major development in Jewish-Christian relations, to be carefully underlined and considered
on this twentieth anniversary—namely, the presence of Judaism as
an academic subject in our higher institutes of learning. And this
brings me to another point I want to make on this particular subject. I have just mentioned the presence of Judaism as an academic
subject in our Catholic places of higher learning. By this I mean two
different things, connected and called to grow together, yet not
identical.

NEED FOR KNOWLEDGE

The first point I want to make is the need (I almost said the dire
need) for proper knowledge of things Jewish in the Catholic academic community. I say: proper knowledge. I should have said,
perhaps, scientific knowledge. If our students, and sometimes even
our teachers, are really to discover and appreciate our Jewish roots,
the Jewish context and Jewish sap of the New Testament and of the
main Christian institutions, and if they are to explore the difficult
problems sometimes posed by more than one biblical text, a per-
functory knowledge, or superficial information, is not enough.
Deep technical study is required. Otherwise, parallels will remain
external, contact more verbal than substantial, problems ignored
or glossed over. What I have said about the Bible is already a world
in itself. What if we bring in the patristic period, with its frequently
negative presentation of Jews and Judaism, and its connections
with earlier classic antisemitism?

Some questions are now too obvious to be just answered with
platitudes, not to say pushed under the rug. Antisemitism has become such an immense tragedy that its roots, its different forms, its
deep challenge to Christians at large, must now be a subject of
dispassionate, careful study. And in this connection the same

Nostra aetate: *A Catholic Retrospective*   25

should be said of the presence of Judaism, mostly—I fear—a negative one, in the history of the church. The subject of anti-Jewish legislation in medieval councils, appalling as it is, should be examined in the light of historical canon law studies. Last, but not least, the positive sides of our common history in the east and the west should be identified, studied, evaluated. Because there are positive sides: Raymond Martin's *Pugio Fidei,* presently being studied by a young scriptor in the Bibliotheca Ambrosiana in Milan, is a case in point.

MAIMONIDES ANNIVERSARY

Another question, an extremely important one, is brought to my mind by another anniversary. This year we celebrate the 850th anniversary of the birth in Spain of Moses Maimonides, the Rambam, as he is called in Jewish tradition. Now, everybody knows that St. Thomas Aquinas knew and often used some of Maimonides' works. However, few people know who Maimonides was, what his intellectual concerns were, the range of his works, and above all how on earth St. Thomas became aware of such writings, why he decided to put them to use and how exactly he used them. I submit that this is a fascinating subject for study in our Catholic theological faculties, this year and for many years after. I add that Jewish institutes of the same or similar level would perhaps find this an interesting subject for research, if it has not come up yet.

Maimonides is a Jewish source. Jewish sources, I have already pointed out, should be better known by Catholic students in theology, philosophy, or canon law, not to mention biblical studies which, in the present context, should be taken for granted.

I have said "better known." Should I simply say "known"? I am afraid that for many of us the Mishna, the Tosefta, the Midrashim and both Talmuds, not to mention the Responsa and the medieval Bible commentaries, remain an uncharted land, in spite of many remarkable efforts in such a difficult field. The Targumim, for example, thanks to the discovery and identification of Manuscript Neofiti 1 in the Vatican Library, and its subsequent publication in Spain and in France, are now more accessible to the average student. Still, there are treasures in their pages, as the work of Fr. Roger Le Déaut has revealed, which remain largely untapped, precisely in the field of Christian origins and the religious context of the New Testament.

All this, however, is not just an internal Catholic, or Christian, matter. It is a matter of collaboration of Christians with the Jews, and of Jews with Christians, and this is already taking place. Judaism can only be taught adequately by Jews. Jewish sources are their heritage and the air they breathe. For some other aspects, Christians are perhaps better equipped. I see in all this at the same time a great open field for common work and a forceful challenge to both our scholarly communities. Let it become one of the results, nay, one of the engagements of the celebration of the twentieth anniversary of *Nostra aetate*. The latter explicitly recommended such studies made in common, in a text I would like to quote verbatim: "Since the spiritual patrimony common to Christians and Jews is so great, this sacred synod wishes to foster and recommend that mutual understanding and respect which is the fruit above all of biblical and theological studies." This recommendation was taken up and enlarged by the 1974 *Guidelines and Suggestions*.

May I express here the wish that such a collaboration should extend further than the presence of one, or even several, Jewish scholars in Catholic institutes, or vice versa, to a more formal link between institutes as such, Jewish and Catholic, like the relationship that already exists between the Pontifical Biblical Institute in Rome and the Hebrew University in Jerusalem.

THEOLOGICAL DIALOGUE

The need for knowledge of things Jewish has brought me, almost unaware, to the subject of collaboration in the field of learning. But there is another form of collaboration in the academic field, a collaboration which is the other aspect of the presence of Judaism in our higher institutes of learning mentioned above. This is theological dialogue. Yes, this pair of words evokes in Jewish memory, that famous tenacious Jewish memory, sad images and a reflex of self-defense. But dialogue is not controversy. Rather it is exactly the contrary. It is listening sympathetically to one another, the better to understand what each one believes, and profit from it. The question then is not if we should have theological dialogue but whether we dare to avoid it. Is this perhaps the consequence of professional deformation or distortion in a Catholic mind, accustomed to look at everything under a doctrinal light, *sub luce theologiae?* Or is it simply the consequence of many years of experience in Jewish-Christian dialogue which makes one aware of the fact that we are always talking "theology" or "religion" (as the Jews would say), even when talking politics?

However that may be, let me state here as clearly as possible that I accept and respect all the reservations that some Jewish representatives, or perhaps many, have for any kind of public exposure of what they believe. This is fully understandable and should be not only respected but also admired. Yet there are some fields in which I believe we could fruitfully listen to each other and exchange ideas with each other at the strictly religious level of our convictions and practice, as we are going to do tomorrow here, at least to some extent. This has already been done in some places, and is planned for others, and I am quite sure it would enormously help to bridge the gap of ignorance, distortion and—sometimes—mistrust. Perhaps, again, this suggestion can be considered a possible consequence of the anniversary celebration.

AWARE OF THEOLOGICAL PROBLEMS

However, I want to add immediately, addressing myself now mainly to Catholics, but also to some extent to the Jews, that such an enterprise, desirable as it may be, cannot in any way substitute for or replace the internal Catholic effort to elaborate a proper theological vision of Judaism.

We are all well aware of the many new and sometimes very entangled theological problems created (or awakened because perhaps they were lying asleep) by the existence and progress of our relations.

Many well-known and renowned scholars, such as Mussner and Thoma, have begun to tackle these problems with some success, but a lot more remains to be done. There are even occasions when the same problems have to be dealt with over and over again, in the light of critiques or new evidence, partially or totally overlooked.

I see this as one of the major tasks of our theological faculties

around the world. Not only should they study Judaism and Jewish
sources, but it is to be hoped that they will study them at first hand
as an indispensable and elementary departing point. But beyond
this, our task is to face adequately, study and try to solve, in all
fidelity to Catholic normative tradition (which we accept and cher-
ish and are called to transmit to those who follow us), the questions
that a renewed vision of Judaism poses to many aspects of Catholic
theology, from christology to ecclesiology, from the liturgy to the
sacraments, from eschatology to the relation with the world and the
witness we are called to offer in it and to it, or rather to the men and
women living here with us, Catholics and Jews.

BECOMING AWARE OF RESPONSIBILITY

We all know that some of the institutions sponsoring this colloquium—and I would here like to mention SIDIC and the Centro
pro Unione—have tried in different ways to foster and inspire the
kind of academic task I have outlined above. Let me express again
my hope that the twentieth anniversary will help our academic
institutions become still more aware of their responsibility and call
in relevant fields of study and the challenge they present. This
would show to all and sundry that *Nostra aetate,* No. 4, that is, the
council, with all the theological weight this word carries for us
Catholics, has really taken root in our lives and in our minds. It is in
this promising context that I would like to see the present anniversary colloquium.

Nostra aetate:
The Fundamental Starting Point
for Jewish-Christian Relations*

It is with great pleasure that I, as president of the Commission for Religious Relations with the Jews, extend my welcome to those here present, Jews and Catholics, to participate in the twelfth meeting of the International Liaison Committee between the Catholic Church, represented by our Commission for Religious Relations with the Jews, and the International Jewish Committee on Interreligious Consultations (IJCIC).

The present meeting is held in Rome, in the premises of the Secretariat for Promoting Christian Unity, which means that, in a certain sense, all of you are our guests. This circumstance, significant in itself, not only enhances the pleasure of receiving you, but also is closely linked to the main scope of the meeting itself.

We are, in effect, meeting in Rome now for the second time, because we wish to commemorate the twentieth anniversary of the promulgation by the Second Vatican Council of the Declaration *Nostra aetate,* the fourth section of which, as we all know, deals with the relationship between the church and the Jewish people.

Today, October 28, happens to be the very date when that document was approved by an extremely large majority of the members of the council, and then officially promulgated by Pope Paul VI and the council, as reads the Latin formula of promulgation.

We are, therefore, in a way celebrating our birthday. It is true, of course, that the International Liaison Committee only took

* Vatican City, 1985; see Bibliography, n. 9.

shape four or five years later, and only met for the first time in December 1971 in Paris. And the Commission now responsible in the holy see for relations with the Jews came into existence in October 1974. However, it is quite obvious that it all began on that October 28. Were it not for that historic paragraph, in all its briefness, and notwithstanding the many critiques moved against it before and after its promulgation, we would not be sitting here this day to celebrate this twentieth anniversary.

I believe that a lesson can be drawn from this.

Documents have always their limits, especially if they are envisaged from the point of view of those who are to receive them and with whom they are mainly concerned. Much less so, of course, if they are looked at from the perspective of those who have wrestled with the text, or texts, and the reactions thereupon, for many years. I was one of them and I think I know very well what this means.

On the other hand, when *Nostra aetate,* 4 is read and pondered, twenty years after, as we intend to do on this occasion, what is in the minds of all of us, Catholics and Jews, are certainly not its limitations, if any, but its extraordinary value, in the light of the preceding attitude, or attitudes, practical and theoretical, in the church, regarding Judaism.

If Jews, during the years elapsed, have better appreciated this newness and virtual uniqueness of the *Nostra aetate* text, we Catholics have to see more how it really conforms with a deeper strand of our tradition, and indeed with the word of God in both Testaments. It could not be otherwise, if it was to be approved by an ecumenical council. Conciliar documents, as I am sure you all know, are held, in Catholic traditional teaching, to come ultimately from the Holy Spirit, who is assisting, illuminating, and, if need be, correcting the human process of reflection and decision.

If, therefore, the Spirit of God is behind the texts of *Nostra aetate,* and also behind *Lumen gentium,* 16 (which should not be forgotten in this connection), then the changed relationship with Judaism is not a question of practical decision, however noble and high-flung our motivations may be for that. It is for us, as Catholics, a question of fidelity to our own vocation, a part of our response to God.

This is why there could never be question of drawing back from *Nostra aetate.* There can only be a question about going forward. Now, to go forward, as I am convinced we have done these last twenty years, one has to be sure of the starting point and constantly look back to it, to reaffirm its fundamental importance and draw inspiration from it.

One reason for the present meeting is precisely this one. We must, on this occasion, look back to *Nostra aetate,* to reaffirm its fundamental importance and to draw renewed inspiration from it. We are all convinced of the fundamental achievement it meant for the Catholic Church, and also perhaps beyond, and of its permanent value.

Let us state a first conclusion from all this: Jewish-Christian relations in the Catholic Church are there to stay, grounded as they are, not on any transient phenomenon of any kind, much less on a kind of guilt complex (what an unreliable foundation would that be!), but on a renewed consciousness of the "mystery" of the church, as *Nostra aetate* starts by saying. Namely, they are grounded in theological convictions, which, for the Catholic Church, is essential. We do not withdraw from such convictions. Our own identity would be at stake here.

Another conclusion I would like to draw is that what has happened since *Nostra aetate* is proof enough of the firmness of our resolve and the coherence of our decision. This is not the place to feed you with statistics or to list positive facts. I will only refer briefly to three significant items, which I believe are extremely revealing.

1. The first one is the constant engagement of the holy see, and of the holy father himself, in reaching out to the Jewish community on the one hand, and in trying to make the Catholic community always more aware of the consequences of *Nostra aetate* on the other hand.

It is not only that the number of Jewish visitors to the holy see and to the holy father—groups and individuals—has grown enormously along the years. There is also the new development of the pope meeting representatives of the Jewish community wherever he happens to be going and where there is a Jewish community willing to be received. This is what I meant by "reaching out."

Obviously, in fact, such encounters are not limited to the person or persons involved, but have much larger, far-reaching consequences.

Regarding our own faithful, you are well aware of what has been done on the part of the holy see. In twenty years we have published two documents, the *Guidelines* and the *Notes,* with the precise aim of permeating all levels of the church with the means and ways to arrive at a renewed presentation of Jews and Judaism in our teaching, but also, deeper still, in our own consciousness.

Now, these documents, each in its own time, have also been found to suffer from limitations. When, however, we look at the first one, the *Guidelines* of 1974, from the vantage point of time (exactly as we have done with *Nostra aetate*), limitations fade into the background, and what is left, and really matters, is the positive aspects of the text and the continuity with the conciliar Declaration.

I believe exactly the same will happen with the *Notes,* if it is not already happening, barely four months after its promulgation. It will be recognized, and this has already been said, on two points that may have seemed insufficient to some, that for the first time the Catholic Church, at the highest level, has told its catechists, its preachers and its teachers to consider the religious link of the Jewish people with the land of their fathers as well as the existence of the state of Israel in the context of international law, and to try to understand the meaning of the *Shoah.*

2. And this brings me to my second example.

Our teaching on Jews and Judaism has already changed. One recent survey, conducted by a group of experts in the United States, bears out the point. As I have said, I will not present statistics. I simply call your attention to the fact. Antisemitism is perhaps still alive. Regretfully it will take long to die out. But it becomes every day more difficult to have it linked with official, approved Catholic teaching. It may draw from other sources, secular or pseudo-religious, and this we have to assess carefully. But we all agree that it is another problem. And as we, in the Catholic Church, have a long experience of anti-Catholicism, coming from many sources, we can perhaps use this experience, as it has been done in certain places such as the United States, to counter the antisemitic plague.

The responses we have received from different Catholic sources, written and oral, public and private, on the *Notes* are extremely revealing in this connection. Either we are told that such suggestions as we offered are already being put into practice, but they are always welcome, or else we are informed of the willingness to pursue the path indicated, so as to be in complete accord with what has become official teaching of the church. And this also in some particularly delicate fields, like, for instance, the relations between the First and the Second Testaments (Section I of the *Notes*).

3. I come now to my third example, the last one, but certainly not the least. I have referred above to the foundation on "theological convictions" of the new relationship between the Catholic Church and Judaism. And when some misgivings have been expressed about the *Guidelines* in their time and more recently about the *Notes,* it has often been in the name of "theology."

(a) Here I would like to make two points. First, "theology" is a pluralistic concept. The title of our Commission seems to me to hint at a certain theological dimension. It is in fact the Commission for Religious Relations with the Jews. "Religious" is normally taken to mean "non-political." And this is true. But it is not all. There is something more which is positive, and not merely negative. And this I believe is precisely the rediscovery and translation into practice of the "link" or "bond" between our two "ways of life," which is grounded, as I believe, in the will of God. When I speak about "theology," I am not referring primarily to a rational, intellectual, reflection on the content of faith, but rather to the way we Catholics try to "walk humbly with our God" (Mi 6:8), according to our own convictions. In this sense there is nothing in the Catholic Church which can be called "alien" to theology, much less Catholic-Jewish relations. To put it briefly: either such relations do have, from our point of view, a real theological character, or they become an exercise in interreligious courtesy. This I would say of any interreligious dialogue, but it must be underlined much more strongly when it is a question of Catholic-Jewish relations.

And here we must sometimes be careful about what we mean with "theological" thinking when we feel that perhaps some statement or some document does not live up to certain "theological" standards. We have to be careful, I insist, not to confuse "accepted theological standards" in the Catholic Church with the personal theological opinions of some scholars, however respectable. These might be good or bad, as the case may be; but they are not, or not yet, "theological standards," which consist for us of the official teaching documents of the church.

(b) I am well aware, and this is my second point on this particular subject, that for many Jews "theology" and "theological dialogue" are problematic terms. I also think I know the reasons—too many sad memories are attached to these and similar expressions. And there is an extremely delicate and utterly respectable feeling that what happens in the realm of faith between God and the human person is not to be made the subject of a conversation with anybody.

This I understand and respect. And I recall vividly, in this connection, a conversation I had in a New York hotel, on March 8, 1971, with Rabbi Joseph Soloveitchik, the venerable Jewish teacher of so many generations of rabbis and, at least indirectly, of very many Jews at large. After having said what I just repeated, only in a more beautiful and moving way, he went on to say that, in any case, "all dialogue between Jews and Christians cannot but be religious and theological because—he continued—you are a priest and I am a rabbi, so can we speak otherwise than at the level of religion? Our culture is certainly a religious one." And then he referred, seeking my approval, which I was only too happy to give, of the permanent validity to both of us of the books of the Old Testament as a "source of hope."

On the occasion of this commemoration it is obvious that we are bound to speak also of what is still ahead of us. As I said before, there is no question of turning back, but only of going forward. Yes, many fields could perhaps be listed in which, either on the Catholic or the Jewish side, more progress could, and indeed should, be expected. I do not think I am the one to start here the discussion on these points. I am sure the participants in this meeting will take up the subject in the following sessions. But I would like, all the same, to stress two points in this connection.

First of all, whatever shortcomings we may be guilty of, on either side, should be seen against the background not only of the progress already made in twenty years, which would be fairly obvious, but much more of the solid, rocklike foundations I referred to in the first part of this speech. Thus, we have at our disposal (I am speaking mainly about the Catholic side), nay in our minds and hearts, as Christians, the rationale and the moving force to go forward. In a certain sense it is only a question of putting into practice —or, if you wish, of coherence.

A second point is about this International Liaison Committee, meeting now in Rome. It is, I submit, the only official linking body we have between the holy see and the Jewish community. Whatever its limitations, it is a symbol and an effective instrument of our relationship. I believe we have still to ponder very carefully how we can make use of it to deepen, foster, apply in many walks of life, such relationship within the "terms of reference" agreed upon in December 1970 in the "Memorandum of Understanding."

By that I do not mean that we should enlarge its membership, or have it changed to become a forum for technical theological discussions, much less a kind of debating society meeting now and then on nice and less nice subjects. It is, in fact, the only place where we are able to meet officially appointed Catholic and Jewish representatives (with asymmetry which is so typical of our relationship), face to face, for three full days, well conscious of the responsibility that the present state of our relationship places on our shoulders, on each side and on both together. Of course, our respective freedom is not impaired and our respective identities should remain untouched and so remain. Even when we are told that "consultations" should be held before doing this or that, or publishing such and such a text, we are all convinced that the final decision, on either side, rests solely with the body or bodies concerned, which may have, as is quite obvious, its own reasons, dependent on its own structures, and finally on its identity, to choose one or the other solution.

But having said as much, there is no question that we are linked for good, and that this "link" or "bond" for the Catholic Church rests on her own identity as church. This we cannot ignore when we meet, and for the twelfth time, in the International Liaison Committee.

Let us try to see very clearly where we are going, how we should move to get there and in which way we can already translate our relationship into concrete forms of collaboration toward all men and women, in a world torn by hate, violence, discrimination and also indifference for the poor, the sick, the elderly and the oppressed.

Our friends here present from different parts of the world, who have joined us for this specific occasion, might help us in the realization of this task before us.

Again, at the end of this already long introductory speech, I am bound to repeat what I have turned to many times during this speech: we are not supposed to do this or that, or not to do it, in the field of Jewish-Christian relationship, out of any sense of expediency, or mere human convenience, but because we believe in the one God of Abraham, Isaac and Jacob, and indeed Jesus Christ, and with all our differences we have been brought together finally, hopefully for good, as Jacob and Esau did one day embrace and reconcile as brothers before God (as it is said in Gn 33:3–4)—a text I would like to restate as an appropriate conclusion to my speech, but at the same time perhaps as an inspiring starting point for our meeting: "He himself [Jacob] went on before them [his wives and children], bowing to the ground seven times, until he came near to his brother. But Esau ran to meet him, and embraced him, and fell on his neck and kissed him, and they wept."

II.

Cardinal Bea
and
Relations with the Jews

Faithful Minister of the
Wisdom of God*

I have been invited to deliver this year's Cardinal Bea Memorial Lecture here at the Westminster Cathedral Conference Centre. I must say that I am doubly thankful for this occasion.

On the one hand, the year 1985 happens to be the twentieth anniversary of the council's Declaration *Nostra aetate,* on the relations between the church and non-Christian religions, which was promulgated by Pope Paul VI on October 28, 1965. Hence the subject chosen for the present lecture: "Vatican II and the Jews—Twenty Years Later."

But, on the other hand, the very title of this series of lectures brings me to the very core of that subject. Cardinal Bea was, in fact, not only the mind behind but, more so, the heart within and even the hand upon the text of the conciliar Declaration we are commemorating. And I am happy to have this occasion of witnessing to this remarkable link between the person and the work, while expressing my hope that this link will never fade away from the memory of the church.

It is quite true, of course, that conciliar documents come, in the last analysis, from the Holy Spirit—and, as Pope John Paul II has said some weeks ago (January 28) to the representatives of the Jewish community in Venezuela, from the divine wisdom. And once promulgated, they belong to the whole church. But this should in no way diminish the role and importance of the person

---

* Lecture given by Cardinal Willebrands at Westminster Cathedral Conference Centre, London, March 10, 1985.

chosen by providence to be an instrument of the wisdom and the Spirit of God—in the present case, Cardinal Augustin Bea, first president of the Secretariat for Promoting Christian Unity.

This reference to Cardinal Bea, as I said, brings me right to the heart of the subject I am invited to speak about. I believe, in fact, that a presentation on "Vatican II and the Jews—Twenty Years Later" should include three different dimensions, so to speak:

- a reference to the past, to the council itself;
- a reference to the present and the immediate past, what has been and is being done after the council;
- a reference to the future, what still remains to be done.

I have thus outlined the sequence of this lecture.

1. WHAT WAS DONE AT THE COUNCIL

I do not think it my task here to narrate history for the sake of history itself. The history of how *Nostra aetate* came about should by now be well known. It has been told, among others, by Cardinal Bea himself in the commentary he wrote on that document. For this, therefore, I refer to that book: *The Church and the Jewish People* by Cardinal Bea (New York, 1966).

What I would like to do here is to highlight some points, historical and theological, which I believe have a bearing on the unique importance of the conciliar Declaration and the impact it has already had and should still have in the church.

The *first* point is the fact that the "Jewish question" was ever given a place on the council's agenda and, despite some (as they are now called) technical incidents, was kept there. That this is an absolute *unicum* should not be obscured by the fact that we now have the Declaration, and have gone a long way to put it into practice. Some councils—it is true—have had Jews and Judaism written into their agendas, mostly in a negative light. Such is the case of the Fourth Lateran Council, which had, however, also its positive side. The council, in fact, specifically forbids forced baptism of the Jews.

But never, I repeat never, before had a systematic, positive, comprehensive, careful and daring presentation of Jews and Judaism been made in the church by a pope or a council. This should never be lost sight of.

There were indeed difficulties and crises. Could it have been otherwise? The remarkable thing would have been if there had been none or if, on the other hand, the difficulties had not been overcome. The former would have meant that there was no problem with the Jews and Judaism; the latter, that the church was not mature enough for a document like *Nostra aetate*. One and the other suppositions have proved to be wrong.

The great merit of John XXIII, as the visionary he was—or the prophet, if you wish—is to have taken, before God, the fateful decision of including the Jewish question in the council's agenda. And a still greater merit is to have kept it there when it had been suppressed. In each of these historical steps, the man called to implement the first decision and the man behind the second was, needless to say, Cardinal Bea. To the pope and the cardinal we therefore owe the conception (so to speak) of the document, as we owe to Pope John's successor in St. Peter's office, Pope Paul VI, and always to the same cardinal, the nurturing and the growing process, a painful growing process indeed, of that small embryo.

The difficulties in the way of the document were mainly of two sorts. This is also enlightening, because they somehow forecast the shape of the things to come.

Some were *theological* difficulties: how to express the role of the Jewish people in relation to the church; how to deal with difficult biblical texts which at first sight might seem intractable for a positive presentation of Judaism; what to do with the intervention of some Jews in the death of Jesus on the cross, and the accusation of deicide?

Others were *political* difficulties. It may seem unexpected that a *conciliar* document, on a *religious* subject, should raise *political* problems. But this is only another instance of the sometimes inextricable interrelation between different realms of the reality we live in. It is also another example of the different and even at times divergent ways in which a selfsame text can be read under different lights. However that may be, Cardinal Bea and myself, as his close collaborator, literally went out of our way to make it crystal clear to all and sundry that the text now called *Nostra aetate* was—and is—religious in its inspiration, religious in its concern and, finally, religious in its orientation.

I have referred again to Cardinal Bea and his action during the council on behalf of *Nostra aetate.* It was his task and his privilege to introduce to the council fathers the four successive stages of the document on the Jews, from first to last—something which he didn't do for *Unitatis redintegratio,* the *Decree on Ecumenism,* not even at the stage when *Nostra aetate* was to be a chapter of that Decree.

In those four presentations, the text of which has been available in English for many years, the cardinal faced and solved the theological, historical and even political difficulties just mentioned, at least to the extent that these last impinged upon the meaning and the wording of the text. It would perhaps not be a waste of time to go over them again even today so as to get a clear idea of what exactly is the weight of each and all of the sentences of *Nostra aetate* in the final draft, and their carefully balanced structure.

The cardinal's presentation obviously convinced the conciliar fathers, as the successive votations demonstrate. The last and decisive one, on October 28, was positive beyond all expectation: only 250 negative votes against 1,763 votes in favor and 10 abstentions.

Who could have foreseen such a vote at the start of the long gestation, five years earlier? It is important to note that the church, through her bishops, was *united* on the question of how to relate to the Jews and Judaism, not torn apart by it. And this has been, and remains, the solid guarantee of the changed, renewed attitude toward Jews and Judaism in the Catholic Church. It is like a house built upon a rock (cf. Mt 7:24ff)—nothing ever can tear it down. More than one comment on *Nostra aetate* at that time, or even more recently, has not taken this sufficiently into account—regrettably so, I must say.

A last point I would like to raise in this first section of my lecture is simply to underline, once more, what I believe are the very real, indeed quite revolutionary, contributions of *Nostra aetate,* as finally promulgated, to a new theological vision of Jews and Judaism and the corresponding new pastoral attitude toward both.

In the *first* place, the church, in the council, "remembers" her "spiritual links with Abraham's stock." There is, therefore, nothing less than a "spiritual link," lying deep in the church's mystery, which creates a kind of family relationship between the people of Israel ("Abraham's stock") and the church. This link can be forgotten or obscured. It has been brought again to the living memory of the church by the council, to remain there. On this living memory the whole edifice of Christian-Jewish relations is built and it receives therefrom its permanent solidity.

Out of this theological affirmation all the rest flows, theologically and pastorally. It is, I am convinced, rather obvious that the council did not intend to make explicit in the few pages of *Nostra aetate* all the possible theological and pastoral implications. This is the work the church has to do, and in fact has already done, and of which stock is taken in this anniversary celebration.

That the council itself was, however, aware of some of these implications is clear from the first sentence in no. 16 (Chapter Two) of *Lumen gentium,* the *Dogmatic Constitution on the Church,* frequently overlooked in this connection, although it is extremely important.

The perspective is here a different one. The central subject is the people of God and the point to be made here is how other "peoples" are connected with this people. The first one is "that people" (*populus ille*) who received the gifts and privileges from God, whence Christ came forth according to the flesh, and who "remains dear [to God] because of the fathers," his gifts and his calling being "without repentance." In this way, the *ethnic* reality of Israel is identified and described *theologically* with a series of quotations from the New Testament. The ring of this passage is unmistakable: it affirms the ongoing reality of Israel as a people, mysteriously chosen by God, and *as such* related to the church. Or shall we put it the other way round: the church related to Israel, Israel being what it is? Both perspectives are complementary. If *Lumen gentium* has chosen the former, *Nostra aetate* has chosen the latter. But both should be kept in mind.

Nostra aetate has also faced two of the major problems, which have vitiated for centuries our relations with Judaism and were part and parcel of what Jules Isaac called, in the title of a famous book, "the teaching of contempt" (*The Teaching of Contempt,* New York, Chicago, San Francisco, 1964). Such a "teaching" was never perhaps so systematic as the title would seem to imply, but there is no doubt that both these points were the main support of it.

These two problems can be formulated as follows: The Jews were guilty of killing Christ and have since remained so. Therefore

they bear upon themselves a kind of original sin with its corresponding condemnation, be it to eternal pilgrimage across the
world and outside the land of Israel, or else to God's equally eternal
disgrace, malediction and reprobation—or, worse still, to all these
put together.

Said like this, it sounds impossible and unspeakable. However,
"deicide" and "damned Jews" said (and sometimes even says)
nothing less.

Both these errors have been rejected by the council. The Jews
are *not* all of them, in that time and since, guilty of killing Christ,
whatever the role of the "leaders of the Jews and their followers" in
the passion. But this careful phrasing *excludes* the people as such
from this guilt.

And it should not be taught in the church that the Jews are,
again as such, subject to God's malediction and reprobation, as if
such were the right meaning of holy scripture.

Therefore, even when faced with difficult or obscure texts in
the New Testament (like 1 Thes 2:15), the Christian, the theologian
and the pastor know now how to interpret such texts and read them
in a light more consonant to the whole message of the entire Bible,
Old and New Testament.

In such a perspective, antisemitism is well nigh impossible. If,
as in the 1974 *Guidelines,* it is "deplored" and not outrightly "condemned," this is only a way of expressing a consequence of the very
harsh premises just exposed. One "deplores" that such forthright,
official interpretation of Catholic teaching has not yet seeped down
to all concerned, or is not heeded to by those outside the Catholic
fold (or indeed the Christian fold). But antisemitic actions, of any
kind, are and have been condemned because of our common
"patrimony." By hitting one brother, the other one is necessarily
hit at the same time. And if one brother is killed, the other one,
according to Genesis 4, is responsible for the killing.

These, then, are some of the highlights of *Nostra aetate.*

2. THE PERIOD AFTER THE COUNCIL

The council was barely over when different and important
initiatives sprang up all over the place to translate into the daily
practice of the church what had been officially promulgated in

Nostra aetate and in *Lumen gentium*. This happened, I am sure, because the conscience of the church had been deeply affected by the wording of the document, but even more so by the fact itself of its existence. It also happened because the other interested party, namely the Jews, or those many (if not all) who are most interested in the attitude of the church toward them, rightly understood that now was an opportunity for them to take the initiative if necessary.

It would be pointless and perhaps even tedious to review the very many documents, decisions and actions published, taken or made in these last twenty years. That history has still to be written. However, those interested may at least follow the highlights of it in several publications in various languages, which gather together the main documents, mostly official, published since then, although none is exactly up-to-date (e.g. *Stepping Stones To Further Jewish-Christian Relations,* ed. H. Croner, New York, 1977; *More Stepping Stones, idem,* New York, 1985; *Le Chiese cristiane e l'Ebraismo (1947–1982),* Casale Monferrato, 1983). Whenever such a publication comes out, it is always one document behind.

Granted, documents are not all. But they are extremely important, nay decisive. Decisions and actions, on the other hand, cannot be catalogued in books. They are mostly arguments for the media, and in these that which is bad, wrong or distorted finds its place much more easily than what is right. However that may be, I would like to refer here briefly to at least some of the more important decisions taken by the holy see for the implementation of *Nostra aetate.*

Already in 1966, the Secretariat for Promoting Christian Unity, whose responsibility it was to follow and promote the implementation, called a Dutch Bible professor, Dr. Cornelius Rijk, to take care of this entirely new task; in fact to have somebody in the Roman curia concerned with relations with Judaism was an absolute novelty. Professor Rijk, under the direction of Cardinal Bea, had to find his own way in a field not yet tilled—or tilled the wrong way. The Sisters of Sion know well what such beginnings meant.

A first need to be met was the preparation and publication of an official document for the application of the conciliar declaration, as foreseen by the rules of the council itself. This document was finally drafted in 1974, under the title *Guidelines and Sugges-*

*tions for Implementing the Conciliar Declaration "Nostra aetate"
n. 4.* It is known to you all. Since it was made public at the beginning of 1975, we can well say that we are now celebrating its tenth
anniversary.

The preparatory work took many years, again because the
field was so new, because the related experiences were not that
many, and, last but not least, because it was addressed to the whole
Catholic Church and therefore had to consider many different situations. All things considered, it is a remarkable piece of work, and I
am sure it has done already, and will do, a lot of good. Some
episcopal conferences (like the NCCB in the United States) have
come out with similar documents when ours was published. Others
followed suit, as most recently (November 1983) the Brazilian episcopal conference. And the Vatican *Guidelines* could profit from
those published before, as also from Cardinal Bea's commentary
on *Nostra aetate,* published first in Italian and translated afterward
in various languages.

But even before the *Guidelines* were made public, our Jewish
friends had approached the holy see and proposed that we start an
official dialogue group with the Jewish community, so as to have a
kind of regular occasion for meeting and facing together many
different issues, some of which had lain between us for centuries.
Those who approached us came from a new Jewish body created
for that aim, the International Jewish Committee on Interreligious
Consultations, mostly known as IJCIC, which at that time brought
together five major Jewish organizations, some of them worldwide.
The holy see accepted their proposal and the so-called International Liaison Committee was born in 1971.

It has met eleven times since, in various places (including Jerusalem and Rome, Toledo and Madrid, and Regensburg in West
Germany) and is about to meet for the twelfth time. It is composed
of official representatives on each side, the Catholic one including
always at least two bishops. It has studied many and difficult, even
conflicting questions, such as mission and proselytism, faith, people and land, violence in the present world, religious freedom, and,
for two sessions, the image of Jews and Judaism in Catholic education and the image of Christianity in Jewish education—an ongoing subject of common concern. The agenda has not yet been exhausted nor will it soon be exhausted.

Similar liaison groups or committees have sprung up since then, nationally and internationally, especially with international church bodies such as the World Council of Churches, the Lutheran World Federation, the Church of England, and even the Orthodox churches. What has now become normal and does not hit the headlines anymore was quite unexpected in 1971, and the fatefulness of the decision then taken by the two related bodies, the holy see and IJCIC, for the first time in history must not be lost sight of. Indeed, it should always be a source of inspiration and a continuing frame of reference for the International Liaison Committee and the task it has already done and is still called to do.

Again in 1974, an important date for Catholic-Jewish relations at the level of the holy see, the Commission for Religious Relations with the Jews was created, linked to, but distinct from, the Secretariat for Promoting Christian Unity. This is obviously another revealing fact. It means, of course, that things had gotten to a certain stage of maturity in which a person and an office in the Secretariat were not enough, not only because of the amount of material work, but much more because of the ever growing and self-asserting importance of the matter to be dealt with, namely, relations with Judaism. It would be true to say that these relations, from the point of view of the holy see, had gone beyond infancy and even adolescence and had entered adulthood. Fr. Rijk had by that time left the Secretariat. Fr. Pierre-Marie de Contenson, O.P. had taken his place and thus became the first secretary of the Commission. In that capacity he signed, along with me, the *Guidelines and Suggestions,* a permanent witness to his commitment in body and soul to Jewish-Christian relations in the church. For, as you know, both he and Fr. Rijk were called rather untimely to the house of our Father in heaven.

I won't describe here the work of the Commission, partly because it is also my own work. I shall only say that I am thoroughly convinced that the Commission has proved to be a remarkable instrument in relations with Jews and Judaism at large, whether organized or not, friendly or unfriendly, approving or disapproving, but mostly, of course, approving and friendly. It has also proved to be necessary for relating with the episcopates around the world, but also with religious orders, theological faculties, parish priests and faithful men and women. And last but not least, it has

found its place and become a necessary instance for matters Jewish
inside the Roman curia, again in itself a remarkable achievement
with many-sided projections and results.

I should not and would not close this second part of my presentation without referring to the pope himself. It can be said, very
truly, that whatever has been done in the holy see for the implementation of *Nostra aetate* comes from the pope, whether it be the
creation of the Commission for Religious Relations with the Jews
or the inauguration of the International Liaison Committee, or the
publication of the *Guidelines*. But if anyone imagines that these are
mostly administrative acts and that the pope would not necessarily
be concerned with such matters, he need only to look at the example personally set by the popes to dispel this idea.

Pope Paul VI expressed his feelings about relations with Judaism when he received the International Liaison Committee on
the occasion of their meeting in Rome in January 1975. This text is
worthwhile reading even now, ten years after. At a different level,
however, not less significant, it was Pope Paul who first started the
series of audiences to Israeli governmental leaders (Mrs. Golda
Meir was the first), which has continued till the present day. And,
last but not least, he was the first pope in many centuries to set foot
in the holy land and the holy city of Jerusalem.

As for Pope John Paul II, his list of audiences to Jewish leaders,
organizations, rabbis and ordinary men and women is simply endless. It must be said that the pope's house is wide open to the Jewish
people at large, no less than it is open to Catholics and other Christians. And many times these audiences are marked by important
speeches which in some way make the point about the state of
Jewish-Christian relations, the road we have traveled and the road
still ahead. While traveling outside Rome, the Pope frequently
meets local Jewish representatives, from Germany to Spain, from
Canada to Venezuela and Peru, from Brazil (twice) to the United
States—and of course here in England. On such occasions the
pope's speech sometimes expresses his thoughts on some aspects of
our relations, or calls the local community to foster its relations
with their Jewish neighbors, or energetically condemns antisemitism. One such speech, the one delivered in Mainz (Germany) on
November 17, 1980, could be read as a blueprint of the path that

dialogue with the Jews should follow. But sometimes it is the Jews present who use the occasion to express to the pope their wishes and desires, or their chief concerns in our mutual relations.

I have just mentioned antisemitism. It will perhaps not be amiss to recall here the many times during these last years when the holy see, mostly on behalf of the pope, has strongly reacted against antisemitic acts of violence, which sadly continue to endanger the peaceful existence of Jews in not a few places, including even Rome. It remains to be seen, however, whether Pope John Paul did not do more against antisemitism and for the promotion of Jewish-Catholic relations in his own diocese of Rome, when he met with the chief rabbi of Rome, Professor Toaff, in the parish church of San Carlo ai Catinari, in February 1981, than when he made his strong condemnation of the attack against the synagogue of Rome on October 10, 1982. However that may be, soon after, in 1983, the diocese of Rome published its remarkable *Guidelines for Relations with Judaism,* short but substantial and to the point.

I shall close this second section by stating something which, I believe, shows well what we have achieved all along these twenty years. I think we have achieved *two main results,* one on the Jewish side, the other on our own. On the Catholic side, notwithstanding all that remains to be done (of this I am well aware as we shall see in a moment), at least this is true: those who chose to ignore *Nostra aetate* and subsequent actions and documents, including the example of the pope, are put in the situation of having to explain their attitudes, theological or pastoral. In other words, an attitude which repeats ancient stereotypes or prejudices, not to say one that is aggressive against Jews and Judaism, has not anymore, and does not find anymore, a right for legitimate existence in the church. It may be there, and it may be frequent still in some places, but it has been put on the defensive. It is not taken for granted, as it was—I fear—twenty years ago.

On the Jewish side, I would only say this: I believe a certain amount of trust has been generated, or at the very least an awareness of the right Jews have to be heard and paid heed to, as such, in the Catholic Church. This means that some, if not all, barriers have been torn down. And it means also, on our side (because both things go hand in hand), that we in the church have become, or are becoming, aware of our responsibility, historical and theological, towards our elder brother, grounded in the "link" the council spoke about.

3. WHAT REMAINS TO BE DONE

Let me start this last section of my presentation by expressing a sobering thought.

I would put it this way: Jewish-Christian relations are an *unending affair,* as are love and brotherhood, but also (regrettably) hate and enmity. The main point is to change the fundamental orientation, from hate to love, from enmity to brotherhood. But also here, it is not a question only of documents, or of particular actions, however highly placed those who act happen to be. It is a question of people, men and women, made of flesh and blood. Still more, it is a question of *hearts.*

Once the foundations had been laid in the council Declaration and the following documents, then the work had to start of helping people change, those who were adults twenty years ago, those who have since become such, those who are still to come—and this all around the world, the Catholic Church becoming more and more true to her name, a universal reality. Now people have their agendas, their priorities, their day-to-day concerns, their cultural and historical inheritance. It is in the midst of all this that we have to go on planting the seed of a new Catholic vision of the Jewish people, in the midst, indeed, of a very diversified, always renewed, Catholic universal community.

This is—I believe—no more, no less, the task we are faced with. It has taken around two thousand years to arrive at *Nostra aetate.* It cannot be expected that everything will be undone, magically, in twenty years, especially when it is a question of people facing people.

In this situation, the immediate task seems to be *twofold*—one mainly on the Catholic side, the other one mostly together with our Jewish brethren.

On our side we could be asked to put our own house in order, namely, to set aside prejudices and to have them replaced by new ideas, in accordance with what is now the official teaching of the church. This is certainly necessary, and this is why Catholic-Jewish relations have to place so much weight on education, whether formal or informal, elementary or advanced, secular or religious, whether through catechetics, preaching, theology and/or public and private deeds. A lot has been done, including the correction of manuals and curricula. A lot remains to be done.

Let me point out one thing among others, but something extremely important, which remains to be done in this particular field. It is fairly easy to dispel prejudices and correct stereotypes, respectfully perhaps but strongly. It is quite another matter to instill new ideas. To this aim, a certain amount of systematizing is needed —or, as the Germans say, *Thematiesierung.* The council Declaration and the following documents have made the main points. Now a certain theological organizing of such points is needed, in themselves, and in relation with other subjects of Catholic teaching and study, like, for instance, exegesis of the Bible. The Jewish question being so central to that teaching, it is certainly not surprising that a long, large and deep effort of reflection is required, to be translated thereafter into manuals, curricula and day-to-day school experience—much more so because, obviously, if it is to be at all useful and permanent, this huge work has to be done with most careful attention to, and inspiration from, the true sources of Catholic doctrine. Adventurous theories and extravagant hypotheses are of no help here. Indeed they are counter-productive.

I must say, and I am happy to do so, that a certain amount of work is being done in this entirely new field. But it is no secret how enormous and momentous is the task still to be done. It is a question of elaborating a new systematic Christian view, or rather theology, of Judaism—nothing less. And I would like, in this connection, to call upon theologians, Bible scholars and other dogmaticians to respond to this urgent challenge.

Simultaneously, but I dare say at a faster pace, the revision of textbooks, manuals and similar works should continue. Here the office for Catholic education could be of much help, in collaboration with the Commission or offices for Catholic-Jewish relations, wherever they exist. And I express here the hope that they become still more numerous than they are now. This last development would help bishops, bishops' conferences and parish priests to keep the Jewish communities in their own areas in their minds, where these exist, and also not to forget them in areas where there are no

Jews. It will also give more credibility to our reaction against antisemitic phenomena, wherever they crop up.

While it is almost universally acknowledged now that present antisemitic attacks have nothing to do with religious prejudices, it is, however, always our own responsibility to condemn them strongly, following the pope's example and that of many bishops everywhere. Therefore we need to have ready at hand the instruments to know, assess and react to what is going on. In this connection Jewish sensibilities should be respected and cared for, although they may not enter into our normal perspectives. I shall name only two here: the recent past history of Jewish suffering during the Nazi persecution, and the Jews' commitment and concern for the land of Israel; this concern is political or secular but also, for many, religious. It belongs, I believe, to an exercise of Christian charity toward one's own brother, with whom we are seeking reconciliation for offenses which are very real, not to gloss lightly over this dimension. To carry the memory of many million deaths is a terrible burden; to have a place under the sun where to live in peace and security, with due respect for the rights of others, is a form of hope. Here we have two important points of reference in the Catholics' day-to-day relation to the Jews.

In fact, it is at this daily level of common living that relations among people of different religions or cultural backgrounds are really placed. We are all convinced, of course, that documents, decisions and deeds at the highest levels of Catholicism, and whatever may be a corresponding level of Judaism, are not only significant but absolutely necessary. A large part of this lecture has been dedicated to making and evaluating this point. But we are equally convinced, or should be, that the real challenge before us is to have those historic acts translated into daily practice and lived out in the lives of human beings. It is readily admitted that a certain amount of divergence between theory, or belief, and behavior is, alas, the common plight of all religious faiths. It is not, however, an excuse to allow matters to remain as they are.

On the Catholic side, with which I am now mainly concerned, I believe there are two main directions to be followed to bridge the gap between belief, or official teaching, and daily practice, always presupposing what I have said about education and its requirements.

The first direction has proved successful in ecumenical relationships, relations namely between Christian churches and communities. It is sometimes called "growing together," but what it really means is that people from different religious backgrounds, in the present case Jews and Christians, who in many places happen to live together, study and work together (ghettos leave only a sad memory), should meet as such. That is to say, they should meet as Jews and Christians, and try to face together, on the basis of what they have in common, as religious men and women, the challenges and issues forming the texture of life in the present world. This implies in its turn that people are religiously committed and that some kind of religious grass-roots organizations, like parishes and synagogues or student groups or whatever, can serve as meeting places and also as irradiating centers. This is already being done in several places with good results. I earnestly hope this will develop elsewhere, and indeed everywhere. Of course the responsibility for this devolves in the first place to the parish priest and the local rabbi, but also, at another level, to the chief rabbi and the local ordinary, or again to some kind of national Jewish organization and the episcopal conference. Each town, province, region or country has to find its own solution, according to local circumstances, which vary greatly from place to place. And we still have to find some other kind of solution, along other lines, for places where there are no Jewish communities, and likewise for Israel, where the Jews form a vast majority. Yet I am convinced that this is a very important way to avoid replacing prejudice and enmity with mutual indifference and mere coexistence, or, what is worse, with another, colder, form of the ancient discriminating practices.

It is also—and this is the second direction I referred to above —the normal presupposition for collaboration, common action, or, if we wish to use a Christian expression, common witness.

Christians and Jews share many religious convictions, which not only conciliar and other documents have made us aware of, but even more so the situation of the present world, where God is absent, human dignity is baffled and oppressed, and hope for the kingdom to come is in danger of becoming an empty word—or an opiate. At different levels of society, whether it be in the case of a local catastrophe, or of some persecuted minority, or still, in a larger perspective, when large sections of the population of a continent languish with famine, or refugees are trying to find for themselves at least a shelter and a bed, Jews and Christians, right across the board, are called in the name of their common biblical heritage to stand up and do something together—also separately, of course, if it proves useful, but mainly together. And this is not only because joint resources become more abundant and more easily organized, but in the first place because we both believe in the God of Abraham, Isaac and Jacob, and of Jesus, and in man his creature and his image. Help and assistance then becomes an act of faith, and, therefore, in the face of the world, but also of God and his angels, a witness to that faith. We all know that this road is already being followed in many places. Let us try to start following it ourselves, if we haven't yet.

I am not blind to the issues such a decision will raise, or has already raised. I shall mention here what I believe is the main such issue, which also becomes, once the twenty years of first encounters have elapsed, one of the major challenges we have to face—if not the greatest. It thus becomes also a significant part of our task for the future. I refer to the *asymmetry* between our Catholic and Jewish communities or, better still, between the church and Judaism. The church is *a church,* a religious community worldwide, oriented mainly to the glory of God and the ministry of salvation of those called to her bosom. It has, as such, no particular ethnic or cultural identity, but every man and woman from any background should feel at home with her. Judaism is a very different matter. While defined by some as an instrument of redemption, it is at the same time, and almost in the same breath, a people with a definite ethnicity, a culture, with an intrinsic reference to a land and a state. These differences should by now be obvious, but it is an open question whether we are well aware, on each side, of all the implications thereof. It means, at the very least, that agendas do not always coincide, priorities are not necessarily the same, and concerns can go very different ways.

Now, if with all this asymmetry we have arrived where we are in our mutual relations, we must gratefully acknowledge that the hand of the Lord is upon us and that we have been abundantly blessed by him.

If the lessons of the past twenty years have taught us, painfully at times, to become more conscious of the differences and the identity proper to each side, it would seem that the task ahead of us must be that of finding ways and means to live together, grow together and witness together, in the respect—and even the appreciation—of such differences.

Catholics are wont to stress the "religious" side of our relationship, as the official title of the holy see's Commission reads, because notwithstanding all political implications and perhaps even entanglements, we are first and foremost a church, a God-oriented community in and through Christ. Jews sometimes stress the political dimensions of their people, because they are one, and no people exists in this world without some form of political identity. Now, if we were not linked as we are, and as Pope John Paul II once said (speech to representatives of Jewish organizations, March 12, 1979) "at the level of our religious identity," it would be well-nigh impossible to establish between us a real religious relationship, namely a brotherhood, given the differences that separate us.

But the fact is that we are linked, and there is no way of denying or obscuring this fact, as we Christians have learned to our loss. So I believe the challenge lying before us in the years ahead, in a world becoming more akin to a desert than to a living place, is to make the most of that link, which is God-given, whatever our differences and divergences. We are divinely called to this, and I fear that if we do not live up to this call we will be faced with severe judgment before the Lord of history. This, I readily grant, may imply for many Catholics, if not all, a real, deep conversion of the heart, or rather a change of it, as Ezekiel prophesied in the sixth century B.C. (Ez 36:26–27)—a conversion indeed made manifest in contrition of many sins committed against the Jewish people.

It is not for me to say what the same decision would imply on the Jewish side. However, I am sure that, whatever that may be, there is only one way to bring us again together, as sons and daughters of Abraham, distinct yet related, asking and receiving forgiveness, reconciled at last. And this is, as in the same vision of Ezekiel, the Spirit of God coming upon us, and, in a way, creating us anew. Because it is only the God of Israel and Jesus, in whom we believe, that can pull all barriers down and put hearts and minds together.

To him we turn, at the end of this lecture, well aware that it will be his gift if, in the years ahead, we shall be able, Christians and Jews, to implement each in his own way, but hopefully together, the vision of *Nostra aetate*.

Cardinal Bea's Attitude
to Relations with the Jews*

It is known that in June 1962 the central preparatory commission of the council had decided not to accept the schema on relations with the Jewish people prepared by the Secretariat for Promoting Christian Unity, and with that the subject was removed from the council's program. It is not known that at the same time the president of the secretariat had written a substantial article for publication in the authoritative Italian Jesuit review *La Civiltà Cattolica* entitled "Are the Jews a Deicide People and 'Cursed by God'?" The article was already set up and had reached the second proof stage when the secretariat asked the cardinal to suppress publication so as not to irritate further the Arab countries. Now at that time the secretariat was a very new organism in the Roman curia and had to safeguard such great subjects as ecumenism and religious freedom, so it was thought better to bow to the anxieties of the secretariat at least for the moment.

Today that article, of which we have the second set of proofs,[1] is a very valuable guide to the cardinal's personal thinking about the matter. While the schema referred to a scarcely filled one printed page, Bea's article tackles the main points of the problem in seventeen closely printed pages. I think it may be interesting to offer some extracts which, in the shape of a thesis, reveal the basic convictions of the president of the secretariat on various aspects of the complex problem.

1. Treatment of these seemed important to the author. With regard to the roots of antisemitism he maintained: "It should not be

* Rome, 1981; see Bibliography, n. 8.

forgotten that this weapon is most often exploited for economic
and social reasons, so that the religious element is only a pretext to
conceal other aims" (l.c. p. 13). But he adds at once: "This does not
explain everything. There is indeed a reason of a psychological,
religious kind: the account of Jesus' passion is continually explained to Christians in the catechism and sermons, and in a sense
relived in the liturgical cycle. This favors the growth of a facile
ambiguity by which, along with spontaneous feelings of sympathy
and love for the innocent Jesus suffering and dying, there arises
insensibly an aversion—to say no more—against the injustice and
the unworthy motives of the persecutors: the envy and other pas-
sions recounted in the gospel" (ibid.). It is important then to examine fully this religious basis and the ambiguity to which it gives rise.

2. For the article's first theme, the accusation of "deicide," the
author first of all explains the concept: "For us Christians Jesus
Christ is certainly the God-man; hence his condemnation and exe-
cution amount, objectively speaking, to a crime of deicide. We
must at once add that the real guilt of deicide could only be im-
puted to those who committed it knowing clearly the divine-
human nature of Christ.[2] The decisive question then is simply this:
What did the sanhedrin and the people who allowed themselves to
be incited by it to call for the condemnation of Jesus really understand about the divine-human nature of Christ?" (l.c. p. 3).

For answer, the writer points to the declaration of the apostles
Peter and Paul, who excuse those responsible as having "acted in
ignorance," "because they did not recognize him nor understand
the utterances of the prophets" (cf. Acts 3:15–17; 8:27). Add too the
prayer for pardon which Christ addressed from the cross to his
Father, giving the reason: "For they know not what they do" (Lk
23:34) (l.c. pp. 3–4). The writer also explains to his Christian
readers the "very great obstacles" which hindered Jesus' contempo-
raries from understanding fully his assertions of his divine dignity
(l.c. pp. 5–6). The cardinal concludes: "The circle of the true actors
in the drama is restricted. . . . The Jews who then lived dispersed
throughout the world cannot be accused of the grave crime of deicide, still less their descendants throughout history" (ibid.).

The accusation of deicide can however be understood in the
broader sense of "killing of the innocent." Here again the author

applied the same words of Peter and Paul and of Jesus himself and concludes: "We too with the apostles, while admitting a certain general guilt in some, without singling out anybody, follow the example of Jesus and hence do not sit in judgment, leaving the thing to the verdict of God alone, and making Jesus' charitable words of excuse our own" (l.c. p. 9). And again he adds: "Even less do we set ourselves as accusers of the Jewish people as such, least of all those who today live dispersed throughout the world" (ibid.).

3. The writer then goes on to examine the conclusion, sometimes drawn from the heavy chastisement inflicted on the Jewish people, that "it is accursed by God" (l.c. p. 10). He answers vigorously: "This is a most grave offense less against the chosen people, than against truth itself, against God's fidelity to his promises, against the Lord's infinite mercy and love" (l.c. p. 11). This is supported especially from Romans 11. In confirmation of his reply the author explains the deeper meaning of the sad vicissitudes of Jewish history: "Even in what seems merely very heavy punishment inflicted by God, his most merciful intentions . . . are hidden; even in suffering, this people is and continues to be a bearer of divine revelation. In its history the severity and the mercy of God are revealed, and the Lord's goodness to other races to which, through no merit of theirs, he has granted a share in the salvation promised directly to Israel. In other words, in its very sufferings the Jewish people remains a valuable instrument of God's merciful designs for mankind; it carries on and fulfills its mission in the world" (l.c. p. 12).

4. We have seen the profound motives the author gives Christians for changing their attitude to the Jewish people. They are not merely humanitarian reasons; they come from the very heart of the Christian message, from the example of charity given by Christ and his apostles, and have that much more force for the Christian reader. The author links them also with the theme, so topical at that moment, of the renewal the church was trying to achieve in the council.

To these motives he adds that of gratitude. Most urgent, he says, is "the duty of charity toward these people who are our ancestors according to the spirit; it is something like the gratitude we owe to those who have given us life, but so much the more profound as the gifts we have received from God through this people are greater, more sublime, more decisive, being spiritual and supernatural. . . . Through the Jewish people we have received the word of God written and preached, the church, Christ himself and his blessed mother, our mother!" (l.c. p. 16).

The writer sums up by quoting the significant words—of which only the last phrase is generally known—spoken by Pius XI in 1938, when in two countries antisemitism was in full swing:

> At the most solemn moment of the mass we recite the prayer which contains the expression "sacrifice of Abel, sacrifice of Abraham, sacrifice of Melchisedek" in three strokes, three times, three steps, the entire religious history of mankind. . . . A magnificent passage. Every time we read it we are seized by an irresistible emotion. The sacrifice of our patriarch Abraham. Note that Abraham is called our patriarch, our ancestor. Antisemitism is incompatible with the thought and the sublime reality expressed in this text. It is alien to us, a movement in which we Christians can have no part. The promise was made to Abraham and to his descendants. It is realized in Christ, and through Christ in us who are members of his mystical body. Through Christ and in Christ we are the spiritual descendants of Abraham. No, it is not possible for Christians to take part in antisemitism. We acknowledge for all the right to defend themselves, to adopt measures of protection against what threatens their legitimate interests. But antisemitism is inadmissible. Spiritually we are Semites.[3]

Hearing these extracts some may regret that the article was not published at the time. That is understandable, but it should be said at once that in spite of everything the article has in a sense borne fruit. I will tell you how. It was to have appeared simultaneously in the German review *Stimmen der Zeit* and in French in the *Nouvelle Revue Théologique* of Louvain as well as *Civiltà Cattolica*. When this last publication was blocked, *Stimmen der Zeit* insisted on having the text. They were told they could have it on condition that someone else signed the article. Thus it came about that Fr. Ludwig von Hertling, S.J., a member of the staff of the review who had in his time taught church history at the Gregorian, agreed to do this. He reworked the materials a little in his own style, but the substance remained. The article came out in October 1962.[4] Von Hertling admitted that he had never had so many reactions to his articles before.

Things did not stop there. The article was ferreted out by a Genoese Jew, Raffaele Nahum, who got permission to have it translated and published in several languages: English, French and Italian. In the autumn of 1963 he had it distributed among the council fathers. By this route the substance of the cardinal's work came to exercise an important influence on the outlook of the council fathers.

Apart from this, more important perhaps was what the preparation of the article meant for Bea personally. He deepened his understanding of the problem and reached the fundamental convictions which were to move him for the future. They inspired him, in December 1962, to propose to John XXIII to reintroduce the subject into the council program—a proposal which succeeded. On the basis of this deeper understanding—leaving aside the fact that the problem was an exegetical one—he reserved to himself the presenting of the draft to the council, and even reserved to himself the preparation of the text of the relatio with which he presented it. In this, far from confining himself to a formal introduction, he expounded the whole problem in all its aspects. In fact the relatio has many points of contact with the article I have been discussing.[5] In other words, the article was the true and profound preparation for sustaining, in the council and in public, with deep conviction and lively commitment, the project of the declaration on non-Christian religions until its final approval. The same preparation inspired his full commentary on the Declaration, which appeared in six languages.[6]

III.

The Pope
and
the Jews

John Paul II and the Jews 1978–1988*

The new pope's first public gesture toward the Jews came on March 12, 1979 when John Paul II received in audience a delegation of the International Jewish Committee for Interreligious Consultations (IJCIC) headed by Philip M. Klutznick, president of the World Jewish Congress. The words he pronounced on that first occasion already made it clear that, continuing along the road opened by the council, he intended to promote the dialogue of the Catholic Church with the Jewish people with both vigor and rigor in a perspective of universal spiritual service: "I believe that both sides must continue their strong efforts to overcome the difficulties of the past, so as to fulfill God's commandment of love and to sustain a truly fruitful and fraternal dialogue that contributes to the good of each of the partners involved and to our better service of humanity. Just how serious and profound a programmatic commitment the pope was expressing at the beginning of his pontificate was to be brought out in a quite unmistakable manner by the admirable flowering of encounters, significant gestures, moments of prayer, theological dialogues and visits that have characterized—and in an altogether unprecedented manner as regards both intensity and quality—the relations between the pope and the Jews during these first ten years of supreme pastoral responsibility for the church.

At the root of this attitude of delicate attention, which recalls Maritain's "thoughtfulness," a human echo of divine predilection, there undoubtedly lies the painful personal experience of the young Karol Wojtyla who, in a Poland smarting under Nazi oppression, witnessed the martyrdom of the Jewish people, as also of his own people. Often the pope has recalled the shoah with accents of great

* Vatican City, 1988; see Bibliography, n. 17.

65

emotion, as on the occasion when, at Auschwitz on June 7, 1979, with a symbolic gesture, he insisted on stopping in front of the tablet that bears the inscription to the Jewish victims exterminated in the camp, saying: "It is not permissible for anyone to pass by this inscription with indifference." It is a dutiful memorial, a meditation about history, a suffered silence; in one respect, it invites us to reflect about the massacre of the Jewish people, evoked in Yiddish in the following words: "Warsaw, Old Warsaw, Jewish Warsaw, Brimful like a temple on a day of feast, Like a market place when a fair is on; Warsaw, with your Jews going about their business, Praying in the synagogues. . . . You are empty now, empty. . . . Not even the dead have remained" (Itzhak Katzenelson, died at Auschwitz, 1944). One can hardly think of these and the memories they evoke without recalling also the heart-rending notes of Ani Ma'amin ("I believe") struck up by the concentration camp survivors in Rome's synagogue on April 13, 1986, when—for the first time after twenty centuries—the pope came to visit the very ancient Jewish community in Rome.

CONDEMNATION OF ANTISEMITISM

From this deep-rooted awareness there springs a second fundamental theme ever present in the pope's teaching: the condemnation of every form of antisemitism and the commitment to fight and extirpate it wherever it may rear its head. The texts that one could quote to bear this out have long since become legion, but among the most important there are his words in Sidney (November 26, 1986): "No valid theological justification could ever be found for acts of discrimination or persecution against Jews," and those of Strasbourg (October 9, 1988): "All antisemitism and racism is opposed to the principles of Christianity, and . . . there exists no justification for them in the cultures that wish to base themselves on these principles. For the same reasons, we must set aside all religious prejudice which history has shown us to be inspired by anti-Jewish stereotypes, or in conflict with the dignity of the human person."

Looking further afield, searching for the reasons underlying the pope's extraordinary commitment, his confidence and benevolence vis-à-vis the Jews, we shall find it in his passion for the an-

nouncement of the gospel, in love for the church and, even more
so, for Christ, *redemptor hominis,* "Jew, crucified and glorified":
"At the dawn of a new millennium, the church in announcing the
gospel of Jesus Christ to Europe discovers ever more, and with joy,
the common values, Christian and Jewish, through which we recognize each other as brothers" (Strasbourg, loc. cit.). And this is said
—as the pope invariably underscores—"within the greatest respect
for Jewish religious identity," without the slightest trace of proselytism, with the intention of mutual spiritual edification, in witness
and in praise of the holy name of God. This relationship between
the church, Jesus Christ and the people of Israel has its roots in the
mystery of the election for salvation, just as the council affirmed
(*Lumen gentium,* 16; *Nostra aetate,* 4), and the Pope does not
hesitate to scrutinize the mystery of the redemption to conclude
that the Jews are "our beloved brothers and, in a certain way, our
elder brothers" (April 13, 1986), "in the faith of Abraham" (December 31, 1986).

And hence his anxiety to promote competent theological research into this aspect of the permanent value of the old covenant,
his constant readiness to receive groups of Jews and Christians
committed in this field. It should here be recalled that it was during
his pontificate, in 1983, that the ancient liturgical prayer "for the
Jews," which after the 1973 reform had been changed to "who were
once the chosen people," was revised a second time and now asserts: "so that thy first-born people of the covenant may attain to
the fullness of redemption."

A FRATERNAL DIALOGUE

To this end, John Paul II keeps exhorting the competent institutions both of the church's central government and at the local
level to do their work with solicitude. Thus the holy see's Commission for Religious Relations with the Jews published a second document about application of the council's directives entitled "Notes
on the Correct Way To Present Jews and Judaism in Preaching
and Catechesis in the Catholic Church," while the International
Catholic-Jewish Liaison Committee met in five plenary sessions
between 1979 and 1985 and in 1988 published the proceedings of
the twelve meetings held between the council and today (*Fifteen*

Years of Catholic-Jewish Dialogue. 1970–1985. Selected Papers).
Nor should one forget the pope's initiative for World Prayer Day
(October 27, 1986), when a Jewish delegation headed by the chief
rabbi of Rome, Professor Elio Toaff, participated in the prayer for
peace at Assisi.

At the local level, no matter where his apostolic pilgrimages
bring him, the pope takes every opportunity of meeting members
of the Jewish communities, arousing interest for the fraternal dialogue, opening new dimensions, soliciting concrete collaboration
in the fields of justice and peace, education of the young, social and
family life, and the right to life and religious liberty. These meetings
have been stepped up at quite an extraordinary rate ever since the
historic visit to the Rome synagogue; in the two years that have
passed there have been as many as ten meetings, at Lyons, Sidney,
Buenos Aires, Cologne, Warsaw, Miami, Los Angeles, La Paz,
Vienna, and Strasbourg.

JERUSALEM AND THE HOLY LAND

Lastly, one can hardly conclude this brief overview without a
reference to Jerusalem and the holy land. Ever since 1979, in the
first audience mentioned above, John Paul II explicitly recalled the
example of Paul VI: "I intend to foster spiritual dialogue and to do
everything in my power for the peace of that land, which is holy for
you as it is for us, with the hope that the city of Jerusalem will be
effectively guaranteed as a center of harmony for the followers of
the three great monotheist religions." On several occasions, twice
in 1980 (at Rome and at Otranto) and in the apostolic letter *Redemptionis Anno* (1984), the pope briefly outlined his conceptions
in connection with Jerusalem and the land of Israel. He recognizes
the uniqueness of Jerusalem: "It is truly a unique city in the world,"
the city of Moriah and Zion, the Kotel, the Aqsa (the farthest temple), and Christ's Passover (September 18, 1980). He prays for the
peace and the reconciliation of the "Jewish people who live in the
state of Israel," but always recalling also "the Palestinian people . . .
all the peoples of the Middle East . . . the Lebanon so sorely tried"
(*Redemptionis Anno*).

On September 1, 1987 at Castel Gandolfo, when receiving a
delegation of world Jewry for the second time, the pope welcomed

its members "as representatives of the Jewish people, to whom the existence of Israel is central." One can thus readily understand the brief judgment expressed by Gerhart M. Rieger, an authoritative Jew, in a recent volume entitled *John Paul II: Ten Years of Pontificate:* "I am firmly convinced that the development of Catholic-Jewish relations is an important chapter of the recent papacy. . . . Let me express the hope that the second decade of the pontificate may continue to be inspired by the ideals of John Paul II as pronounced in his memorable speech in the Rome synagogue, furthering Catholic-Jewish relations in full respect of the identity of both our communities."

IV.

Thematic Essays
(1977–1990)

Catechesis and Judaism*

It seems important that, in a discussion on catechesis, especially for young people and children, as is going on in this assembly of the synod, the question of the image of Judaism in catechetical teaching is raised. The reason is twofold: on the one hand, it is impossible—theologically and practically—to present Christianity without referring to Judaism, at least as it is found in the pages of the Old Testament, and also as it really was at the time of the New Testament, and, on the other hand, because the image of Judaism used to illustrate Christianity in Christian teaching is seldom exact, faithful and respectful of the theological and historical reality of Judaism.

For these reasons it seems useful to offer some material, taken from official documents of the church, on how to present Judaism in our catechetical teaching.

The Second Vatican Council, after a general presentation of the relations between Christianity and Judaism, states (cf. Declaration *Nostra aetate,* "De ecclesiae habitudine ad religiones non-christianas," n. 4): "Ideo curent omnes ne in catechesi et in verbi Dei praedicatione habenda quidquam doceant, quod cum veritate evangelica et spiritu Christi non congruat."

This principle appears as a conclusion of the previous developments in which some very practical points emerge, which are taken up by the recent *Guidelines and Suggestions for Implementing the Conciliar Declaration "Nostra aetate" (n. 4),* published by the Commission for Religious Relations with the Jews, on December 1, 1974.

1. A first point of great importance is the relation of one Tes-

* Vatican City, 1977; see Bibliography, n. 3.

tament to the other. A catechesis which would not found the revelation of the New Testament upon the revelation of the Old Testament would be a false one. Indeed it would be in serious danger of incurring the Marcionite heresy, because, as the Second Vatican Council says: "Ecclesia enim Christi agnoscit fidei et electionis suae initia iam apud Patriarchas, Moysen et Prophetas, iuxta salutare Dei mysterium, inveniri." And the *Guidelines* (Par. III) say specifically: "The Old Testament and the Jewish tradition founded on it must not be set against the New Testament in such a way that the former seems to constitute a religion of only justice, fear and legalism, with no appeal to the love of God and neighbor (cf. Dt 6:5; Lv 19:18; Mt 22:34–40)." In fact: "The New Testament is profoundly marked by its relation to the Old." The continuity of both Testaments in God's plan, with all respect for the plenitude found in the New Testament, must be a guiding principle in cathechesis.

2. Another point of great practical value regards the presentation of Judaism in the time of the New Testament and as a necessary background for the interpretation of the gospels. On these points the *Guidelines* state: "Judaism in the time of Christ and the apostles was a complex reality, embracing many different trends, many spiritual, religious, social and cultural values." Therefore all simplification in the presentation of the facts, groups and persons mentioned in the New Testament must be carefully avoided. The *Guidelines* say in another place (II): "With respect to liturgical readings, care will be taken to see that homilies based on them will not distort their meaning, especially when it is a question of passages which seem to show the Jewish people as such in an unfavorable light." And, in a note (I), two important references are made: "Thus the formula 'the Jews' in St. John sometimes according to the context means 'the leaders of the Jews,' or 'the adversaries of Jesus,' terms which express better the thought of the evangelist and avoid appearing to arraign the Jewish people as such. Another example is the use of the words 'Pharisee' and 'Pharisaism' which have taken on a largely pejorative meaning." Apropos the last question, scholars distinguish at least seven classes of Pharisees for the time of the New Testament.

3. There is still another delicate point regarding the interpretation of the New Testament which was taken up by the council and the *Guidelines*. It is the responsibility for the death of Jesus.

This point comes out necessarily in any catechesis on the life of our Lord or the history of redemption. On this the council has this to say: "Etsi auctoritates Iudaeorum cum suis asseclis mortem Christi urserunt, tamen ea quae in passione Eius perpetrata sunt nec omnibus indistincte Iudaeis tunc viventibus, nec Iudaeis hodiernis imputari possunt." And it goes on to say: "Ceterum Christus, uti semper tenuit et tenet Ecclesia, propter peccata omnium hominum voluntarie passionem suam et mortem immensa caritate obiit, ut omnes salutem consequantur," thus giving the exact theological meaning of the death of our Lord. The *Guidelines* (III) repeat the first quote as one of the "facts" that "deserve to be recalled."

4. As a consequence of this last point, another reference made by the council is quite worth recalling here for the use of catechesis. It brings the question of the image of the Jewish people for Christians. The text says: "Licet autem Ecclesia sit novus populus Dei, Iudaei tamen neque ut a Deo reprobati neque ut maledicti exhibeantur, quasi hoc ex Sacris Litteris sequatur." Already the Dogmatic Constitution on the Church *Lumen gentium* had said (n. 16): "In primis quidem populus ille cui data fuerunt testamenta et promissa et ex quo Christus ortus est secundum carnem (cf. Rom 9:4–5), populus secundum electionem carissimus propter patres: sine poenitentia sunt dona et vocationes Dei (cf. Rom 11:28–29)." On this the *Guidelines* comment appropriately (III): "The history of Judaism did not end with the destruction of Jerusalem, but rather went on to develop a religious tradition. And although we believe that the importance and meaning of that tradition were deeply affected by the coming of Christ, it is still nonetheless rich in religious values." Therefore, Judaism should not be presented as a dead or useless religion.

Grounded upon these facts, the Commission for Religious Relations with the Jews, created by the holy father in October 1974, tries to relate to the episcopal conferences to serve them in this important matter of the implementation of the conciliar Declaration *Nostra aetate* (n. 4). But it also has tried to relate to Judaism in an official way so as to bring about the desired reconciliation between both religions which have so much in common. To this end a Liaison Committee was created, even before the existence of the Commission itself, with the main Jewish organizations, which is already in the sixth session. Many important questions have been discussed frankly and fraternally in these sessions. It is relevant to note for the present discussion that the following meeting, fixed for next year, has as its main subject the image of each religion in the teaching system of the other one.

We sincerely hope, with the help of our Lord, that these facts and ideas will promote a better image in the catechetical teaching of the Roman Catholic Church as well as a growing and more fraternal relationship among all the "sons of Abraham" (cf. Rom 4:11–12).

Are the New Testament and Christianity Antisemitic?*

It is a pleasure and an honor for me, as president of the holy see's Commission for Religious Relations with the Jews, to lecture in this Oxford Society, at the same podium at which many illustrious personalities have already spoken. Let me express the hope at the outset that in this year, during which we celebrate the twentieth anniversary of the promulgation of the conciliar Declaration *Nostra aetate* on the relations between the church and the non-Christian religions, precisely my talk may help to improve still more the relations between the church and the Jewish people, and also eventually to dispel certain stereotypes sometimes heard about the church and her teaching of Judaism. Along these lines it would be good to keep in mind the words of Pope John Paul II spoken during his visit to the great synagogue of Rome on April 13, 1986:

> It is necessary to say that the path undertaken is still at the beginning, and therefore a considerable amount of time will still be needed, notwithstanding the great efforts already made on both sides, to remove all forms of prejudice, even subtle ones, to readjust every manner of self-expression and therefore to present always and everywhere, to ourselves and to others, the true face of the Jews and of Judaism, as likewise of Christians and of Christianity, and this at every level of outlook, teaching and communication (*Information Service,* 60, 1986/ 1–II, pp. 27–28).

Before entering into the substance of the response I intend to give to this question, I think it necessary to dwell for a moment on

* Oxford, 1985 and Rome, 1986; see Bibliography, nn. 10 and 14.

77

the context and terms of the question, on its wider and more general meaning, asking thereby an even more radical question: "Are the New Testament and Christianity antisemitic?"

1. One could ask, to begin with: What does the word "Christianity" mean in this context? Does it mean a body of belief and practice or, as the time-honored Latin expression goes, *fides et mores?*

2. Does it mean, instead, a certain cultural world, more or less inspired by such belief and practices?

3. Again, does it mean a group of men and women, in a certain moment of history, who are held to be somehow linked to the Christian faith?

These three meanings, while connected among themselves, do not exactly overlap. In the same way it could also be asked: What does "antisemitic" mean in the question above?

1. Is it the original "racist" sense, intended by W. Marr, who first coined the term in the last years of the nineteenth century (1879)?

2. Or is it meant in a broader sense, including prejudices and stereotypes against Jews and Judaism, more or less religiously inspired?

3. Or is it meant in a yet broader sense, with political overtones?

In the face of all this, I am convinced that to answer in a straightforward way the question in the title of this lecture, some ambiguities ought first to be dispelled. In order to do this in an orderly fashion, I shall proceed step by step. First, however, I shall propose a kind of thesis, namely: If "Christianity" is taken to mean the distinctive body of Christian faith and practice, as professed and lived out, albeit imperfectly, in the Christian churches, it cannot be said that Christianity is "antisemitic."

But I must immediately add that "antisemitic," in the last sentence of this thesis, should be understood in the first and in the second sense spelled out above (racism, religious prejudice).

Let me now try to prove, or illustrate, this thesis:

1. As the normative text for Christianity is the Bible, as the word of God, and particularly (but not exclusively) the New Testament part of the Bible, I would like to start by considering the fundamental question: Is the *New Testament* antisemitic?

As you are well aware, this question has been answered in the affirmative, and, it is only honest to say, more by Christian than by Jewish scholars.

Regarding this question, the following points should be carefully weighed:

   (a) The New Testament (=NT) contains a series of "prosemitic" statements, which I would like quickly to refer to here, without in any way listing them all:

In the gospel of Luke we find two extremely important hymns of praise, one attributed to Mary (the *Magnificat*) and the other to the priest Zechariah (the *Benedictus*). Both of these are fully intelligible only in the Jewish context of passionate waiting for a savior.

In the first canticle, the *Magnificat,* the Virgin Mary rejoices because the Lord "has helped his servant Israel in remembrance of his mercy" (Lk 1:54).

In the second canticle, the *Benedictus,* the father of John the Baptist blesses "the Lord God of Israel, for he has looked favorably on his people and redeemed them" (Lk 1:68).

These affirmations, which follow each other and are intertwined, are based on the Old Testament literary form of *midrash.* They cannot be understood without an extremely positive attitude toward the mystery of Israel and its election in relation to the eternal covenant of salvation for all peoples.

The same could be said for the canticle of Simeon in Luke 2:29–32, and, even if it is less explicit, for the affirmation of John 4:22: "Salvation is from the Jews."

Paul twice goes out of his way to profess his attachment to Judaism: in Romans 9:1–5, of which I shall only quote verbatim this verse: "Indeed, I could even wish to be separated from Christ (*anathema*, in the Greek text) for the sake of my brothers, my kinsmen, the Israelites," and in Philippians 3:4–6: "I was circumcised on the eighth day, being of the stock of Israel, a Hebrew of Hebrew origin."

And, last but not least, Luke's (a Gentile!) remarkably positive presentation of the Jewish way of worship, and/or the Jewish way of life, in his narrative of the infancy of Christ (cf. Lk 2:21, 22–38, etc.), and in his narrative of the nascent church (cf. Acts 3:1; 5:41–42). Are not both these careful descriptions, parallel one to the other, a way of affirming the Jewish matrix of the Lord and his church, however artful Luke's literary construction may be thought to be?

(b) At a still *deeper* level, the writers of the NT quite consciously place Jesus and his mission in the continuation of the Old Testament (=OT) *and* the contemporary Jewish tradition. Before I get to the specific points following hereafter, I would like to stress this last reference to the "Jewish tradition." It should be borne in mind that between the last books of the OT in Hebrew (and Aramaic), or Greek, and the first written texts of the NT there is a whole period, called for this reason "intertestamental," with a rich and varied literature and with oral traditions, some of which have been revealed to us by the so-called Dead Sea Scrolls and other recent manuscript discoveries. This variegated body, or rather bodies, of Jewish religious and cultural expression should be considered carefully when the relationship between the Second and the First Testament is assessed: between one and the other, or more concretely between the last OT writings and Jesus, stands all this multiple oral and literary material, which sometimes helps to explain what in the Jewish background of the NT does not find a clear enough explanation in the OT.

I shall also list here—as I did above—some text or themes, without at all trying to be exhaustive.

Jesus' Jewish origins and attachments are revealed, not dissimulated, even to the Gentiles, who knew, most of them at least, next to nothing about Judaism. The text to be highlighted in this connection is Romans 1:1–4 ("The Son of God, descended from *David* according to the flesh"). Luke, chapters 1 and 2, already mentioned, belong here too. Thus the most ancient kerygmatic presentation of Jesus, Son of man and Son of God, included an explicit reference to his Jewishness.

Jesus' mission was directed in the first place to Israel. The gospel writers are very much aware of this and even make an explicit formulation of this point when it is a question of opening up that mission to the Gentiles. See Matthew 15:24 in the story of the Canaanite woman: "My mission is only to the lost sheep of the house of Israel." The apostles, also in their first mission, are enjoined to do exactly the same: "Do not visit pagan territory and do not enter a Samaritan town. Go instead after the lost sheep of the house of Israel" (Mt 10:5–6).

This order of mission was scrupulously kept by the apostles after the resurrection, as it is easy to see in the book of Acts, where Paul always starts his apostolic visits in the local synagogue (e.g. 13:5 and passim), but also in the programmatic assertion of the same Paul in Romans 1:17: "[The gospel] is the power of God leading . . . to salvation, the Jew first, then the Greek."

It could be said, quite truly, that this preference or priority (if not exclusiveness, in Jesus' own mission) is expressed later on by Paul in his well-known parable of the wild olive branches grafted onto the good olive tree (cf. Rom 11:12ff).

In this same connection, one should point to all such texts where the NT writer finds the confirmation of, or, if you wish, the foundation of Jesus' identity and mission, in "the law, the prophets and the psalms" (Lk 24:44 etc.).

May I add here that this is why the universal church, as articulated by Irenaeus in the east and Tertullian in the west, so decidedly and unhesitatingly rejected Marcion and Marcionism. If one tries to cut off the NT from the OT, it will soon be obvious that also the NT goes asunder. Thus Paul found it quite natural to affirm, at the end of chapter 3 of Romans: "Are we then abolishing the law by means of faith? Not at all! On the contrary, we are confirming the law" (v. 31), as the law confirms Christ.

Let us conclude this reflection on the person and the mission of Jesus with a few words from the *Notes:*

> Jesus was and always remained a Jew. . . . Jesus is fully a man of his time and of his environment—the Jewish Palestinian one of the first century, the anxieties and hopes of which he shared. This cannot but underline the reality of the incarnation and the very meaning of the history of salvation (*Notes,* III, 20).

(c) It would be rather easy to extend the former section to the main concepts, imagery and language of the NT. They come first and foremost from the OT.

There was a time in biblical scholarship when the trend was to read and interpret the NT writing in the light of Greek, or rather late Hellenistic, culture and religion. This trend has not entirely died out. But I think it is only fair to say that what is seen and appreciated now by scholars is the deep, essential Jewish character of the NT. To illustrate briefly this change of orientation, I shall mention just two items:

(a) the interpretation of the book of Revelation in the light of biblical apocalyptic imagery, taken almost intact from Isaiah 6, Ezekiel 1 and 10, and Daniel (*passim*), with besides a real influx from Jewish apocalyptic writings. Moreover, the entire structure of the book of Revelation draws upon and describes many elements from the liturgy of the heavenly Jerusalem, referring to the indispensable model of the solemn liturgy of the temple. Thus it is impossible to read and understand these texts without a knowledge of and respect for the liturgical and apocalyptic-messianic tradition of Judaism.

(b) messianic titles, however, reinterpreted and given a new meaning in the NT, *all* come from the OT, or the Hebrew Bible, while a title like "Son of man," notwithstanding the many problems connected with it, has some kind of relation to the same title in contemporary Jewish apocalyptic literature (the Book of Enoch).

At this point we could perhaps draw a first, provisional, conclusion: To affirm that the NT is "antisemitic" would be tantamount to affirming that it is, in itself, contradictory. In fact, it is not at all easy to find a book more "semitic" or more Jewish than the NT. To try to tear off from the NT its "semitic" substance would simply mean to destroy it, lock, stock and barrel. I recall here again Marcion's self-defeating enterprise and the church's reaction against it.

Now Christianity, in the first sense indicated above, embodies the NT.

2. But let us make another more difficult step: Does the NT contain "antisemitic" statements? No doubt, while affirming with utmost energy, as I just did, the Jewishness of Jesus and of the writings witnessing to him, I must—in all honesty—face the objections which might spring from the texts of those same books, and see if they would make us change my thesis.

Let me consider some of them at least, first by listing them, then by trying to deal with the challenge they present.

(a) There are in the NT some affirmations which, at first sight, seem, at the very least, critical of and negative toward the Jews, such as 1 Thessalonians 2:14–16: "For you, brothers and sisters, became imitators of the churches of God in Christ Jesus that are in Judea, for you suffered the same things from your own compatriots as they did from the Jews, who killed both the Lord Jesus and the prophets, and drove us out; they displease God and oppose everyone by hindering us from speaking to the Gentiles so that they may be saved. Thus they have constantly been filling up the measure of their sins; but God's wrath has overtaken them at last"), and Matthew 27:25: "Let his blood be on us and on our children."

(b) Some texts, if not complete books, of the NT present "the Jews" in an unfavorable light. The case in point, as is known to all, is the gospel of John, where "the Jews" appear mostly (but not always) as the *opposers* of Jesus' person and mission, entirely closed to both and indeed because of an obvious lack of good will (or "blindness"; cf. the story of the man born blind in chapter 9, which could be taken as paradigmatic).

(c) The Pharisees are also frequently (but again not always) pictured as forming a very negative, hypocritical, falsely religious group, a presentation which, unfortunately, has contributed to giving to that name, in many languages, a decisively derogatory ring —quite unjustly, in the opinion of many, not only Jews but also Christians.

What could, or should, be said of such texts and pictures, to which more could be added?

In fact, it must be admitted that texts such as these have had a long-lasting negative effect on the Christian view of Jews and Judaism. In fact, it must also be admitted that they have had "antisemitic" consequences. Still, if we are to keep to the terms of the question which gives its title to this lecture, it cannot be said, because of this, that either the NT or Christianity as such (in the sense explained above) is "antisemitic." These texts and descriptions do not, in any way, cancel or modify the other, positive thrust of the NT regarding matters Jewish. It is true that they are there, and have to be explained (not explained away), but they do not put into question the fundamental Jewishness, not only of Jesus, but of the NT *as such,* Paul included. Indeed, it is in light of this basic Jewishness that such texts should be read and interpreted, and not, most certainly not, the other way around.

It is here perhaps that a certain Christian tradition may be found to be defective. For centuries an image of Jews and Judaism has been projected which was inspired mostly, if not exclusively, by such negative references. The positive thrust was never forgotten (as I shall point out later on); what we are trying to do now, after the Declaration *Nostra aetate,* No. 4, and the 1974 *Guidelines and Suggestions* for its implementation, is to link with that truer, normative past, always living in the NT, according to the spirit and the principles expressed in the fourth chapter of the *Notes:* "The Jews and the New Testament."

After having said this, I now turn to the problematic texts and descriptions I have referred to:

(a) If "the Jews" are criticized, I am not aware of any radical condemnation, or even criticism, of Judaism, as it was known and practiced at that time. Even Paul's severe critique of the law presupposes always that the law is "good" in itself, which he says explicitly, at least twice (cf. Rom 7:7. 12; 1 Tim 1:8). The epistle to the Hebrews speaks mostly about what we have called later the "ceremonial" law and that aspect of the Mosaic covenant (not the Abrahamic one) which deals with worship (cf. e.g. 8:13).

(b) This is why it was not held to be contradictory, much less "un-Christian," to participate in the temple worship and ceremonies, even after the resurrection, let alone before (cf. e.g. Acts 3:1; Jn 10:21 and *passim*), even by Paul himself (cf. Acts 21:26ff). This of course ended with the complete separation between Judaism and Christianity. But still it was never canceled from our sources, or rather not omitted when those were put into writing, which happened many years after the facts.

(c) It cannot be said that Paul's text in 1 Thessalonians 2:15, notwithstanding its harsh language, implies that *all* the Jews then and since are guilty of the death of Christ. However this text may be explained, it most certainly does not mean this. "Deicide" has never been taught by the NT (nor the Christian church as such, for that matter). Paul says very clearly in 1 Corinthians 2:8: "None of the rulers of this age knew the mystery: if they had known it, they would never have crucified the Lord of glory." The same Paul is quite conscious that Jesus died "because of our sins" (Rom 4:25), "in accordance with the scriptures" (1 Cor 15:3). And at this theological level, it is we, the believers in Christ, who truly crucify him, then, and again when we are unfaithful to him. This was said, in sculptural terms, in the letter to the Hebrews (6:4–6) and taken up, to be learned by all concerned, in the catechism of the Council of Trent (Pars I, quaest. V, cap. XI). The passage in Hebrews to which the catechism text explicitly refers may be quoted here: "For when men have once been enlightened and have tasted the heavenly gift and become sharers in the Holy Spirit . . . and then have fallen away, it is impossible to make them repent again, since *they are crucifying the Son of God* for themselves and holding him up to contempt."

It is to be noted too that in the profession of faith, the Credo, which all Christians recite frequently, especially in the celebration of the central sacraments of the faith, baptism and eucharist, and which they hold as their distinctive mark, Jesus is said to have suffered "under Pontius Pilate," with no mention being made of the Jews. This profession of faith, as is well known, comes from the very earliest times of the Christian church. This, of course, does not solve historical questions about *who* is responsible for *what* in the death of Jesus. Here, as you are well aware, there are different interpretations of the gospel evidence, according to the different degrees of weight it is given by individual exegetes and Bible scholars. I shall not enter here into such a discussion. Suffice it to say that many interpreters, if not most, hold that some intervention of the Jewish leaders is required to adequately explain what is found in an admittedly difficult and much worked over account, which we know in three, if not four, different versions (the synoptics and John). It is also generally accepted that the final decision rested with the Roman procurator, the Jewish leaders being deprived at that time of the right of sentencing somebody to death (*ius gladii*). And it must be added that it is not altogether clear (as sometimes said) that Pontius Pilate, as an irresolute weakling, was pushed or forced to the fateful decision of crucifying Jesus by an angry, excited Jewish mob. He was not that kind of man, according to what we know from other sources. He certainly knew what he was doing and did it with conscious will of humiliating the Jews and their authorities: "Look at your king" (Jn 19:14), he says to them when he is about to condemn Jesus to death after having had him scourged. And exactly the same description he wanted written on *titulus crucis* for all to see and ponder, refusing moreover to have it changed when the authorities ask him to do so, for good reason: "What I have written, I have written" (Jn 19:22).

It is this considered opinion which has been taken up by the Second Vatican Council, in *Nostra aetate,* No. 4, when it says: "True, the Jewish authorities and those who followed their lead pressed for the death of Christ." But this is not to place any blame on the Jewish people as such, whether in that time or thereafter. Rather the contrary, because the council goes on to say: "Still, what happened in his passion cannot be charged against all the Jews, without distinction, of that time, nor against the Jews of to-day" (ibid.).

At the historical level, we observe that the authors of the gospels give support to this idea when they report that it was necessary to await favorable circumstances for the secret arrest of Jesus, because the crowd of Jews would certainly not have permitted the arrest of a prophet in public (Lk 22:2 and parallels in Jn 18:3, Mk 14:49, Mt 26:4–5). The same great number of people with crying women among them followed Jesus to Calvary, as Luke testifies (23:27).

Theologically, this is a decisive statement, with magisterial (conciliar) authority. It should lay to rest any controversy on this particular point still existing among Catholics.

The conciliar statement, which implies a certain reading of scripture and the scriptural data, gives us the key to interpret Matthew 27:25, "Let his blood be on us and on our children." Whatever the right meaning of this text (and the explanation for its presence *only* in Matthew), it is certainly *not* that all the Jews, till the end of time, if not converted, carry upon themselves the guilt for the death of Christ and are punished for it.

In any case, the blood of Jesus is blood which cries out not for revenge, but for forgiveness (cf. Franz Mussner, *Traktat über die Juden,* München: Kosel 1979, pp. 309–310); it is blood which redeems, according to the reference to Isaiah 53:11, and thus "for all," as it has been translated in the eucharistic prayer ("shed for you and for all").

This is blood for expiation, which refers to the aspersion ceremony of Kippur (Lv 16:3–18) performed by the high priest. A typological interpretation of this and many other important elements is provided in the letter to the Hebrews. But an exploration of the question of a correct typology as called for in Chapter II of the *Notes* would require another conference.

(d) For the same reason, it cannot be said, *according* to NT teaching, that all "Jews" (that is, the Jewish people) stand under damnation and therefore are, again as such, rejected by God. The council, also on this delicate point, has given us the clue for a correct reading of holy scripture, by saying, "The Jews should not be presented as rejected or accursed by God, as if this followed from the holy scriptures" (*Nostra aetate,* No. 4). "The Lord will judge each one 'according to his own works,' Jews and Christians alike (cf. Rom 2:6)" (John Paul II, Discourse at the Synagogue in Rome, *Information Service,* 60, p. 27).

Negative and ambiguous texts, which seem to mean this, are to be read in the light of the general positive thrust of the NT regarding Judaism, to which I have referred above, but also in the light of more positive, unambiguous texts, which say the opposite, like Romans 9:1–5, already quoted, and Romans 11:1–2: "I ask, then, has God rejected his people? Of course not. . . . No, God has not rejected his people whom he foreknew."

(e) For the "Jews" in the gospel of John, some kind of anti-Judaism at some stage of the gospel redaction would be admitted. Still, that this is not at all the whole picture of Jews and Judaism in the Johannine gospel is proved by the fact of the very positive references to be found in that gospel. Some were quoted earlier, like John 4:22, "salvation comes from the Jews," and others were alluded to.

So the picture is a mixed one, to say the least. On the other hand, it seems clear enough that, at the time of the final redaction of the gospel, the community reflected and embodied in the last redaction considers itself a religious body different from Judaism and looks at it from outside. One should add here: and from a distance. A certain rift, and a painful one, for that matter, had certainly taken place some time before. It is quite possible, if not probable, that some sections of the gospel reflect such hard feelings toward the "mother" community from which nascent Christianity had disassociated itself, not without conflicts. This accounts for a certain measure of what I called "anti-Judaism" in the gospel of John. But I would insist that "anti-Judaism," at least of this particular brand, is not exactly "antisemitism" in the senses spelled out at the beginning of this lecture.

However, such an "anti-Judaism" could, and perhaps did, in

the course of history, nurture the seeds of real antisemitic actions and prejudices. This is why we churchmen must be so careful to interpret rightly texts and terms and trends as those quoted, and keep a vigilant eye on what is done (or not done) around us in their presentation and explanation. The *Notes* (IV, 29A) encourage taking the complicated historical context into account in order to avoid using antisemitic expressions "when preparing catechesis and homilies for the last weeks of Lent and holy week."

I would submit that the same set of principles, *mutatis mutandis,* should be applied to a correct reading of the gospel of Matthew.

(f) Lastly, the Pharisees. Here I shall be very short. I am convinced, in fact, that from what can be known through sound scholarship level, there is no question that the Pharisees, as such, were certainly not the hypocritical, repulsive bigots that a certain Christian (and also secular) tradition has made them to be. This is a caricature, and a very nasty one indeed. Again, one has only to look carefully at the text itself of the NT to find, alongside negative references, many positive ones. Gamaliel was a Pharisee (Acts 5:34) and so was Nicodemus (Jn 3:1ff; 19:39). The Pharisees warn Jesus that Herod is trying to kill him, and this in Luke (13:31), who is not kind to them. They are never mentioned in the actual account of the passion and crucifixion, while other groupings are frequently named. To convey of them a quite negative, almost diabolic picture is unfair and unhistorical, whatever the failures of many or even most of them, which also the Babylonian Talmud recognizes: of seven classes of Pharisees there described in a famous text, only one is approved of.

For this reason, the *Guidelines and Suggestions for Implementing the Conciliar Declaration "Nostra Aetate" (n. 4),* published in 1974 by our Commission for Religious Relations with the Jews, refer specifically either to the Pharisees and the "Jews" in St. John's gospel and give briefly some orientations on how to interpret these expressions rightly, so as to "avoid appearing to arraign the Jewish people as such," or to the whole of the Pharisaic movement, whose rightful heir present Judaism considers itself to be. Jesus himself—as mentioned in the 1985 *Notes* (III, 24–25)—had Pharisees as friends and shared many teachings with them, especially with the moderate Pharisee school of Rabbi Hillel. In a similar vein, St. Paul took pride in the Pharisaic formation he had received.

3. A *third* step could be made here, so as to give an answer to those who believe, for one reason or another, that the distinctive Christian profession of faith, namely the one in Jesus as "Christ," or messiah, is of itself "antisemitic." They hold that such a profession would, in fact, imply almost automatically the depreciation of the Jewish religion. If it is said that the messiah has already come, Judaism has no true right to exist. Therefore, all antisemitic prejudices are validated. To this I would say the following. First, we must once again be careful not to jump from one set of assertions or convictions to another, of an entirely different order. Professions of faith are one thing; social and even religious attitudes, especially if tinged with prejudices, are quite another. This is not to say that there might not be—and unfortunately there has been—a connection between one and the other. But the whole point is that this should not be so in the first place, and it raises a constant challenge to all religions, as professed and lived out by their faithful, namely: to constantly keep a severe check on possible, but as such unwarranted, conclusions from what we believe or practice. This, I gather, is one of the major contributions of the Second Vatican Council, and not only in the field of Jewish-Christian relations.

Second, I would strongly argue that the affirmation just mentioned is simply not true. It *does not* follow from the Christian profession of faith that Judaism, let alone the Jewish people, is not worthy of any respect and that, in consequence, the door is wide open for antisemitism. Referring back to the much discussed question of typological interpretations, I would like to give another example and to suggest a methodology. The best example provided to us by the NT is from the letter to the Hebrews. Here the typological applications do not lead to contempt for the Hebrew scriptures, nor is it ever affirmed that the Mosaic covenant has been abrogated. It remains "old," and therefore good like "old wine," a "treasure" which the wise scribe draws upon along with the "new things." If the author affirms that the old covenant "will soon disappear" (Heb 8:13), it is a question of an imminence more eschatological than chronological, which does not call into question that covenant's validity or vitality, nor does it wish to reduce it to an empty shadow. This eschaton which erupts into history is the risen Christ, which always refers to the mystery of the covenant of love with Israel.

Drawing an immediate application of this principle, I would note that in this sense "we continue to use the expression *Old Testament* because it is traditional (cf. already 2 Cor 3:14), but also because 'old' does not mean 'out of date' or 'outworn.' In any case, it is the permanent value of the OT as a source of Christian revelation that is emphasized here (cf. *Dei verbum,* 3)" (*Notes* II, footnote).

The Christian profession of faith is a *positive* one: it looks to Jesus as the Christ. It does not refer to anything else. If it suggests a reference to Judaism, it is again a positive one, as said above, because it is from Judaism that we receive the notions of messiah and messianism, and this establishes a link between both religions. It is a link which asks for reflection and deepening, pointing as it does to a kind of common hope, for Judaism is always hoping for the coming of the messiah and/or the messianic age. For Christians, in fact, if the messiah has already come, it is also an article of our profession of faith that he is nonetheless expected in a second coming. Thus the Christ-messiah links us to Judaism, because he was, and remains, a Jew, and with him Judaism enters into Christianity through the main door.

Yes, we Christians are utterly convinced that this Christ, whose human identity we receive from Judaism, is, since his resurrection, the Lord and center of the world and history. We believe him to be the Son of God. This, of course, divides us from Judaism.

We must say then that the same Jesus who brings us together divides us. This is true, and there is no point in blurring the distinction. Nevertheless, the fact of our "link" remains forever, and this means that even in our separation, we are mysteriously "linked" together, as *Nostra aetate,* No. 4, says in its first sentence. This means that, far from being intrinsically antisemitic, the Christ is, so to speak, intrinsically "pro-semitic" and, properly understood, leads not to depreciation of the Jewish people or the Jewish religion, but, on the contrary, to a deep appreciation of both—very deep, in fact, because it is grounded not in any external conjunctural circumstance of some kind, but in the very distinctive identity of Christianity. It would be useful to cite again, thus summarizing these considerations, what the Holy Father clearly stated at the Roman synagogue:

> No one is unaware that the fundamental difference from the very beginning has been the attachment of us Catholics to the person and teaching of Jesus of Nazareth, a son of your people, from which were also born the Virgin Mary, the apostles . . . and the greater part of the first Christian community. But this attachment is located in the order of faith. . . . This is the reason why we wish to deepen dialogue . . . taking as a fundamental basis the elements of revelation which we have in common . . ." (*Information Service*, 60, p. 28).

It cannot be said, therefore, that Christianity, as a normative body of belief and practice embodied in the NT, is antisemitic. The question of our title, thus far, must therefore be answered *in the negative.*

4. I would not like, however, to seem to dodge a further question. If Christianity *as such* is not antisemitic (in the first of the three senses listed above), could it perhaps be said that Christianity is, or has been proved to be, antisemitic in any of the two other meanings? Here one has to be very honest, and acknowledge quite openly:

(a) Some, and perhaps many, *interpretations* of Christianity, throughout the ages, have been unjust and prejudiced against Judaism;

(b) Sometimes such misguided interpretations have been translated into practice, legal or otherwise, seriously discriminating, attacking, oppressing, and even violently mishandling Jews, to the point of physical suppression;

(c) This has obviously nourished, in the Greco-Roman world, a form of antisemitism, coming from pre-Christian sources, to which, for instance, Josephus Flavius (*Contra Apionem*) and Philo (*Legatio ad Caium*) refer. But it has also quickly developed into a form of antisemitism of its own.

Now, having acknowledged all this and even more that could and should be acknowledged, I would like to state very clearly that a careful distinction must be drawn between this kind of "Christianity"—or perhaps "Christendom"—and the more fundamental, basic meaning of the same word, to which I have been referring up till now. The Christian body of belief and practice is one thing. Historical and cultural realizations of that body of belief and practice are quite another. It must be admitted, therefore, that most, if not all, historical embodiments of Christianity, this side of history, do not easily live up, socially and culturally, to the requirements of our own religious profession. In this, I fear, we are not alone. I wonder if any other religion, in the course of history, has been able to create in its own geographical context a world *entirely* faithful to its ideals.

Christianity, however, is a very special case, in this connection, because I do not think it has been given to any other religion (not even Islam), as it has been given to us, to rule and mold and give a shape, for such a protracted period in history, to such an important section of humanity. A mixed blessing, indeed! One can point to many achievements, no doubt. But deficiencies and limitations only appear thus in a more painful light. Our only excuse, if any, is that men and women are very seldom up to the task assigned them by the very faith they profess, and profess sincerely. This is why we Catholics value so much our saints. In a way they atone for the weakness of the rest.

Some very nasty forms of antisemitism are part of such deficiencies. It is a grace of God that we are now much more aware of them. But it is a greater grace still that we are convinced that our own identity (Christianity in the first meaning listed above) not only does not approve of such deviations, but positively condemns them and requires of us to go the opposite way, namely, to love, respect and, if need be, help and protect our Jewish brother.

When all this is said and done, I think there is still room to show that, notwithstanding our negative record, some trends at least of what Christianity really means for Judaism have persisted along the ages, even in the darkest moments. I shall only mention here a few points, without entering into any deep analysis. But I am convinced that careful historico-theological analysis could bear them up and perhaps even add some others.

(a) The notion, however dim, of a certain indebtedness to Judaism has never been lost in the Christian tradition. This indebtedness has perhaps been interpreted in the wrong way, but the trend was there, and it is partly on this basis that the present change has been built. I add that the consciousness of this debt has been particularly alive in liturgy and in biblical scholarship. Examples would be easy to find for both.

(b) There has always been a clear conviction, at least at the theological and juridical levels of the church, and therefore in the places where decisions are made, that, for instance:

- Jews should not be baptized against their will, and this goes as far back as St. Gregory the Great (end of the sixth century);
- there was no excuse for wantonly killing Jews, or otherwise oppressing them physically, much less exterminating them. Popes and prelates and saints, like St. Bernard, vigorously opposed the massacre of Jews by crusaders on their way to the east;
- popes have strongly condemned the so-called "blood libel," namely the perverse idea that Jews needed the blood of a Christian infant or boy for the eastern rites and murdered them in consequence. The cult of such imaginary "martyrs" was never approved of and at times severely disapproved, as in the case of Simon of Trent by Sixtus IV, or for a similar case in Poland by Benedict XIV.

Further, I would add to this that condemnations of antisemitism in the more modern "racist" variety have been expressed in the Catholic Church much before the Second Vatican Council. I shall only mention in this connection the decree of the Congregation of the Holy Office, on March 25, 1928, under Pius XI (cf. *AAS* 20, 1928, p. 104), explicitly condemning antisemitism under that name in a context which seemingly refers more to France than to Weimar Germany.

The same Pius XI dedicated a whole encyclical to the evil of racism, and to bring the point home he did not hesitate to have it published in German, contrary to the time-honored Roman preference for Latin. Entitled *Mit brennender Sorge* in 1937, it was preceded by a whole series of instructions and orientations by holy see offices about how to counter, in Catholic education, the dangers of racist theories, which then meant in the first place antisemitism. It was the same Pius XI who said, in September 1938, to a group of Belgian journalists: "We refer, in the eucharistic prayer of the mass, to Abraham our father in faith; thus we are all spiritually Semites."

The opposition to antisemitism, then rampant, is obvious. If anything, such reactions prove the truth of the central assertion of this lecture: the New Testament, and, more generally, Christianity, is *not* antisemitic.

But, as an appropriate conclusion to this lecture, I feel I should go a step further. It is not enough just to say that Christianity is not antisemitic. Whatever our historical record, and I am well aware of the deficiencies of men and women of the Catholic faith, in this point (as in others), I must say here that antisemitism, as this word is understood today, is simply *anti-Christian*. And this, I believe, is the real decisive thrust of all I had to say tonight. Thank you.

Unity Between Old
and New Covenant[1]*

INTRODUCTION

Centrality of the Word of God

When one proposes to reflect about the old and the new covenant, one must face up to the word, starting from our own everyday words, expressions of meanings, and arriving at the transcendental word, creator of meaning. In the Bible, human words are perennially the expression of the word of salvation, albeit in different ways according to Saint Augustine's saying: *Novum in Vetere latet, in Novo Vetus patet* (*Quaestiones in Heptateucum* 2.73: "the New is veiled in the Old, in the New the Old is revealed"). Using the terms of modern hermeneutics, those of Fuchs or Ebeling, the disciples of Bultmann for example, we could say that the word that God addresses to man is a language of the love that redeems and saves and thereby renders the words of human history significant and meaningful.

If we were to use the term "metaphor" to describe words and events laden with symbolism, with mystery, with the dynamics of salvation, we could say that the Old Testament appears to us as an anthology of the metaphors of the word, and the New Testament as word of the metaphors; both are "inheritance" and "covenant," *rota intra rotam* (Saint Ambrose, *De Spiritu Sancto* III, 162), according to the full meaning of the word *diathēkē* (Testament). Word of man and word of God, the one God whose name alone is holy, and whom we Christians yet invoke with three holy names,

* Munich, 1987; see Bibliography, n. 15.

Father, Son, and Spirit: the confrontation and example of the old and venerable Judaic tradition appears before us right from the beginning of our reflection. Word, faith and action: the word (Heb. *dābār*, cf. *Dictionnaire de la Bible,* Supplement V, 488–495) that is celebrated and comes to life in the liturgy, expression of faith, action of grace and memorial, in which "wherever two or three are gathered together: there is present the glory of the Shekhinah" (cf. Mt 18:20), that is to say, "the Word has become flesh and has dwelt among us" (Jn 1:14).

One can readily understand the truth of the Jewish affirmation that the loving study of the living word of the living God (this is the Talmud Torah) is the highest form of prayer and sacrifice, the one that leads into the very heart of God. The teachings of Martin Buber (*Je et tu,* Paris 1938) and Abraham Joshua Heschel can give us more than just a little fleeting help in our search that is both harkening and obedience, hermeneutics and theological synthesis.

Prior to every confrontation, however, there is a fundamental experience of the heart of man that seeks the encounter with the absolute, and of the inexpressible that reveals itself—like the consuming fire of Mount Sinai—to those who seek, as we are told by poet Jehudah Halevy, enamored of Jerusalem (he died with the name of the holy city on his lips) and celebrated by Heinrich Heine in his *Hebräische Melodien:* "If I could contemplate thy face in my heart! . . . As the heart longs for flowing streams, so longs my soul for thee, O God" (Ps 42:1).

The fundamental and central value of this encounter has been fully recovered and expressed in the Constitution *Dei verbum* of the Second Vatican Council in reference to Christ the redeemer: "In sacris enim libris Pater qui in caelis est filiis suis peramanter occurrit et cum eis sermonem confert" (DV, Chapter VI, No. 21: "In the sacred books the Father who is in heaven comes lovingly to meet his children, and talks with them"), and the announcement of the word of God is continuously spread "ut societas nostra sit cum Patre et cum Filio eius Jesu Christo" (1 Jn 1:2–3, cited in the Prologue of *Dei Verbum:* "that our fellowship be with the Father and with his Son Jesus Christ"), according to the glad tidings of the apostle John.

THE HISTORICAL DIMENSION

But this communion is not a purely spiritual or metaphysical fact, to be understood in an abstract or philosophical manner. It is once again the *Constitution on Divine Revelation* (Chapter I, no. 2) that states that this economy of the revelation manifests itself in the history of salvation (*historia salutis*) by means of facts and words (*gestis verbisque*). More recently, the Jewish philosopher Michael Wyschogrod likewise underscored, and very forcefully, the importance of history in Judaism and, more particularly, the Judaism of the Bible (*The Body of Faith,* 1983).

And a substantially analogous affirmation at the Christian historico-dogmatic level was made thirty years ago by Karl Barth in *Kirchliche Dogmatik:* In Jesus Christ the divine election in favor of Israel became an event of human history, and God's being a Jew in Jesus Christ forms part of the self-revelation of the Son of God (II/2, No. 32: IV, 1, 178). This historical dimension, so strongly underscored in recent years, corresponds to a feature that was traditionally present already in evangelical times, in Philo for example, as Walter Volker noted (*Fortschritt und Vollendung bei Philo von Alexandrien,* 1938), and that continued in Irenaeus and in some fundamental lines of the Antiochene school, against the trends of the gnostics and the neoplatonists.

When we take the historical perspective seriously in our question as to the relationship between the Old and the New Covenant, we could not but examine with extreme care and attention also the Jewish conception of the sacred scripture, the Islamic approach, and the various points of view that characterize the Latin and eastern Christian traditions and those of the churches that came out of the reformation. Nor indeed is this mode of proceeding either new or original. It is wholly in keeping with the great school of the church fathers and the masters of scholasticism, because the method of Saint Thomas Aquinas started precisely from the viewpoint of these different traditions of faith and speculative analysis, as for example when considering inspiration in scripture and the distinction between "philosopher" and believers "habentes legem" in the *Summa contra Gentiles:* the latter are precisely *"Iudaei et Saraceni,"* while the *"rationales"* (or epicurei) are spokesmen of the reasons of logic and of metaphysics, as, for example, Avicenna and Averroes (cf. P. Marc in *S. Thomae Aquinatis Liber de Veritate Catholicae Fidei contra errores Infidelium qui dicitur Summa Contra Gentiles,* Turin and Paris 1967, Vol. I, Introduction).

And thus, in coming to grips with our topic of the relationship between the "old" and the "new" covenant, I should like to start from these methodological propositions, though obviously enriched by the contributions and the problems that form part of our everyday following the birth and the growth of refined exegetical and hermeneutical methods and the historico-critical and comparative analyses carried out by modern scholars.

A search of this kind will be of evangelical, ecumenical and interreligious value at one and the same time. Indeed, it could make it possible to spread the word of God among contemporary humanity, in accordance with the program of *Aggiornamento* or "updating" proposed by the council in the theological, pastoral and spiritual sense; as regards the ecumenical and—more generally—interreligious aspect, we know how greatly this has increased in importance in recent years, as was well brought out on the occasion of the prayer for peace at Assisi on October 27, 1986, and we shall put our dialogue on clear and solid foundations, without equivocations or misunderstanding, if we confront each other jointly in the matter of divine revelation.

I. THE JEWISH PERSPECTIVE

"Hear, O Israel"

Dietrich Bonhoeffer, writing to a friend from prison, said that "the Christian is the man of the Old Testament." But are not the Jews also men of the Old Testament? We cannot therefore use this category to indicate the Jewish perspective.

The traditional Hebrew term to indicate the scriptures is not "testament" but "sacred books" (*Sifrê qodesh*) or "sacred proclamation" (*Miqrā qodesh*), but also "oral" (she be-'al-peh) tradition, according to Saint Jerome. This manner of indicating scripture clearly expresses a particular conception of God and of his work of salvation: the unity and uniqueness of scripture appears as a mirror of the oneness of God and the people called to harken to, to obey, to the love of God and of one's neighbor.

This conception of scripture is comprehensive, pluri-dimensional: it is dynamic, according to the dynamic of the Spirit of prophecy, and therefore open to the future; it is inserted in the tradition, the history and the liturgical celebration of the entire community and the people in making its "memorial" of the "magnalia Dei." The center of this memorial is the covenant, the alliance of Mount Sinai, in the arc of God's action that extends from the Passover to Pentecost (Shavu'ot), and is projected toward the future, as is well expressed by Isaiah: "For out of Zion shall go forth the law, and the word of the Lord from Jerusalem" (Is 2:3).

Only within the community of faith, in the people of the covenant, is the written and oral word of God alive, at work, continuously meditated with love and practiced with at times heroic fidelity. The law of the covenant becomes Torah in the pregnant sense of the rule of life as the condition for remaining within the covenant; one can speak of a Torah that existed even before the creation, as a Logos, as hypostatized and subsisting Wisdom-Word (Memrah) in the Aramaic targumim (cf. *Dictionnaire de la Bible, Supplement,* V, 465–468).

Ephraim Urbach, in his *The Sages* (Jerusalem, 1979[2]), a fundamental work for understanding the Judaism of the first and second century A.D., reminds us that among the Jews of Alexandria the term Nómos was the exact counterpart of Torah in the pregnant sense. On the other hand, the individual precepts, the precepts of the Torah, were terms that can also be expressed by Torot (plural of Torah), according to the Alexandrine conception.

Michael Wyschogrod,[2] on the other hand, deems Nómos to be an inexact and reductive translation of Torah, even though—in substance—he does not differ from Urbach nor, as we shall see, from Sanders and Neusner. From Wyschogrod we receive the suggestion of verifying the Jewish conception of the Torah and of grace, availing ourselves of the texts of the Siddur[3] and of prayer, which constitute an important font of theological reflection. Here too, in fact, we have the principle: "*lex orandi, lex credendi.*"

It is most interesting to study the various interpretations of the covenant and scripture that characterize the different currents of Judaism in the early centuries: both Ed Parish Sanders and Jacob

Neusner give us different images in referring to the Mishnah, the Leviticus Rabbah, and Palestinian Judaic literature.[4]

Sanders assumes a position different from the line of Thackeray, Weber, Bousset, Billerbeck and Bultmann, all of whom underscore the opposition between Judaic legalism and salvation by grace; rather, he further develops some affirmations made by Montefiore, Parkes and Daines and devotes himself to an analysis of rabbinic literature with a view to discovering its basic conception in the matter of the theology of the covenant-election-alliance, in relation with Paul and New Testament research. He concludes from this analysis that, according to the masters of the Mishnah (the "Tannaites"), the pact includes both benediction and commandments; it is not only law, but also promise. There is no "legalism," because God loves by grace and chooses by grace, and human obedience is an appropriate response to confirm that man intends to live within the ambit of the covenant, in order to receive the gift of salvation. Jewish scholars object that Sanders reads the Hebrew texts as seen in a Pauline perspective, and that this vitiates his conclusion.

Neusner, for his part, showed that in the first and second century A.D. (i.e. at the time when the Christians drew up the sacred writings of the New Testament), Judaism, too, had a reaction that seems to me to be very similar to the Christian one. Indeed, the editing of the Mishnah seems to Neusner[5] as intended to create a new text, a text as sacred as the Torah, the prophets and the Ketuvîm; this constitutes the distinctive character of the Mishnah with respect to other writings, the Targumin for example, which place themselves quite consciously at a more subordinate level than scripture.

Neusner's conclusion drawn from his analysis of the Leviticus Rabbah seems far clearer: "Judaism is not the religion of the Old Testament: Judaism *is* Judaism. Scripture is comprised in Judaism because it is the religion 'of the one Torah of Moses, our rabbi,' and scripture forms part of this Torah. Taken as a whole, the entire Torah is the divine revelation of the rules of life: about creation, and also about society and history" (op. cit. p. 64).

II. THE CHRISTIAN PERSPECTIVE

A. *In the New Testament*

I have dedicated a certain amount of space to expounding the Jewish perspective, because it seems to me to be more important for us than is commonly thought.

If we now place ourselves within the Christian perspective, we shall note—first of all—that in the Jewish Bible that was received by the early Christians there was not, nor could there be, any reference to the "Old" Testament as a collection of sacred scripture (prior to Christ). In Jeremiah there is mention of "foedus novum" (Jer 31:31), but this consists of the Torah written not on tablets of stone but "on their hearts" (Jer 31:33).

Jesus calls the sacred Jewish writings "Lex Moysi, prophetae et psalmi" (Lk 24:44). Paul and the letter to the Hebrews resume the context of Jeremiah 31:31 (cf. 2 Cor 3:14; Heb 8:8). According to Hebrews 8:13 and in this sense, therefore, this law would be on the point of disappearance: just how difficult it is to interpret this affirmation will be shown also by the fact that we are not concerned with "abolition" but with fulfillment, this in keeping with the words of Jesus "I have come not to abolish [the law], but to fulfill it" (Mt 5:17).

What is certainly close to disappearing is the veil, the envelope, the velamen (2 Cor 2:13) that hides the interpretation without veils of words, "the day that dawns upon us from on high" (Lk 1:78) and overcomes the darkness. If—in relation to the sacred texts—we were to interpret in the sense of abolition, we would arrive at the Marcionite heresy that denies value to the Jewish Bible, and that is something we cannot approve, as is well shown by Irenaeus.

Saint Paul is certainly in the line of the continuity of the covenant (or the covenants), as becomes apparent in Romans 9:4 and 11:27, since in the first passage he affirms that to Israel belong in the present: the light of glory (which is light also in the interpretation of scripture) and "the covenants," though without specifying which or how many. For a more ample treatment, I would refer you to Franz Mussner, *Die Kraft der Wurzel,* Chapter III, which faces up to the argument also in the Protestant perspective of Israel's salvation by grace.

For the first Christian generation, therefore, the term "New Testament" must have meant, above all, reference to Christ's action that in the celebration of his passover-death-resurrection-pentecost renews and makes come true Israel's passover in Egypt. Guided by Christ and the Spirit, the apostles put the new scriptures to paper by rereading the old in a new way: the outcome of this is what some people have defined as a midrash (i.e. edifying explanation) of the Jewish Bible in the light of the paschal Christ.

Christ appears as the fulfillment of the scriptures (cf. Mk 14:49: "Day after day I was with you in the temple teaching, and you did not seize me. But let the scriptures be fulfilled"; Jn 19:30: "It is finished"). The scriptures are interpreted on the basis of Christ's historical experience in the passion and the redeeming passover.

These few remarks seem to suggest that in an analysis of the relationship between the Old and the New Testament we must also bear in mind some important considerations regarding the covenant and, consequently, the promise and the gift of salvation connected therewith. These are considerations that touch upon themes common to Christians and Jews. Franz Mussner, in the work I mentioned a little earlier (Chapter V, par. 5), substantially presents the interesting thesis of Ed Parish Sanders in *Paul and Palestinian Judaism* and accepts it.

B. The Church Fathers

Many people hold that the fathers, though they generally—but not always—recognize the texts of the Old Testament as being of great value, tend to see themselves obliged to consider them as bound up with the salvific economy of the figures rather than with that of the fullness of redemption, thus depriving them of autonomous consistency to the benefit of the "allegoric" sense. The great variety and complexity of the historical and cultural situations and the dogmatic and philosophic controversies characteristic of the days in which the fathers wrote do not permit the drawing of hasty conclusions. Probably a more profound knowledge of Talmudic sources would also prove precious in connection with this problem, as has already been demonstrated by some recent studies that refer to these works: cf. Johann Maier, *Jesus von Nazareth in der Talmudischen Überlieferung,* Darmstadt 1978.

I shall therefore limit myself to proposing the reading of a few brief texts that I deem to be particularly significant.

Among the fathers of the second century, great interest seems to me to attach to the perspective in which Justin Martyr speaks of the scriptures in the liturgical context and, more particularly, of the eucharistic memorials: "The apostles, in the memories they have left and called gospels, have handed down to us that Jesus commanded as follows: 'Having taken the bread and rendered thanks, he said: This is my body. . . .' And on the day named after the Sun there shall be a congregation. All those who live in the city or in the country shall convene in the same place, and there shall be read the memories of the apostles or the writings of the prophets . . ." (I *Apologia,* 66–67).

Irenaeus, too, proceeds in accordance with an association of ideas of the same order and, in his *Adversus Haereses* IV, 9–16, considers the manifold relations between law and gospel and then passes on to presenting the meaning of the sacrifices that are fulfilled in the eucharist (IV, 17–18). Irenaeus opposes the Valentinians and the Marcionites, supporters of the gnostic dualism, in the name of the unity of the divine plan of salvation that manifests itself in the two covenants (IV, 34; V, 22, 1–2): "since God is one, and he will justify the circumcised on the ground of their faith and the uncircumcised through their faith" (Rom 3:30).

We know how greatly Origen appreciated the exegetical science of the learned Alexandrine Jews, though he was well aware of the substantial differences of faith. Just like him, and perhaps even more so, Jerome willingly followed the conclusions of the Jews regarding holy scripture, to the point of doubting the canonicity of some books deemed to be apocryphal according to the Jewish canon. But Origen and Jerome held wholly opposite opinions about the Jewish Christians who accepted scripture as being totally binding also as regards the precepts of the Torah. While Origen—in his *Commentaries to the Romans*—says that they should be viewed with benevolence, Jerome (*Ad Augustinium,* Ep. 112, 13–15) condemned them, and in this respect differed also from Augustine.

The fathers, as we know, greatly developed exegesis of the Old

Testament in the typical, accommodated, and allegorical senses. On the other hand, the Antiochene school insisted on the literal and historic sense: in the fourth and fifth centuries, at the same time as the Jewish masters fixed the text of the Masorah, greater attention was also being paid to the literal sense.

In Saint Ambrose we note that the moral and pastoral-pedagogic perspective occupies a particularly prominent place in evaluating the Old Testament: "Mare est Scriptura divina. ... Habes quod primum bibas, habes quod secundum, habes quod postremum" (Epist. 2,3: "Divine Scripture is a sea. ... There is a part to drink first, second, and last"). "Sed ordine suo bibe, primum in vetere Testamento, cito fac ut bibas et in novo Testamento" (Expl. ps. I,33: "[Drink this Word] but drink it in keeping with its order, first in the O.T. and then immediately in the N.T."). In this way the Christian is "tamquam perfectus eruditus in lege, confirmatus in evangelio" (Epist. 74,9: "Perfectly instructed in the law, confirmed in the gospel").

Among the eastern fathers, I shall cite only—by way of example—Saint John Damascene who, in his treatise entitled *The Orthodox Faith,* dedicates the greater part to expounding the mystery of the three divine hypostases and the salvific economy culminating in the incarnation and the resurrection of Jesus Christ. Here is how he treats the argument of the Jewish scriptures and the people of Israel within this general context:

> The divine is ineffable and incomprehensible. ... Nevertheless, God has certainly not left us in complete ignorance, because each one of us has—by nature—sown within himself the awareness that there is a God. Creation itself . . . proclaims the magnificence of the divine nature. Moreover, the law and the prophets, and then his only-begotten Son, the Lord, our God and Savior Jesus Christ, have revealed to us the knowledge of God, so that we can attain it. And thus, we accept, know and practice devoutly everything that has been transmitted to us by the law and the prophets, by the apostles and the evangelists, and do not seek further" (*The Orthodox Faith,* I,1).[6]

In keeping with this general perspective, not even the least negative sign can be found in this work of John Damascene as regards the Jewish scriptures; and even when he is concerned with the genealogy of the Theotokos, the mother of God descending from Pantera and Bar-Pantera, there is no anti-Jewish polemic in parallel with the Talmud passage (cf. Talmud Jerushalmi, *Avoda Zara* II, 2; Origen, *Contra Celsum,* 1,32) that speaks of Ben-Pantera as the father of Jesus (cf. *The Orthodox Faith,* IV, 14).

Indeed, to the contrary, John Damascene writes as follows: "Baptism circumcises us of every foreskin that covers us from birth, that is to say, of sin. Spiritually we become Israelites and people of God" (IV, 10). There is never the least suggestion of a replacement of the "ancient Israel" or of diminishing the Old Testament.

The ethical and pastoral perspective we have seen in Damascene seems to us to recall that of Ambrose.

In conclusion, therefore, the fathers undoubtedly looked at the Old Testament from within the Catholic tradition that was forming with them, but this does not mean that the Old Testament appeared to them as a source of materials to be used outside their original context, thereby doing violence to the primary and fundamental literal or historical sense.

We could say that the apostles looked to the Old Testament in order to write the New Testament in the light of the paschal Christ, and the fathers, receiving in this way the entire set of sacred scriptures, began their interpretations of these texts, employing the instruments furnished them by their Jewish tradition and by the classical tradition, though always remaining within the community of faith.

EXCURSUS

Karaitism and Islam

As we pass from the patristic period to the medieval period, there are at least two phenomena that seem to me to merit attention: Karaitism and Islam, and this on account of both their relation with each other and their attitude to the letter and the spirit of the sacred scriptures.

A. Karaitism

Treated in a recent study by the Frenchman Simon Szyszman (*Le Karaïsme,* Lausanne 1980), Karaitism appears to have been a heterodox Judaic movement closely related to the Masoretes and affirming the sole and central importance of the written Torah, refusing all oral tradition.

The fundamental principle is that each one must interpret the precepts according to his own capacities and without being conditioned by authorities or external competencies, basing himself rigorously on the written text, a principle that contributed to the development of the masoretic method in the second half of the first millennium.

The Aleppo Codex, the oldest manuscript of the complete Bible, an ideal model of the masoretic *textus receptus*, is said to be the fruit of the great school of the Karait masoretes of the Ben Asher family of Tiberias (eighth to tenth century A.D.).

B. Islam

The oneness of revelation is an incontestable dogma in Islam, so that Muhammad calls on Jews and Christians to return to the original purity of the divine message that God (Allah) in Islam and through the thought of Muhammad, "Seal of Prophets," restores to its maximum fidelity.

The covenant (*mithaq*) is offered to all who believe in the scriptures: "God has promised it, with a solemn and binding promise, in the Torah and in the Gospel and in the Koran" (Koran, Surah IX, 111).

The oneness of God and his covenant is also unity of the scriptures: "God! There is no other God but he. . . . He revealed to you the Book, with the Truth, thereby confirming what was revealed before, and revealed first the Torah and the Gospel as a guide for men, and has now revealed salvation" (III, 3–4).

But only the Koran has the value of the word of God in the absolute, direct and literal sense; other sacred Arab writings, the Hadit and the Syrah in point, are sacred writings—together with the Torah, the gospels and the apocrypha—but at a lower level.

Muhammad is Ahmad (LXI, 6), i.e. the Praised One, the "Counselor" promised by Jesus (cf. Jn 14:16–17): his importance as the Prophet therefore also underscores the importance of the prophetic element and of inspiration in the scripture and the revelations.

These brief remarks may well help us to an understanding of certain developments in medieval thought, especially, for example, the way Saint Thomas developed the theory of inspiration using as his starting point the Moreh Nevuchim by Maimonides and the theories of knowledge in God formulated by the Arab philosophers 'Al Farabi and Avicenna. The influence of 'Al-Ghazzali was to manifest itself on another front, that of Muslim mysticism, this philosopher holding the sacred book to be a transposition of the eternal word that must yet not be confused with it: it is the human expression of a divine message. In 'Aqida, 'Al-Ghazzali expresses himself in the following terms: "The Koran is read aloud with the tongue, it is written in the books, reposes in the hearts, but in truth it is eternal, subsisting in the essence of God Almighty."

III. THE MIDDLE AGES

De Lubac, who in 1959 introduced a completely new manner of viewing medieval Christian exegesis (*L'Exegese Medievale*), offers us a profound and interesting approach to the medieval sources. For example he reminds us that Pascasius Radbertus (+ ca. 865) liked to apply exegetical categories of "sacramentum" and "mysterium" to the scriptures, and presents us with the radical novelty of Joachim of Fiore (1132–1202), who saw the period of the Old and New Testaments as two wholly analogous and homogeneous contiguous epochs, that of the "littera veteris testamenti" and of the "littera novi testamenti," with the book of Revelation as their key of interpretation.

Navigating in the vast ocean of medieval allegory, we feel the wind of the Franciscan renewal with its four senses of scripture, to which there correspond the four epochs of the history of salvation:

(1) the literal sense, which has its counterpart in the epoch of *nature;*
(2) the allegorical sense, which has its counterpart in the epoch of the *law;*
(3) the anagogical sense, which has its counterpart in the epoch of the *prophets;*
(4) the tropological sense, which has its counterpart in the epoch of the *gospel.*

The unique, universal, and necessary rule is Christ. Object of all scripture, he is also the sole exegete of scripture, the "verbum abbreviatum" that epitomizes the whole of scripture. To navigate in the ocean of scripture, one has to make use of the helm of the cross with supreme humility.

We have thus come to Saint Thomas, who in various places (*Quodlibet*, VII, art. 1–3; *Commentary on the Galatians* VI, Lecture 6; *Summa Theologiae* I, 1 art. 10) summarizes with great clarity and genius the positions of twelve centuries of Christian exegesis. He distinguishes four senses:

(1) sensus litteralis;
(2) sensus moralis seu tropologicus;
(3) sensus typicus seu allegoricus (the O.T. as figure of the N.T.);
(4) sensus anagogicus (O.T. and N.T. both as figures of the church triumphant).

Saint Thomas introduces the dynamics of the theology of history into exegesis in a systematic manner, dynamics that link allegory and analogy to the future Christ: just as the Christ of the passover and the church represents the future with respect to the Old Testament so also the total Christ of eschatological plenitude is the future with respect to the New Testament.

It seems to me that Nicholas of Lyra (1270–1340?) merits a singular place and significance with his *Postillae in Universa Biblia* (1322–1330): on account of his fidelity to the patristic tradition and his vast knowledge of the medieval Jewish exegetes, he constitutes even for us a solid point of reference and a valid example of an approach to scripture and its presentation.

Concluding, we can therefore say that the middle ages were in a line of continuity with the patristic orientation, but that this period sought further insight into scripture in terms of systematic theology, and enriched it with an eschatological opening toward the future.

IV. THE RENAISSANCE

As regards the humanistic period of the renaissance, it seems to me to be important to recall at least the great movement of the

"Christian qabbalah," recently studied by Hayyim Wirszubski (Flavius Mithridates, *Sermo de Passione Domini,* Jerusalem 1963). It refers us not only to the great Jewish mysticism, but also to the method of "gematria" in biblical exegesis. Though it was known to the fathers (Augustine explains the number of "153 large fish" in the miraculous draught of fishes in the following terms: $1 + 2 + 3 + 4 + 5 + 6 + 7 + 8 + 9 + 10 + 11 + 12 + 13 + 14 + 15 + 16 + 17 = 153$; Marcel Simon (*Verus Israel,* Paris 1948) noted in this connection that 153 is the equivalent of the eighteenth number, symbol of the "living" God (in Hebrew, the letter Hay = 18); this mysticism is not a simple exercise in rhetoric, but presupposes the existence of a profound unity in the scriptures. In this connection reference should be made to the vast literary production of Gersom Sholem and the investigation of mysticism in Daniélou's *Théologie du Judéo-Christianisme.*

V. THE REFORMATION PERIOD

Despite his passage from a first phase of open benevolence vis-à-vis the Jews to a second phase of violent persecution, Luther never changed his fundamentally positive attitude toward the Jewish scriptures, faithful to his motto "sola scriptura." In particular, he deemed direct reference to Hebrew to be essential, agreeing with interpretations of such medieval exegetists as Rashi and Qimhi, and accepting also the attitude of Reuchlin, who deemed the Talmud to be useful in biblical criticism: "Quod per talmudicas traditiones sacrae scripturae depravationes optime corriguntur" ("The talmudic traditions make it possible for corrupt passages of the sacred scriptures to be optimally corrected") (Fr. Galatino Colonna, *De Arcanis,* 1518, c. IV).

Although Calvin claimed christological exegesis of the Old Testament to be legitimate, he put very precise limits on the liberty of the exegete in seeing a christological testimony in any passage of Israel's scripture, this in defense of the literal and historical "sensus genuinus."[7] His interpretation, even when christological, conserves the tension toward the future; this function of announcement and of witness conserves its validity. Another interesting element is his affirmation of the close link that exists between the testimony of the Spirit and that of the Bible.

VI. THE MODERN AND CONTEMPORARY PERIOD

I do not think that we can limit ourselves to considering the relations between the Old and the New Testament only in the light of the evolution of literary criticism and hermeneutics during the last three centuries. Furthermore, new studies of the history of the exegesis of this period are more than ever desirable and useful for our problem.[8]

If we wanted to grasp some particularly significant line in the vast panorama of studies, a current in which we are ourselves inserted, one could perhaps indicate the salutary reaction of the so-called "Scandinavian" school of critical exegesis and use of historical criticism (Sigmund Mowinckel, Ivan Engnell, Aaage Bentzen), and especially Harold Riesenfeld's Uppsala school which reacted to Wellhausen's school—though without denying the value of the historico-critical method—in a manner[9] that seems to me to be substantially consistent with the conclusions of Sanders, Neusner, and Mussner, whom I mentioned earlier. According to the conclusions of this school, supported also by archeology and the history of religions in the Middle East, the Old Testament stands at the center of a religious or, more precisely, a cultural experience that comprises the whole of Israel's history.

Within this context, the most recurrent interpretative categories are those of the word of God as event, and historical incarnation, as revelation of the ineffable, as law of life (Torah) and of sanctity, presence of glory and salvation (Shekhinah), as account, memorial and cultural benediction (*Berakhah* and *Zikkaron*), as wisdom and prophecy of the kingdom of the messiah, king of peace and obedient servant.

Against this background one can readily understand the importance and richness of the affirmations of the Second Vatican Council (*Dei verbum* 14–16) concerning the Old Testament:

> In carefully planning and preparing the salvation of the whole human race, the God of supreme love, by a special dispensation, chose for himself a people to whom he might entrust his promises. First he entered into a covenant with Abraham (cf. Gen 15:18) and, through Moses, with the people of Israel (cf. Ex 24:8). To this people which he had acquired for himself, he so manifested himself through words and deeds as the one true

and living God that Israel came to know by experience the ways of God with men, and with God himself speaking to them through the mouth of the prophets, Israel daily gained a deeper and clearer understanding of his ways and made them more widely known among the nations (cf. Ps 21:28–29; 95:1–3; Is 2:1–4; Jer 3:17). The plan of salvation, foretold by the sacred authors, recounted and explained by them, is found as the true word of God in the books of the Old Testament; these books, therefore, written under divine inspiration, remain permanently valuable. 'For whatever things have been written have been written for our instruction, that through the patience and the consolation afforded by the scriptures we may have hope' (Rom 15:4).

The present trends of theological and biblical hermeneutics, which have assumed such great importance, above all, in Protestant reflections (Bultmann, Barth, Fuchs, Ebeling, Gadamer), seem to me to be going in the same direction. In the Catholic camp these interpretative principles, which are of importance also for grasping the relations between the Old Testament and the New, have been accepted very broadly in the Constitution *Dei verbum* (No. 12) of Vatican Council II: "The interpreter must investigate what meaning the sacred writer intended to express and actually expressed in particular circumstances as he used contemporary literary forms in accordance with the situation of his own time and culture."

The centrality of the liturgical celebration, in particular of the paschal mystery in the eucharist, as the vital and interpretative context in which, in Christ and by means of Christ, one understands the profound unity of all the scriptures, has also been adequately underscored by the council in the Constitution *Sacrosanctum concilium* (No. 24): "Sacred scripture is of paramount importance in the celebration of the liturgy. . . . It is Christ himself who speaks when the holy scriptures are read in the church" (No. 7). This presence of the word is found "praecellenti modo" in the writings of the New Testament (*Dei verbum* 17). "In the earthly liturgy, we, by way of foretaste, share in that heavenly liturgy which is celebrated in the Holy City of Jerusalem" (*Sacrosanctum concilium*, No. 8). And the Constitution *Dei verbum* likewise recalls (No. 21) that "The church has always venerated the divine scripture just as she venerates the body of the Lord, since from the table of both the word of God and the body of Christ she unceasingly receives and offers to the faithful the bread of life, especially in the sacred liturgy."

Moving from these general perspectives to more particular applications, I would now like to recall some aspects that have been underscored in recent declarations of the churches and the Catholic magisterium. I do not propose to give a systematic presentation, but merely an invitation for a systematic examination of some lines of research that I have tried to set out rather summarily.

The council declaration *Nostra aetate* speaks of the "great spiritual patrimony" common to Christians and Jews. Ten years later, a Catholic document (*Guidelines and Suggestions for Implementing the Conciliar Declaration 'Nostra aetate' No. 4,* December 1, 1974) and an Evangelical one (*Christen und Juden,* May 24, 1975) have underscored among these "common roots" the Jewish sacred scriptures (*Christen und Juden* 1,2), whose value has not been obliterated by the further interpretation of the New Testament. "When commenting on biblical texts, emphasis will be laid on the continuity of our faith with that of the earlier covenant, in the perspective of the promises, without minimizing those elements of Christianity which are original. We believe that those promises were fulfilled with the first coming of Christ. But it is nonetheless true that we still await their perfect fulfillment in his glorious return at the end of time" (*Guidelines and Suggestions,* para. II). In connection with the eschatological perspective of the fulfillment of the scriptures, cf. also *Christen und Juden* I,6.

The evangelical document (I,1) also recalls and develops the central point of the faith of the Old Testament: the one God, a point that we find also with an interesting annotation in the document of the International Theological Commission (Rome, October 20, 1980), Para. II B: "The faith of the Old Testament proclaims an absolute transcendence of God." On the other hand, the New Testament presents "the event of Jesus Christ": the whole of the patristic christological theology seeks the conciliation of transcendence and immanence as attested by the Old and the New Testament.

This manner of understanding the relationship between Old and New Testament in the theological and christological perspective seems in keeping with the thesis of Bullinger, as is recalled in the recent document entitled *Reformed Theology and the Jewish People* (Geneva, World Alliance of Reformed Churches, 1986, pp. 11–12).

In particular, the thesis that the merciful grace of the Father is present in the economy of salvation as testified in the Old Testament is accepted and borne out by the document of the reformed churches, by the scientific analyses of Sanders I have already discussed, and in a very ample and profound manner by the entire section III, 4 of the encyclical of John Paul II, *Dives in misericordia* (November 30, 1980), as far as "mercy in the Old Testament" is concerned.

We can see that the central affirmation of the faith of Islam described above also converges on this point of the one and merciful (*Raḥman*) God.

These theses are found again in the "Fundamental Theological Points of the Dialogue Between Jews and Christians" of the Central Committee of German Catholics (April 24, 1979), where the note of the ethical centrality of the Old Testament also very clearly comes to the fore: "Among the fundamental exigencies of the biblical revelation common to Jews and Christians there is the absolute respect for the life of others." The consequent moral obligation founded on the Old Testament is a constant feature of the Jewish-Christian dialogue, and was recently recalled by John Paul II in the synagogue of Rome and on the occasion of the beatification of Edith Stein on May 1, 1987 in Cologne.

The Jewish philosopher Emmanuel Levinas expresses himself as follows: "The oral Torah speaks 'in spirit and truth' even when it seems to crush verses and letters of the written Torah. It explains the ethical sense of the letter as extreme intelligibility of man and even of the cosmic. . . . The sanctity for which that [Israel] longs will be given it by the living God" (*Du Sacre au Saint—Cinq nouvelles lectures talmudiques,* Paris, 1977). We could here recall the moral and pastoral endorsement that Saint Ambrose and other fathers already lavished on the Old Testament.

In these brief remarks I hope to have shown some possible lines of present-day interpretation of the manifold relations between Old and New Testament. Nothing prevents us from calling them first covenant and second covenant, as some people are proposing, although one can say, in a certain sense, that there have been many covenants. The scriptures as a whole would thus appear as "the books of the covenants." But would one not thereby lose the sense of the unity of the economy of salvation of God, of the Spirit? And therefore, rightly as it would seem to me, the document *Plures nostrae aetatis* concerned with the Bible and christology (*Bible et Christologie,* Paris, Du Cerf, 1984), prefers to speak of but one covenant, the first, renewed in Jesus: "With the first, the law was given to the people of God; with the new, the Spirit of the Lord was showered on every being" (Para. 2.2.2.2).

It would therefore be very interesting indeed if scholars, taking due account of these orientations, were to seek today this very necessary synthesis, just as Saint Thomas, with a humble and lucid intelligence (*intellectus*) of faith, drew up a synthesis for his own day and age. That, at least, is my hope and good wish for your illustrious university.

Relations Between the Church and Judaism*

I would like to recall once again, for my part adding to what those who preceded me, H. E. Monsignor Rossano and Dr. Gerhart Riegner, so rightly emphasized, how important it was for our generation to work in close contact and harmony with the great fathers and protagonists of the council: Pope John XXIII, Pope Paul VI, Cardinal Bea, and how the council, in its deepest and most authentic spirit, was a coherent maturation of ideas already present in the preceding pontificates of Pius XI and Pius XII. The volume (*Fifteen Years of Dialogue,* Vatican City–Rome, 1988) which we have the honor of presenting this evening bears witness to this maturation, which was so rich, so exceptional and so extraordinary that it signaled a true, historic, turning point in relations between the Catholic Church and Judaism. For this we are particularly grateful to Monsignor Rossano and to the Director of the Libreria Editrice Vaticana, Fr. Giustino Farnedi, O.S.B., for having included this worthy publication in the prestigious collection of theological and philosophical studies, a collection which also contains several fundamental works of Karol Wojtyla, Pope John Paul II. I would also like to thank the technical director of the Tipografia Poliglotta Vaticana, Mr. Antonio Maggiotto, and his collaborators, as well as Professor Jean Halperin, Consultant of the World Jewish Congress, and all the others who contributed to the production of this work.

It is not by chance, perhaps, that just a few weeks ago another great work was officially presented, the systematic biography of Augustin Bea, written by Fr. Stjepan Schmidt, S.J. This too gives public witness to the path followed, in the first years after the council, for the fulfillment of No. 4 of the Declaration *Nostra aetate.* It is

---

* Rome, 1988; see Bibliography, n. 18.

not by chance, but rather providential coincidence that this year marks both the twentieth anniversary of the passing away of the "cardinal of Unity" as well as the twenty-fifth anniversary of the death of Pope John and the succession of Giovanni Battista Montini in the pontificate. In 1981 we honored the centenary of the birth of Cardinal Bea with a symposium, whose Acts, published in 1983, constitute another important historical source.

The last months of Pope Roncalli's life were of vital importance for the fate of *Nostra aetate*. In fact, in February 1963, as Fr. Schmidt points out in his book, the Secretariat for Christian Unity in its plenary meeting took up the theme of the Jews, according to the disposition given by the pope on December 13, 1962, with a view to the elaboration of a conciliar document.

If we recall that the proposal to set forth such a document had earlier been removed from the council's schedule and was reintroduced only after this decisive intervention of the pope, then we can understand why John XXIII has been so rightly described as "doubly father" (cf. St. Schmidt) of *Nostra aetate*. Faithfully interpreting the spirit of dialogue which animated the pope's actions, Cardinal Bea, a few months later, on March 31, 1963, met in New York with representatives of Jewish civil and religious organizations of various orientations (cf. St. Schmidt, *Agostino Bea,* pp. 466–467, 569).

This volume, which is here before us, condenses the fruit of all that was carried out in the succeeding twenty years and especially since 1970, with the launching of the International Liaison Committee, destined to take its place as an effective instrument of religious dialogue between the Catholic Church and Judaism.

Throughout these twenty years of progress many people worked along with us, and the names of the principal protagonists —one hundred and twenty-eight of them—are listed at the beginning of the book. Some of them are no longer with us, and we would like to remember them. They are Professor Cornelius Rijk, Fr. Pierre-Marie de Contenson, O.P., Professor Sidney Hoening, Monsignor Charles Moeller, our dear Zachariah Shuster, and, finally, Joseph Lichten, Knight Commander of Saint Gregory the Great, who passed away December 15, 1987.

Others will deepen the historical research of this impassioned and sometimes tormented journey, or will highlight several fundamental characteristics (developing the suggestions put forth by the previous illustrious speakers). I would like here to briefly try to turn our gaze to the future, almost to throw into the darkness ahead of us a torch which might illuminate and anticipate the path others will follow. I find comfort and faith for this effort in the humble yet firm example of the pope, whose teaching in this regard has become increasingly clear, explicit and profound, especially in recent years, and has been accompanied by meaningful and unequivocal gestures of reconciliation and affection toward the Jews, "our elder brothers in the faith of Abraham": it is for this that we owe the pope our most sincere thanks.

As a point of departure for these considerations, out of necessity rather brief, we can look to the emblematic address of the holy father during his visit to the temple of Rome two years ago. The text of the papal discourse, which has happily been published at the end of this volume, represents in a certain sense, the conclusion of a great, intense period—"Fifteen Years of Dialogue," in fact—but also, and perhaps to an even greater extent, represents the synthesis of this same period and the prophetic inauguration of a new period, a richer phase, almost a second voyage of discovery in more open waters, and thus with even greater risks. We are already living in this second period, and we must live it with full consciousness and responsibility.

In the two years since the visit to the synagogue we have also witnessed the great World Day of Prayer for Peace at Assisi. The fruits of that event have, in part, taken root before our eyes. At the same time the pope, for his part, has intensified his meetings with Jewish communities around the world, never missing an opportunity to deepen understanding or clarify this or that point, a point which perhaps needed theological clarification or application in the fields of ethics or justice, or simply on a more general ecumenical plane.

Out of this recent development, so rich and dynamic, I would like to pick out five programmatic points, asking the experts to reflect on them within a complete and organic synthesis, in the hope that they might also be, for all of you, a stimulus to concrete action.

The points are these: (1) a commitment against antisemitism; (2) a reflection on the shoah; (3) a mature dialogue; (4) a common religious basis and hope, mutually recognizing each other's essential characteristics and substantial differences; (5) a common commitment for justice and peace.

1. A COMMITMENT AGAINST ANTISEMITISM

The commitment against antisemitism, already programmatically spelled out in the disapproval expressed by the Second Vatican Council, has now been made even more explicit, concrete, and vigilant. We will carefully search for any remaining causes of potential antisemitism in the persistence of religious stereotypes or in prejudicial and incorrect attitudes, and also in publications which are either implicitly or openly antisemitic.

Nonetheless in the past, in particular historical circumstances, there have been episodes of antisemitism which were erroneously referred to religious motivations. Today we condemn them, and affirm that neither the New Testament nor Christianity as such must inspire antisemitic gestures and feelings. Speaking to the Jewish community of Sydney on November 26, 1986, Pope John Paul declared that there are no theological justifications for antisemitism. The commission which I head has already released two important documents, which should be known and applied by all Catholics—*Guidelines,* published in 1974, and *Notes,* published in 1985.

The common commitment against antisemitism, in another sense, is also part of the larger commitment for human rights, which I will speak about shortly.

2. A REFLECTION ON THE SHOAH

Connected, and yet distinct from the previous issue, this will be a mature and complete reflection on the period of atrocious persecution and suffering inflicted on European Jews during the Second World War. This period is called by its name in Hebrew, the Shoah. To bow one's head often just in religious silence before this endless abyss of pain and evil is only a right and proper sign of respect to the living memory of so many innocent victims, as Pope John Paul II has often said, recalling that they were exterminated because of their Jewish origins and identity, in the name of a perverse and diabolical ideology, an ideology both dehumanizing and anti-religious. Cardinal Lustiger has written: "Le centre de cette idéologie, c'etait la persecution du peuple juif, parce que peuple messianique" ("The center of this ideology was the persecution of the Jewish people because they were a messianic people") (*Le choix de Dieu,* Paris 1987, p. 126). With this, far from any possible hint of banalization or exploitation, we hope to carry out an act of reconciliation and spiritual conversion, before God and our Jewish brothers, for the good of all humanity.

3. A MATURE DIALOGUE

This volume, in the multiplicity of the themes it deals with and in a genuine spirit of esteem and an objective search for the truth in all its aspects, all seen from the different points of view of various authors, constitutes in and of itself a concrete example of mature dialogue, conscious of the limits and the objectives that dialogue proposes, respectful of the religious identity of both sides in dialogue, as much on the personal level as on the broader level of a meeting between two communities of faith. At the same time there seems to be a clear need inside the church to broaden our knowledge of a theology of Judaism which adequately takes these recent developments into account. Both courses were strongly encouraged by the pope in his letter of August 8, 1987 to Archbishop John May: "The more we try to be faithful, in loving obedience, to the God of the covenant, the creator and savior, contemplating in prayer his wonderful plan of redemption and loving our neighbor as ourselves, the deeper will be the roots of our dialogue and the more abundant its results."

4. A FOUNDATION AND A COMMON RELIGIOUS HOPE: MUTUALLY RECOGNIZING EACH OTHER'S ESSENTIAL CHARACTERISTICS AND SUBSTANTIAL DIFFERENCES

Through dialogue and common reflection we hope to be able to reach a better understanding and to be able to expound the many common elements which unite us at the root level of our shared religious identity, elements such as the faith of Abraham and the patriarchs, the commitment of faith and to the gift of the covenant,

the call to holiness and the ethical imperative of the commandments, veneration of the holy scriptures, the tradition of prayer, of
hospitality and love for our neighbor, respect and responsibility
toward all creation, and the desire for peace and the welfare of all
humanity, without discrimination.

Conscious of these common roots, we Christians will be able,
in an open and respectful dialogue, to fully express our faith in
Christ the universal redeemer in terms which, while recognizing the
substantial differences with the Jewish faith, lead us not to hostility
or mutual isolation, but rather to a fraternal emulation in fulfilling
all that we believe essential to the mission and witness of the church
in the world. Likewise, we hope that on the Jewish side, taking into
proper consideration the "asymmetries" which qualify our relations, it might still be possible to continue an analogous effort of
conceptual clarification and opening to religious cooperation.

We will thus be able to clarify, without fear of being misunder-
stood, that our Christian faith does not exclude either hope or
responsibility in building the kingdom of God. The hope and expectation for the kingdom of heaven had become even more intense at the time of Jesus. "That there might soon be a King over
us" was and still is the daily prayer from the "Eighteen Blessings" of
the devout Israelite who calls for justice, peace and salvation from
the God of the covenant. This messianic hope, which today still
resonates in the heart of each Jew and leads to a concrete commitment, constitutes as well one of those values of the "great spiritual
patrimony common to Christians and Jews" (*Redemptor hominis,*
n. 11), although this value may be lived and expressed in different
ways according to the faith of the church and the faith of the Jewish
people.

On the other hand, no one is excluded from the redeeming
embrace of Christ who, on the cross, offered his life for the sins of
everyone, and no longer, as the council teaches (*Nostra aetate,* n. 4)
can the historical responsibility of Christ's passion be "blamed on
all those Jews then living nor to the Jews of our own day."

Homilies, especially during Holy Week and the paschal trid-
uum, should hold to these principles, in conformity with the *Guidelines* published by our Commission in 1974 and the *Notes* published in 1985.

In a more general way, it will certainly be of great value to us

Christians to ask ourselves what exactly are the meanings and implications of the affirmation of John Paul II that "the old covenant was never revoked." Two other recently published documents will also be able to help us in this reflection: the document "Plures nostrae aetatis" on the Bible and christology (*Bible et Christologie,* Cerf, Paris 1984) and the document "In hac relatione" on *Selected Themes of Ecclesiology,* published October 7, 1985 by the International Theological Commission. This last text leads us to consider the "novelty" of the church as a "people of the Trinity" (cf. par. 3.2) on a pilgrimage through history, and as "a communion of faith, hope and charity" (par. 6.1). Within this perspective, limiting itself to dealing only with certain questions—among them the issue of inculturation—the document leaves open and unprejudiced the possibility of a reflection on the "mystery of Israel" (using the expression Jacques Maritain was so fond of) and on the Jewish people as a "community of faith" and "people of God," a reflection in keeping with the train of thought which emerges from the development of Catholic-Jewish dialogue, to which the volume we are presenting today bears witness.

5. A COMMON COMMITMENT TO JUSTICE AND PEACE

Among the programmatic points which the International Liaison Committee for Catholic-Jewish cooperation has emphasized since the beginning and reconfirmed at each plenary session is cooperation in various fields: education, ethics, the defense of human rights and religious liberty, the promotion of justice and peace.

I want to reaffirm that commitment, which will find even more efficient and concrete forms of expression. In the field of education, I hope it will take place through the various Centers of Judeo-Christian Studies (several have already been founded in different countries: in the United States at Seton Hall University, in Switzerland at Lucerne's Faculty of Theology, in Israel at the ancient Monastery of Ratisbonne), and also developing in a more articulated way the courses and cultural exchanges which have for years been successfully organized by the Pontifical Universities of Rome.

Of the many points which could be touched on in the field of justice and peace, I would like to express the prayer and hope that it might be possible to contribute, by means of our religious dialogue, to the construction of a peace which respects the rights of all, wherever our two communities may find themselves living together, and especially in that land, so dear to Jews, Christians and Muslims, the holy land, land of the fathers, and of the holy city of Jerusalem, for the Jewish people which lives in the state of Israel and for the Palestinian people.

Thanks to the commitment of all of us to end violence and injustice in every corner of the globe—according to the message of the prophets of Israel and on the religious foundation of our common brotherhood, deriving from the common fatherhood of God recognized by Jews and Christians—we express the wish that, overcoming every painful misunderstanding, the invocation of the Psalm might be fulfilled:

> Let your servants see what you can do for them,
> let their children see your glory.
> May the sweetness of the Lord be on us!
> Make all we do succeed (Ps 90:16–17).

The Church and Modern Antisemitism[1]*

It is a great pleasure and, indeed, an honor for me to have this opportunity of addressing you today. I wish to begin by recalling two events which are very significant for our theme: "The Church Facing Modern Antisemitism." They took place fifty and twenty-five years ago respectively.

The first is the tragic prelude to the "final solution," the attacks against the Jews in the German Reich in the night of November 9–10, 1938, the "Pogromnach" (Kristallnacht).[2]

The second took place twenty-five years after the horror of the shoah, in which we saw the most terrible and diabolical aspects of antisemitism. The Catholic Church, developing a series of previous condemnations of antisemitism, on November 18–19, 1963, a few months after the death of Pope John XXIII, at the Second Vatican Council, started discussion on a document concerning the Jews.[3] We were at the beginning of the pontificate of Paul VI who, following the hope and the spirit of Pope John XXIII, would approve in 1965 the final Declaration *Nostra aetate,* section 4 of which states: "The Church . . . deplores[4] the hatred, persecution, and displays of antisemitism directed against the Jews at any time and from any source."

Why and how did the council decide to speak about Jews and antisemitism? We know today that this theme was suggested to Pope John XXIII by Professor Jules Isaac (1877–1964) during an audience of June 13, 1960.[5] After this audience, the pope referred Isaac to Cardinal Bea, and on October 26 of the same year the

* Aberdeen and London, 1988; see Bibliography, n. 19.

cardinal had another important meeting with the then president of
the World Jewish Congress, Nahum Goldman.[6]

Malcolm Hay was, from 1950, a close and sincere friend of
Jules Isaac, after having read his *Jésus et Israël*. Both are examples
of men who devoted themselves to the study of a tradition other
than their own so as to promote respect for the Jews among Christian people. Hay, a Catholic, fervently studied Hebrew and Jewish
culture; Isaac, a Jewish historian, under Nazi oppression under-
took theological and biblical research. Their examples of commitment to the truth and to hope in the fruits of sincere dialogue
between Jews and Christians influenced the attitude of the church
over these last forty years.

Pope John Paul II, in his consistent and untiring efforts to
spread the teaching of the Vatican Council on Jews and Judaism,
takes every opportunity of offering reflections and reactions on
antisemitism. Let me recall just a few of his recent statements,
which reveal the context in which I will put my lecture this evening.

Visiting the great Roman synagogue (April 13, 1986), the pope
clearly recognized "that the acts of discrimination, unjustified limi-
tation of religious freedom, oppression also on the level of civil
freedom in regard to the Jews were, from an objective point of view,
gravely deplorable manifestations." The pope also quoted *Nostra
aetate* and honored the memory of the victims of the shoah. Writing to Archbishop John May of St. Louis (August 8, 1987) John
Paul II affirmed:

> There is no doubt that the sufferings endured by the Jews are
> also for the Catholic Church a motive of sincere sorrow, espe-
> cially when one thinks of the indifference and sometimes the
> resentment which, in particular historical circumstances, have
> divided Jews and Christians. Indeed this evokes in us still
> firmer resolutions to cooperate for justice and true peace.

In his address, this year, to Jewish representatives in Vienna
(June 24, 1988) the pope underlined the religious dimension of our
Christian reflection on Jewish sufferings, and added:

The process of complete reconciliation between Jews and Christians has to be carried on in full force on all levels of relationship between our communities. Collaboration and common studies should help to explore in a deeper way the significance of the shoah. The causes which are responsible for antisemitism or which still more universally lead to so-called "holy wars" must be discovered and, if at all possible, removed. From what we see happening in the ecumenical sphere, I am confident that it will be possible to speak openly among ourselves about the rivalries, the radicalism and conflicts of the past. We must try to recognize them also in their historical conditions and overcome them by our common efforts for peace, for a consistent witness of faith and the promotion of the moral values which should characterize individuals and nations.[7]

All these references indicate the perspective of the considerations that will follow. My reflections continue the spirit and the conclusions of a lecture I delivered to the Oxford Union Society on March 13, 1985.[8] There I suggested a distinction between "the Christian body of belief and practice" and the "historical embodiments of Christianity." In relation to the first concept of "Christianity" I concluded that "antisemitism is simply anti-Christian"; referring to the second concept, I recognized that "some very nasty forms of antisemitism are part of . . . deficiencies" of Christianity.

And so we come to our subject matter. Taking up the preliminary distinction between the historical and the meta-historical (spiritual or divine) dimension of "Christianity," we can apply the same principle to the "church." Consequently, I will first of all examine historically the attitude of the church to modern antisemitism. Secondly, I will consider, in the light of Christian faith principles, the reasons for this attitude.

The concept of "modern antisemitism" impels us to distinguish between the cultural, racial and socio-economic aspects of antisemitism as developed during these last hundred years, and the religious anti-Judaic elements in antisemitism. These latter have had long centuries of development. It is thus that I prefer to maintain the three terms of anti-Judaism, antisemitism and anti-

Zionism, avoiding ambiguities, generalizations or confusions in terminology and in the historical and religious events that such terms evoke.

HISTORICAL OVERVIEW (1840–1928)

Since I am not an historian, I will limit myself to recalling here only some of the most relevant events which have happened since the beginning of emancipation, starting at the accusation of ritual murder made against the Jews in Damascus (1840), up to the decree of the holy office in 1928, when the apostolic see condemned antisemitism. But let me also identify myself with the wish of the Christian historian François Delpech, that from deeper dialogue between Jewish and Christian historians in this matter—and, I would add, from similar dialogues also in the field of ethics, philosophy or religion—a more complete knowledge of the historical facts will help us to formulate correct judgments about this period.[9]

It has been observed that the episodes of Jewish hatred in the second half of the nineteenth century present generally a new form, less religious, more political and more particularly racial than the previous.[10]

In this judgment, the French historian Delpech follows conclusions already expressed by Bernard Lazare in 1894.[11] I have already cited the so-called Damascus affair, which, together with the scandal of the kidnaping and baptizing of the Jewish child Mortara, led to the foundation of L'Alliance Israelite Universelle (1860). In both events religious convictions and prejudices were at work, and in consequence of the reaction from the Jewish side, there was counteraction in Christian circles, in strongly polemical and anti-Jewish terms.

But the confusion and the mixture of religious with other non-religious causes of Jewish hatred, already present in those episodes, becomes more evident in various events that took place in different European countries:

- in 1863, after the fall of the Polish revolution, anti-Jewish pamphlets were published in Poland;
- in 1878, in Germany, the Protestant pastor Adolf Stocker, and

the journalist Wilhelm Marr (who created the term antisemitism), founded the first political anti-Jewish party in Berlin;

- in 1881, after the killing of the czar, the Russian pogroms began;
- in 1886 Drumont published his antisemitic book *France Juive;*
- in 1894 the Dreyfus Affair broke out: it was, as Péguy realized, a notable crisis in three histories—in the history of Israel, in the history of France, and in the history of Christianity;[12]
- in England, but also in the United States, the English teacher Edward Freeman was very active; he was judged by Hay to be one of the early pioneers of Nazi doctrine.[13]

To provide a really balanced judgment, this short historical overview must be supplemented by other elements specifically concerning the Christian attitude and reactions to antisemitism in modern times.

In 1870 the French brothers Joseph and Augustin Lémann, inspired by sincere love for the Jews together with a strong commitment to their conversion, prepared a project concerning the preeminent position of the Jews in the church to be submitted to the fathers of the First Vatican Council. Before the anticipated dispersal of the council, the project received the support of 510 conciliar fathers out of 1,087.[14]

In 1892 we can recall the efforts of Pope Leo XIII to moderate antisemitic attacks through his public letter, "calling upon all right-thinking men in France, including Protestants and Jews, to unite together against the enemies of religion and society."[15] One can also take into account many Catholic voices that in various countries supported "semitism" (as they called it) against antisemitism. I already quoted the example of Péguy who was said to have "defended the Jews because he loved them."[16] But the clearest exposition of a positive theory against antisemitism was expressed by two Italian priests, Semeria and Bonomelli. The latter subsequently became bishop of Cremona. The terms of their condemnation are the same as found in post-Vatican II Catholic teaching. After spending three months in European countries, Bonomelli discussed the antisemitic theories he came across in Germany, France and Austria, and concluded:

- the people of Israel are "a mystery";

- the economic reason for antisemitism is not a reason;
- the racial reason for antisemitism is "absurd";
- antisemitism "is not Christian";
- the Jews of today are "in no way guilty for the death of Jesus."[17]

In Germany the young Jesuit Augustin Bea condemned the racial reason for antisemitism in an article published in 1920.[18] Let me conclude this first historical section with an analysis of the apostolic see's attitudes. Pius XI in 1926 condemned the Action Française, in whose programs both anti-Christian and antisemitic doctrines played a significant part, and in 1928 the church condemned antisemitism with the usual very strong terms of that time: "reprobat, ita vel maxime damnat." This decree of the holy office, issued on March 25, 1928,[19] had the title *De consociatione vulgo 'Amici Israel' abolenda.* It referred to an association of so-called "Friends of Israel" which it sought to suppress. The program of the "Friends of Israel," set out in the Latin booklet *Pax super Israel* (Peace to Israel), included: (1) modification of the prayer Pro perfidis Judaeis on Good Friday; (2) repudiation of the accusation of deicide; (3) suppression of the liturgical celebrations related to legends of ritual murders. Nineteen cardinals belonged to this society, including five holy office consultants and Merry del Val, secretary of state of Pius X, together with 278 bishops and 3,000 priests.[20]

The Decree declares:

1. that the original profound spirit of the society was *laudabile* (praiseworthy);
2. that in this spirit the apostolic see condemns antisemitism; but
3. nevertheless the evolution of the society "Amici Israel" does not correspond with the church's sentiments or the teaching of the fathers or with sacred liturgy, so it must be abolished.

An anonymous commentary to the decree was published in *La Civiltà Cattolica.*[21] To each of the three points of the decree the commentary adds some clarification:

1. Love for the Jews involves prayers and action for their conversion, in forms that must not increase scandals or polemics.

2. Christian condemnation of antisemitism has therefore specific moral and Christian motivations.
3. The abolition of the society "Amici Israel" is not a condemnation of serious writers who defend the Jews against antisemitic attacks. Libels, such as the Protocols of Zion, are falsifications; polemical writings are not encouraged.

At the end is added a long and confused paragraph concerning the "Judaic danger," written in terms which are not helpful to our reflections, and reveal in fact the persistence of prejudices against the Jews.

The evolution of Catholic teaching after the Second Vatican Council enables us at this time to evaluate the holy office's decree in a more balanced way.

1. It was a positive step to affirm that the Christian love for Israel is the reason for the condemnation of antisemitism; such condemnation in fact in subsequent years encouraged many Christian writers in their defense of Jews against antisemitic attacks.

2. The rejection of the program of "Pax super Israel," particularly of the three above quoted points (which were later adopted during and after the pontificate of John XXIII) can be explained both historically and theologically: historically, because in regard to the Jews, economic, social, political and religious considerations continued to be confused; theologically, in that the absence of positive reflections on the values of Judaism—as developed only after the Second Vatican Council and *Nostra aetate*—was the obstacle to eliminating and repudiating the basic elements of the "teaching of contempt" present in the church.

Dr. Gerhart Riegner, in another recent lecture,[22] clearly set out further reflections on the failure of development in the field of Christian-Jewish relations, particularly in Germany during the period I have examined.

THE PERIOD 1928–1942

Again, I am not an expert, in the technical sense, of the history of this period, and my overview takes its inspiration from a reflection on history in the light of faith, and of course also from my own experience.

During the years preceding the systematic, dehumanizing Nazi attempt to destroy the European Jews, between 1928 and 1942, we see an escalation of antisemitism promoted by the Nazi regime. For its propaganda, not only racial, economic, nationalist prejudices, but also the old anti-Jewish stereotypes, stemming particularly from the influence of Christian writers during and after the middle ages, were widely employed: accusations of ritual murders, collective guilt, "deicide," immorality, passion plays as popular expressions of Jewish hatred, and so on.

In addition to such anti-Jewish prejudices, other extrinsic obstacles stood in the way of a more massive Christian reaction to the increase of Nazi antisemitism: for example the anti-communist polemic and the accord of the Vatican with Germany (1933). Nevertheless, one must bear in mind the opposition to antisemitism, led in France by Catholics (Maritain, Mounier), in Germany by Protestants (Karl Barth and especially Dietrich Bonhoeffer); after the promulgation of the encyclical *Mit brennender Sorge* (1937), Pius XI in the Vatican was deeply sensitive to this defense of the Jews, and accepted the suggestion of Edith Stein and J. Veraart to write an encyclical against antisemitism.[23] After the pope's death (February 10, 1939), his successor Pius XII in part continued his project in the promulgation (October 27, 1939) of his first encyclical, *Summi pontificatus,* condemning extreme nationalism, state idolatry, totalitarianism and racism as being responsible for the war.

The strong opposition of the Vatican to Austria's annexation is also well known. Bishop Henri de Lubac recently put together a long series of interventions against antisemitism; in particular let me recall the common protest of Cardinals Verdier (Paris), Van Roey (Malines) and Schuster (Milan) after the ruthless pogrom of the Kristallnacht (November 9–10, 1938)[24] as well as the words and action of Father Bernhard Lichtenberg, who later died on the way to Dachau.

It will be of interest for our evaluation to quote here some authors concerned with this period. Aaron Steinberg's two essays were published in Yiddish in 1934 and 1939. In the first, Steinberg clearly observed that "the deeper motive of Nazi antisemitism is its anti-Christian, politico-cultural Pan-Germanism."[25] He appreciated the battle of Protestant preachers (Friedrich Bodelschwingh,

Martin Niemöller) against Nazi idolatry and in defense of the Jews, as well as of Cardinal Michael von Faulhaber of Munich in his sermons on "Judaism, Christendom and Germanism."[26] Steinberg also recalls that the book of Alfred Rosenberg, *Der Mythos des XX. Jahrhunderts* (1930), was condemned by the Vatican (but not so *Mein Kampf*).[27] In his second essay, in 1939, he concluded, dramatically before the shoah, with words still relevant: "If we accept the support of Christianity while we are spiritually strong and armed, then we can accept it freely and without fear. What is more, we can then accept it as equals, for in a deeper sense Christianity today needs our good will no less than we need its concern."[28]

THE SHOAH (1942–1945)

After this prophetic voice came the diabolical storm of the shoah, for which no ancient words and concepts (holocaust, churban) nor silence could possibly describe the indescribable and inconceivable horror of the scientific, modern extermination of an entire people, the Jewish people. How can we judge this catastrophic event, and therefore the attitude of the church during those terrible years of persecution? This question is very sensitive and complex, nonetheless serious and important for the present and future state of Jewish-Christian relations, and for western civilization.

One of the first lessons, or imperatives, we can learn from this catastrophic destruction of European Jews is the imperative of the remembrance: "There is no reconciliation without remembrance."[29]

Another point can be reflection on the Jewish destiny and its uniqueness, which can be regarded as having an exemplary value.[30] As Cardinal Hume recently declared at the Holocaust Conference: "The political and racial philosophies of National Socialism may have been consigned to the past, but the soil in which they took root is to be found in other countries and other times. It could yet yield other harvests of hate."[31]

For this reason, it is a positive step to develop holocaust studies at various levels: religious, moral, historical, scientific, as for example the most recent held in Oxford (July 10–13, 1988).[32] Concerning the particular point of the holy see's interventions during the persecution, let me add the references to two studies by Jewish scholars, the first by Pinchas Lapide,[33] and the second, recently published in a new Italian edition by the late Joseph Licthen.[34]

Since, as it seems to me, no definitive historical or theological analysis on the shoah has yet been written, it is difficult actually to propose ultimate conclusions. Nevertheless, at least we can be cautious in avoiding historical oversimplifications, extreme philosophical generalizations and radical or paradoxical conclusions in the theological field. The recent exhaustive research of Raul Hilberg is the latest helpful example we have in the field of history.[35]

On the other side, let me present some conclusions, or observations, of Cardinals Martini and Lustiger, from a religious perspective. Cardinal Martini, in his paper delivered last year at the "Workshop on Antisemitism" in Philadelphia, affirmed that "theology now is invited ever more insistently since the shoah to be confronted with the history and the experience of faith of the Jews at Auschwitz."[36]

Another interesting annotation is made by Cardinal Lustiger: "The center of this [Nazi] ideology was the persecution of the chosen people, the Jewish people, as a messianic people."[37] The pagan Nazi "messianism" was the opposite of the doctrines of messianism and redemption as affirmed in Judaism and in Christianity.

AFTER THE SHOAH (1945–1988)

Immediately after the end of the Second World War, in 1946, an International Council of Christians and Jews (ICCJ) was set up. Among its members were the Jew Jules Isaac and the Catholic Jacques Maritain. The ICCJ promoted an international conference against antisemitism (Seelisberg, July 30–August 5, 1947), which ended with a call to the churches, in which ten points were suggested for combating antisemitism in Christian civilization. It was this same program that Jules Isaac presented to Pope John XXIII in 1962, thus exercising great influence on the conciliar Declaration *Nostra aetate,* no. 4.

The trend toward the condemnation of antisemitism, already expressed in many statements of various Christian churches before the Vatican Council, had a significant increase after 1965. In 1970 a permanent International Liaison Committee (ILC) between the

Roman Catholic Church and the world Jewish community was created in Rome. The question of antisemitism had a first place on its agenda.[38] Pope Paul VI, in his address to the ILC and to the recently created Commission for Religious Relations with the Jews, on January 10, 1975 solemnly reaffirmed this point.[39] The same condemnation of antisemitism was clearly repeated by the two documents published by the Commission—in 1974 (*Guidelines*)[40] and in 1985 (*Notes*),[41] and by the XII Plenary Session of the ILC in 1985, this last with particular reference to the shoah.[42] The pontificate of Pope John Paul II gave a very significant impulse to Catholic reflection on antisemitism and on the shoah, as was clear when on June 7, 1979 the holy father visited and prayed in the death camp at Auschwitz. His gestures, his words, his moments of silent prayer were so frequent, moving and impressive, that nobody up to now has succeeded in presenting a full and organic synthesis of the pope's mind and teaching in this matter.[43] This may account for some misunderstanding or manipulations of the events by the media, and for people sometimes not being completely confident in the sincerity of the church's attitude toward the Jews and Judaism.

CONCLUSION

I would try now to offer some conclusions from my words so far, and to indicate some programmatic points. A first point relates to methodology. The point of view of the church is not merely historical, although history constitutes the "body" of its experience. To use an analogy: as the Greek and Roman historians such as Thucydides and Tacitus examined the events of the *historia magistra vitae,* the church analyzes the events of the *historia salutis,* i.e. it looks at history in the light of its faith in Jesus Christ, son of David, Kyrios and redeemer.

The style of pure, technical analysis of history can be in some cases academic and abstract in a way that risks the trivialization of tragic events like the shoah. On the other hand, we are also conscious of the risk, implicit in our Christian perspective, of "dejudaization" of the events of the Jewish history. We take both risks, with the aim of course of overcoming them.

One of the main questions of history is the question of the

"causes" of the events. In this context can be put the search for the "roots" of modern antisemitism, and one can speak with truth also of "Christian" roots.

But when our perspective is religious, the reference to "Christian" roots of antisemitism is very ambiguous, since it can be interpreted—as is affirmed by some authors—as implying that antisemitism is a basic element of Christianity, which is not true and is a very damaging affirmation.

After these two preliminary clarifications, we can affirm that the church's attitude to modern antisemitism was—with some exceptions—of condemnation, both before and after the shoah—nevertheless, with a notable difference, since before the shoah there was no general reflection on the causes of antisemitism, neither in cultural nor in theological terms. After the shoah such reflection in Christian culture began principally in a spiritual perspective, less in historical perspective, although this second was also developed.

With particular regard to Nazi antisemitism, it can be said that Christian opposition could have been, on some occasions at least, stronger and more massive, but we cannot forget that there was opposition, sometimes in cooperation with Jews. Among the causes that worked against a strong general reaction were:

■ Before 1939, there was a failure of the Christian culture to develop any rational systematic analysis of the non-religious components of antisemitism and the complementary lack of positive teaching concerning Jews and Judaism in Catholic theology. More generally, anti-Jewish prejudices were still active, stemming from the medieval "teaching of contempt" which was a source of stereotypes and of popular hatreds.
■ After the beginning of the war, we must remember, however, how difficult it was to speak out, given the polemic propaganda and oppression of the German military regime. Nonetheless, in many cases Christians condemned publicly the Nazi persecution and saved Jews with great risk and even at the cost of their lives, as John Paul II recently recalled on different occasions.[44]

The evolution of the Catholic Church's attitude in search of the causes of antisemitism was determined, after 1945, by close dialogue with the Jews and with other churches and ecclesial communities. This evolution has had various dimensions.

1. *Theological dimension:* the Christian people must respect and love the Jewish people, since it remains beloved by God (see *Nostra aetate,* no. 4).

2. *Rational-juridical dimension:* antisemitism is condemned as one of the expressions of discrimination and hatred against people for reason of race, nation, religion, culture (see Declaration of Human Rights, 1948).

3. *Historico-philosophical dimension:* the absolute hatred of the Jews, as appears in the Nazi persecution and ideology, argues for a continuous serious inquiry into Christian history and culture, in order to eradicate anti-Jewish prejudices with erroneous theological motivations.

4. *Ethical dimension:* for all the previous reasons, we share common responsibility today for remembering the victims of antisemitism and for combating any expression of anti-Jewish hatred. Not only this, but also we must develop and expand reflection on Judaism in the various above-mentioned dimensions, in a pluralistic and democratic way. This has been our study in the twenty-five years after the Second Vatican Council and we must continue to pursue it.

Jewish and Christian Witnesses to the Living God*

For all of us, the life of Abraham is an example of dialogue with God, of faith, and of witness.

We see how Abraham was engaged in dialogue with God in the story of his reception of the guests at the oak of Mamre (Gen 18). He exemplified faith in God even to the point of offering Isaac, his only son (Gen 22; Heb 11:17).

He was a witness among the pagans that God demands an obedient response from the human person in solidarity with others (cf. Qur'an 60:4).

This is why the church, with her supreme teaching authority, declared at the Second Vatican Council that Christians "are included in the same patriarch's call" as sons and daughters of Abraham according to faith (Gal 3:7; *Nostra aetate* 4). God revealed himself to Abraham and established a covenant with him for the blessing of his stock and all the nations on earth. Consequently, we Catholics think of the Jews, Abraham's stock, as our "elder brothers in the faith of Abraham" (John Paul II at the "Gesú" Church in Rome, December 31, 1986).

Muslims also revere Abraham as a prophet and "friend of God" (Halil Allah), as a model of wholehearted gift of self to God (*Islam,* lt. *oblatio*) in hope and confident expectation, which implies complete submission to God's inscrutable decrees (*Nostra aetate* 3). For this reason, "we are especially brothers in God, who created us and whom we are trying to reach, in our own ways, through faith, prayer and worship, through the keeping of his law and through submission to his design" (John Paul II, to the representatives of Muslim community, Davao 1981).

* São Paulo, 1989; see Bibliography, n. 21.

This is the root of our common spiritual bond, and of our common responsibility to promote human dignity, peace and freedom according to the high ethical standards God has given to us. For this reason, in thanking you for honoring Dr. Gerhart Riegner and me with the "Patriarch Abraham Award," I feel both a sense of gratitude to almighty God, and a renewed sense of commitment to his commandment to love every human being.

Among God's many gifts and graces is religious and human freedom, that is, the complete liberation of men and women. This is part of God's universal plan of merciful redemption, a plan which demands a response from us. So it was when the people of Israel were delivered from slavery at Passover. Then they received the beginnings of the redemption, but its fulfillment only came fifty days later with the gift of the Torah which included commandments of universal value. It is precisely this gift that we celebrate at Shavuot, a celebration which is taking place this very week; Jesus Christ confirmed in the new covenant the deep values of the first covenant.

In what ways can we Christians and Jews cooperate in this responsibility to work for the "mending of the world" (the *tikkun y'olam be-malkhuth Shadday*), to make this world a better place while serving the kingdom of heaven?

In his recent encyclical *Sollicitudo rei socialis* (December 30, 1987), John Paul II suggested that all people, "by their civic activity, by contributing to economic and political decisions and by personal commitment to national and international undertakings," implement "the measures inspired by solidarity and love of preference for the poor." Then the pope addressed an appeal "to the Jewish people, who share with us the inheritance of Abraham, our father in faith (Rom 4:11), as well as to the Muslims who, like us, believe in the just and merciful God" (II, 47).

I would also like to recall the suggestions made in the recent document, "The Church and Racism: Toward a More Fraternal Society," issued by the Pontifical Commission "Iustitia et Pax" on November 3, 1988. By means of our solidarity, we must avoid every form of modern racism, such as antisemitism, discriminatory legislation, and bio-engineering manipulation, from which genocide, ethnocide, and radical and social discrimination flow. There are times when, in Abraham's footsteps, our witness will require us even to be ready for martyrdom. Indeed, this was the spiritual meaning of Abraham's willingness to offer his child to God at Moriah, and of Jesus' self-offering on the cross. In this spirit, we are particularly grateful to you, Mrs. Jehan Sadat, for your presence among us today. We remember here your husband, Anwar al-Sadat, who had the courageous peace initiative in going to Jerusalem.

Another area of collaboration involves the integrity of creation. Every creature on earth—in the skies, in the sea, everywhere—sings the glory of God, and can contribute to our happiness. But we should regard all these creatures and all of creation not with a spirit of exploitation or rapacity (this was, in fact, the first human sin in the garden of Eden), but with a spirit of respect for God's wonderful mirabilia. This goal will be attained more easily if we cooperate in trying to find solutions to economic and developmental problems affecting both individual persons and nations.

This wonderful hope we have for the development of better relations between us as peoples living the faith of Abraham finds particular expression in the Jewish-Christian dialogue. When we consider the great change in our attitudes toward one another that took place after the Second Vatican Council, we look back with great sorrow upon the long history of divisions, polemics, and misunderstandings which kept us apart for so long. Who could have foreseen that our relationship would change so much for the better in such a brief time?

Immediately after the council, a Vatican Office for Jewish Relations was established. This was followed in 1974 by the institution of the holy see's Commission for Religious Relations with the Jews, whose work would be assisted by a number of permanent consultants. In 1970 a permanent International Liaison Committee (ILC) was created, including five Catholic members appointed with the approval of the holy father, and five Jewish members representing the "International Jewish Committee on Interreligious Consultations" (IJCIC).

Between 1970 and 1985, the International Liaison Committee held twelve meetings, and papers given at these meetings have been published jointly by the Vatican and Lateran Presses. The holy see's Commission, for its part, published two important documents, in 1974 and 1985. The way was prepared for this activity by many Christian-Jewish encounters which took place before the council. One of them, the Seelisberg conference in 1946, benefited from important contributions by Jacques Maritain and Jules Isaac, both of whom influenced the thinking of Pope John XXIII and Cardinal Augustin Bea, the first head of the Vatican Commission.

We should never retrace the steps we have made during and after the Second Vatican Council, but go forward and develop further and deeper our relations in the light of faith and with confidence in Abraham's God who brings us together toward a better world for the benefit of all humanity.

The depth of this rediscovered brotherhood between Jews and Christians has been shown in the teachings and gestures of Pope John Paul II, particularly in his visit to the great Roman synagogue, and in his invitation to Jewish and other religious leaders to pray for peace at Assisi in 1986. But also, important developments in relations between Jews and Christians in Latin America make me very confident about the future. With hope and joy I have learned of your progress in the Continental Department of CELAM (Conselho Episcopal Latino-Americano) in Bogota, and of the initiatives at the national level under the auspices of the Conference of Brazilian Bishops' Commission for religious dialogue between Catholics and Jews. I hope these initiatives, which have important ecumenical implications, will also have great impact on interfaith activity.

Moreover, your 1985 Panamerican Conference (I Conferencia Panamericana de Relações Católico-judaicas, São Paulo, Novembro de 1985), The Day of Prayer of Peace in October 1986, and the recently introduced courses on Judaism at the Catholic seminary at São Paulo have been greatly appreciated.

Let me conclude with a quotation from your meaningful document, "Guia para o diálogo católico-judaico no Brasil" (Guide for the Catholic-Jewish Dialogue in Brazil): "All of us are heirs of the Second Vatican Council. The council irreversibly altered the way in which we look upon each other, determined to travel the path toward a future marked by brotherhood, harmony, and peace." Through your prayer and spiritual conversion, and through your common witness and action in Brazil, may God's blessing that was promised to Abraham's stock come down upon your nation, and upon all the nations and peoples of the world, for the glory of God, as the psalmist sings:

> The princes of the people gather
> as the people of the God of Abraham,
> For the shields of the earth belong to God:
> he is highly exalted (Ps 47:10).

Religious Pluralism and the Second Vatican Council*

It is both a privilege and a joy for me to be with you this morning, at the Twelfth National Workshop on Christian-Jewish Relations. I gratefully accepted your invitation to speak on the theme of "Religious Pluralism and the Second Vatican Council." But before entering into this subject, I would like to engage in a brief etymological analysis of "religious pluralism." "Pluralism," although of Latin origin, is fundamentally an English word. "Religious," however, as a basically Latin word, requires a look at its meaning in some classical and Christian Latin authors.

In philosophy the term "pluralism" was used in opposition to "monism," indicating a theory according to which the world is composed of a multiplicity of individual, independent entities which cannot be considered simply as forms or phenomena of a unique and absolute reality.

Used as a sociological concept, we find in Webster's *Ninth New Collegiate Dictionary* the following description: "a state of society in which members of diverse ethnic, racial, religious, or social groups maintain an autonomous participation in and development of their traditional culture or special interest within the confines of a common civilization."

Religious pluralism considers the diversity in society according to the relation to God which a person accepts and confesses. The Latin term *religio* is etymologically derived from *re-legare* or *re-eligere,* but all three meanings describe a relation to the divine:

(1) Cicero in *De natura deorum:* "qui omnia quae ad Cultum

* Chicago, 1990; see Bibliography, n. 25.

141

deorum pertinerent diligenter retractarent et tamquam relegerent, sunt dicti 'religiosi' " (those who reconsider and so to say reread (and/or recollect) continuously and zealously all things that belong to the cult of the gods, are said to be "religious") (*De natura deorum,* 2,72).

(2) In the same sense St. Isidore of Seville: "religio a relegendo ea quae sunt divini cultus" (Religion comes from re-reading (and/or recollecting) what belongs to divine cult) (*Etymologiae X ad litt. R*).

(3) St. Augustine derives "religio" from "re-eligere": "Deum re-eligere debemus quem amiseramus negligentes" (We should choose God again, whom we have neglected and lost) (*De Civitate Dei* X, 4), as well as from "re-ligare": "Religat nos religio uni omnipotenti Deo" (Religion binds us to the one almighty God) (*De vera religione,* Cap. LV, n. iii). This etymology had his preference and was also favored by Lactantius (*Divinae Institutiones* IV, 28).

The word "religio" has always expressed a relationship with the divine, with God and, in Christian literature, a bond with God. Religious pluralism supposes a diversity among human beings, precisely in what they have in common, namely their relationship with God, their search for God, their way to God. Is their goal, in the end, the same? Have they nothing in common on the way? The diversities that we find in religious pluralism are very different in content and depth. I would group these into three categories: Religious pluralism among Catholics; Religious pluralism among Christians of different communions; Religious pluralism among Christian and non-Christian religions.

Concerning the first category we may ask the question: is religious pluralism possible within the boundaries of the same church? I raise the question especially with regard to the Roman Catholic Church. It could be lucidly argued that she is accurately defined by dogma, but also tightly governed by canon law, in such a way that real pluralism seems impossible. At the same time we see, for example, a great variety in religious life for men and women, from monastic life in its various forms and expressions to active engagement, inspired by religious principles, in all fields of human life and society. But we see here a great variety of organic life within the same body rather than real pluralism. This variety of life within the same body has been eloquently described by St. Paul in his letters to the Romans and to the Corinthians (Rom 12 and 1 Cor 12). The diversity is functional (Rom 12:4), "a manifestation of the Spirit for the common good" (1 Cor 12:7).

A greater diversity developed from the beginning within the one Christian community between Christians in the east, of oriental culture, whether they be Greek, Syriac, Chaldean, Coptic, or Armenian, and Christians in the west, of Latin culture. The Christian Church of Jewish origin and tradition had already disappeared as a particular church. A strong process of inculturation caused differences between east and west in all forms and expressions of the Christian faith. The Second Vatican Council speaks of a particular church or churches of the eastern rites. The term "rite" more specifically indicates the celebration of the sacramental, especially the eucharistic, liturgy. Since "the liturgy is the summit toward which the life and activity of the church is directed and it is at the same time the fountain from which her power flows" (cf. *Constitution on the Sacred Liturgy,* 10), the word "rite" stands for the church as a whole. In a wider sense, therefore, the term "rite" includes church order, canon law, discipline, theology, spirituality. It is in this wider sense that the council normally uses the word.

In a conversation on ecumenical matters, Pope Paul VI once said to me: "Why do you not write something on a typology of the different churches?" I used the opportunity afforded by the invitation to deliver an address in Cambridge, England, at the opening of the Week of Prayer for Christian Unity in 1970. There I briefly developed this idea: "Where there is a long coherent tradition commanding men's love and loyalty, creating and sustaining a harmonious and organic whole of complementary elements, each of which supports and strengthens the other, you have the reality of a typos."

I mentioned several such complementary elements, for example:

- a characteristic theological method and approach;
- a characteristic liturgical expression;
- a spiritual and devotional tradition;
- a characteristic canonical discipline.

Through the combination of all of these a typos can be specified. It goes beyond external differences; it touches people's distinctive experience of the divine mystery, their contemplation and action, their joys and sorrows, their art and behavior. For me, this is more than a functional variety. We find here a diversity which causes religious pluralism even within visible boundaries of the one church. The Second Vatican Council's *Decree on Ecumenism* (UR) says: "For many centuries, the churches of east and west *went their own ways,* though a brotherly communion of faith and sacramental life bound them together," and "The heritage handed down by the apostles was received in different forms and ways" (n. 14). In the *Constitution on the Church* we read: "By divine providence it has come about that various churches, established in various places by the apostles and their successors, have in the course of time coalesced into several groups, organically united, which, preserving the unity of faith, enjoy their own discipline, their own liturgical usage and their own theological and spiritual heritage" (n. 23). These deeply rooted realities, and not territorial or national boundaries, determine a typology of churches. This is the well-defined, and at the same time real, possibility of religious pluralism within the ecclesial communion of the Catholic Church. Obviously, the very existence of such diversities, which created different types of churches, "added to external causes and to mutual failure of understanding and charity," and thus, as the *Decree on Ecumenism* states, they also "set the stage for separations" (n. 14). Today the words "Orthodox" and "Catholic" indicate two churches which are not in full communion of faith, life and order with each other. Separation continues to exist. However we should not forget the words of Pope Paul VI when he said that we remain in a nearly full communion (*communio quasi completa*).

Here we arrive at the second category of my reflection: religious pluralism in the Christian world. Through the ecumenical movement we have learned to call each other brothers and sisters in Christ, and that is really what we are. At the same time the diversities are many and sometimes they go deep.

Indeed, they are numerous, innumerable. But as a result of the ecumenical movement, Christians have founded worldwide organizations in which they have come together on the basis of a common interpretation of the gospel. This sense of togetherness has grown into a sense of family, of communion in Christ. Besides the Roman Catholic Church and the Orthodox Church we have

- the Ancient Eastern Churches of the Armenians;
- the Copts, the Syrians who live in full communion with each other;
- the Anglican Communion;
- the Old Catholics (Union of Utrecht);
- the Lutheran World Federation;
- the World Alliance of Reformed Churches (Presbyterians);
- the World Methodist Council;
- the Disciples of Christ;
- the Baptist World Alliance;
- the Pentecostals;
- the Evangelicals.

Most of their member churches are also members of the World Council of Churches. They all confess Jesus Christ as Lord and Savior, but in this very confession they look at each other with both a "yes" and a "no." St. Paul describes in his lapidary style what should fully unite all Christians: "one Lord, one faith, one baptism." It is significant that in Greek he plays on the threefold gender of the unique "one." Christians have become divided by not responding to the unity which is given in Christ and which he wanted to be achieved among his disciples. "I am the good Shepherd. I know my own and my own know me, as the Father knows me and I know the Father. . . . So there shall be one flock and one shepherd" (Jn 10). The same idea is expressed even more profoundly in the prayer for unity: "that they may all be one, even as thou, Father, art in me, and I in thee, that they also may be one in us" (Jn 17:21).

The pluralism which we find among Christians is not what defines them as such. In the present pluralism among Christians "the elemental spirits of the world" (cf. Gal 4:3; Col 2:8) still work in us. We oppose different interpretations of Christ against each other and, in this way, dividing ourselves we divide Christ. Paul pointed out this danger to the Corinthians and emotionally asks: "Is Christ divided?" (1 Cor 1:13). Communion in Christ, which for Christians is not a psychological or sentimental attitude, but an objective reality of faith, should bring them to full communion among themselves. However this is very different from uniformity. Paul speaks of "varieties of gifts but the same Spirit . . . varieties of service but the same Lord . . . varieties of working, but it is the same

God who inspires them all in everyone" (1 Cor 12:4–6). We find here again that mysterious threefold unity: Spirit–Lord–God.

The council teaches: "This is the sacred mystery of the unity of the church, in Christ and through Christ, with the Holy Spirit energizing a variety of functions. The highest exemplar and source of this mystery is the unity, in the Trinity of persons, of one God, the Father and the Son in the Holy Spirit" (UR, n. 2). The variety we have been endowed with gives life to the body, the church. All Christians confess Christ as the head of the body, the church. At the same time, they differ from one another by reason of the nature and seriousness of questions of faith concerning various areas, especially ecclesiology. Therefore, among Christians, while there still exists and lives a real communion, it is very incomplete and not corresponding to the unity of which Christ speaks in the prayer for unity quoted above. There is a Christian religious pluralism which fails to bind us together in full communion. In the one ecumenical movement we are studying together the one apostolic faith, its consequences and demands for full communion.

The Second Vatican Council elaborated Catholic principles of ecumenism, not a Catholic ecumenism. It recognized and promoted Catholic participation in the ecumenical movement, which is a gift of the Holy Spirit to all Christians: "The Lord of ages . . . has begun to bestow more generously upon divided Christians remorse over their divisions and a longing for unity" (*Unitatis redintegratio,* n. 1). The council accepted and promoted religious pluralism starting from our common heritage, urging us to transform differences that separate into that harmonious manifold unity of which Ignatius, the successor of Peter in Antioch and martyr in Rome, speaks so beautifully in his letters. Let me give some concrete examples, where, still living in a religious pluralism that causes division and separation, in our time we came from No to Yes. From a period in which the reading of holy scripture was restricted for Catholic lay people and the use of translations made under the auspices of non-Catholic Bible Societies was prohibited (these restrictions were not directed against the Bible, but against Protestants), we have now joined in widespread cooperation in hundreds of projects to prepare common translations, and in fraternal competition in spreading the text of the Bible, in response to the Second Vatican Council's statement: "Easy access to sacred scripture should be provided for all the Christian faithful" (*Dei verbum,* n. 22). Where formerly common prayer with other Christians was prohibited or restricted to praying the "Our Father," the council now says: "In special circumstances such as prayer services 'for unity' and during ecumenical gatherings, it is allowable, indeed desirable, that Catholics should join in prayer with their separated brethren" (*Unitatis redintegratio,* n. 8). This practice has developed in a happy way, and since the unity of the church is a "sacred mystery," sharing the word of God and common prayer are the most effective means for promoting a healthy religious pluralism among Christians in search of full communion.

Other examples could be given, especially on the local and national level, into which I cannot go on this occasion. But it should be clear that religious pluralism exists among Christians, and is considered by Catholics and most Christians with a sense of duty as needing to be transcended. We must move from the present state into full communion of faith, of sacramental life, of ecclesial structure, without destroying a sound pluralism. The council says: "While preserving unity in essentials, let all members of the church . . . preserve a proper freedom in the various forms of spiritual life and discipline, in the variety of liturgical rites, and even in the theological elaboration of revealed truth. In all things let charity be exercised" (*Unitatis redintegratio,* n. 4).

Religious pluralism among Christians is quite different from pluralism of religions. The question is: How shall we conceive of religious pluralism in all religions, or, to be more specific for our purposes: What have all the peoples, all the nations, belonging to any of the great religions which we find in the world (being all of them creatures of the one God and stemming from one Father), what have they in common in their search for God, on their way to God? What are the elements which we appreciate as "religious," so that we can talk not only about pluralism but actually about religious pluralism?

Christianity as an historic reality is a young religion. During the time of the apostles, the followers of Jesus, in Antioch, were called Christians for the first time. Christianity considers itself to be the fulfillment of the promise given by the creator to the first human couple. Judaism goes back to the origin of the Torah. But in the first traces of human life and culture which we find in archaeological evidence we also have signs of religion.

Today we find the great religions spread all over the earth. Besides Christianity we have Judaism, Islam, Hinduism, Buddhism, and the popular African traditions, to mention only the greatest and well-known ones. In the great urban centers of all countries you will find all of them.

Recently, Jacob Neusner wrote: "The single most important problem facing religion for the next hundred years, as for the last, is an intellectual one: how to think through differences, how to account, within one's own faith and framework, for the outsider, indeed, for many outsiders, thinking about the other in religion: it is necessary, but is it possible?" (*Modern Theology* 6:3 April 1990, pp. 273–285). The problem was put to the fathers of the Second Vatican Council on more than one occasion (*Lumen gentium,* n. 16; *Gaudium et spes,* nn. 19–20; *Declaration on the Relationship of the Church to Non-Christian Religions*), and studied more thoroughly in relation to Judaism, more tentatively regarding the other non-Christian religions.

Cardinal Bea declared in his presentation to the council: "If I am not mistaken, this is the first time that a council has solemnly explained the principles (of non-Christian religions)."

The initiative came from Pope John XXIII. Originally it was limited to the Jews. As apostolic delegate in Turkey and Bulgaria, he was able to grasp the real meaning of the "transportation to the east" of the Jews, and personally did everything in his power to save Jewish lives. But there was more than sympathy here. When in October 1960 he received a group of American Jews, he greeted them with the words: "I am Joseph, your brother." In a certain way Pope John anticipated the words of Pope John Paul II in the synagogue of Rome: "You are our most beloved brothers and one might say, in a certain sense, our elder brothers."

Later the Declaration was amplified, and also included the great non-Christian religions. Bishops from Africa and Asia insisted on this broader vision. Living together often as a small minority with people of other faiths, they asked for a word of the church, an appreciation of these religions in relation to Christianity.

The theological principles involved are given by St. Paul in his first letter to Timothy: "God our Savior desires all men to be saved and to come to the knowledge of the truth. For there is one God, and there is one mediator between God and men, the man Christ Jesus, who gave himself as a ransom for all" (1 Tim 2:3–7). In this text three are mentioned: God, Christ Jesus, and the apostle Paul in their universal relation to mankind (the church).

A related idea is found in the letter to the Colossians: "He is the image of the invisible God. . . . All things were created through him and for him. . . . In him all things hold together. . . . He is the head of the body, the church" (Col 1:15–18). The key words are "he" and "all," affirming the universality of the mission of Christ.

And in the gospel of John: "In the beginning was the Word, and the Word was with God, and the Word was God. . . . In him was life, and the life was the light of all people. . . . The true light that enlightens everyone" (Jn 1:1–6).

The knowledge of God which we find in other religions is not only based upon natural reason and intelligence (cf. Rom 1:20) but flows also from the light that came to the world in Jesus Christ. The fathers of the first centuries of church history spoke of the *semina verbi,* the seeds of the word. They lived in a world of non-Christian religions. In his famous discourse at the Areopagus in Athens, Paul addressed himself directly to the pagans, quoting from their own poets and thinkers. It is easy to find beautiful words about the omnipotence and mercifulness of God in the Koran, or to quote verses from the Vedas and Upanishads on the love of God and our unity in him, which sound like Christian mystics or even like the words of holy scripture in the New as well as the Old Testament, although they belong to a different context. Are they not the seeds of the word which bear fruit in the soul of all people? In the Christian view they are mediated by Christ from God to mankind, and by Christ from the human being to God.

The Jews venerate the scriptures which Christians have received from them and which both, Jews and Christians, venerate as holy and divinely inspired. Therefore, in Judaism we find not only *semina verbi,* but divine revelation, as it is given in the books of the Torah (Pentateuch), Nevi'im (Prophets), Ketuvim.

They tell us the history of salvation, God speaking to Abraham and Moses. The *Constitution on Divine Revelation* of the Second Vatican Council teaches: "These books give expression to a lively sense of God; they are a storehouse of sublime teaching on God and of sound wisdom on human life as well as a wonderful treasury of prayers; in them, too, the mystery of our salvation is present in a hidden way" (*Dei verbum,* n. 15).

In the *Guidelines* for implementing the Declaration *Nostra aetate* more precisely as it speaks on our relation to Judaism, a very important principle is stated: "Christians . . . must strive to learn by what essential traits the Jews define themselves in the light of their own religious experience" (Preamble). This applies of course also to our relationships with other religions. Only with respect to such matters of principle can we develop sound relationships and dialogue with "the other." It will also make us rethink the truth about ourselves. It will prevent us from thinking about the other solely in terms of ourselves. The Second Vatican Council has laid the foundation of "a Christian theology of the other in terms of the other—or believing Jews" (Neusner). It showed good will and good intentions, and hinted that we should also work in the same direction in regard to other non-Christian religions. The reason for the difference is, on the one hand, the desire of so many fathers of the council to have a word about this, and, on the other hand, the lack of preparation for it. The secretariat, now Pontifical Council for Interreligious Dialogue, was created to pursue this task.

After long and sometimes dramatic discussions, the Second Vatican Council issued a Declaration on another principle which is also important for our subject: the principle of religious liberty. Religious liberty is a natural right of the human person, based on his dignity. It protects the person against external pressure or coercion. The subject of religious liberty is both the physical human person and moral persons, such as religious communities. Religious liberty demands acknowledgment, respect, protection, and promotion from the authorities. It also has its limits regarding other persons and the common welfare. The children of God, who receive this liberty as a gift from God, their creator and savior, through Christ in the Holy Spirit, assert it within the church as well as within the world, always for the sake of the world and the church (cf. J. Courtney Murray, in his Introduction to the Declaration in W.M. Abbott, ed., *Documents of Vatican II,* p. 674). The Declaration recorded the theological development from tolerance to respect for the human person in one of his fundamental rights. It opened the way toward new confidence in ecumenical relationships and in relationships with other religions, toward open and respectful dialogue in a common search for religious truth, which will allow us to cooperate in building a new world and society in which justice and peace will prevail. In a world in which there is pluralism of religions, religious liberty must be acknowledged and practiced. At the same time, because all religion comes from God and tends toward him, we may, with his grace, in a dialogue of love and truth, come nearer to him and nearer to each other.

The world day of prayer for peace in Assisi (October 27, 1986) marked a culminating point in relations between world religions. Prayer is more than dialogue; although there was no common prayer, except between Christians in the ecumenical prayer service in the Cathedral of San Rufino, we stood together in prayer. Assisi provided a solemn and public image of what is possible in religious pluralism. What happened in Assisi continues in a less visible way when all over the world prayers rise to the one God, Father of us all.

Salvation and Redemption: Themes of a Common Faith*

"The Declaration on the Relationship of the Church to Non-Christian Religions, *Nostra aetate,* n. 4, endorses and promotes dialogue between Christians and Jews, just as the Decree on Ecumenism endorses and promotes dialogue between the separated Christian groups." This was rightly acknowledged in the first edition of *The Documents of Vatican II* (New York: The America Press 1966, p. 665, n. 21), commenting on the following words: "Since the spiritual patrimony common to Christians and Jews is thus so great, this sacred synod wishes to foster and recommend that mutual understanding and respect which is the fruit above all of biblical and theological studies, and of brotherly dialogues" (*Nostra aetate,* n. 4).

The chosen topic for this colloquium is central for theological studies. Salvation and redemption are, in fact, among the most significant themes of our common deposit of faith. The *Notes* (I:7) recognized the primacy of this theme, and at the same time they indicate the necessity of further reflection. Stating that the church and Judaism cannot be seen as two parallel ways of salvation, they understand parallelism in the sense of classic mathematics, according to which parallel lines will never meet. However, we hope to share, at least at the end of times, the salvation which God has reserved for all the righteous, as the psalm says: "This is the gate of the Lord, the righteous shall enter through it" (Ps 118:20). In that sense I understand also the words of Jesus: "So there shall be one flock and one shepherd" (Jn 10:16). In the *Guidelines* we affirmed

---

* Rome, 1986; see Bibliography, n. 13.

the church must witness to Christ as the redeemer for all, "while maintaining the strictest respect for religious liberty in line with the teaching of the Second Vatican Council (Declaration *Dignitatis humanae*)" (*Guidelines,* 1).

I wanted to make these remarks in order to show how much our theme is a delicate one. Indeed, at the same moment in which we express in very similar ways and terms our conception of salvation and the action of our saving God, we cannot but recognize that there are a certain number of substantial divergences which are characteristic for each part. Both of us, in fact, implore salvation from the Father with the same words: *Hosha-nah* ("Save us, O God!"), and the Jews end the celebration of *Sukkot* with the day of *Hosha-nah Rabbah* or "of the Great Hosannah," imploring to be inscribed and sealed in the book of life. We Christians repeat the same invocation in the eucharistic celebration, which is the memorial of Christ's passover and implies also the salvific memorial (*zikkaron*) of Israel's liberation from Egypt, and of every subsequent event of salvation. Thus we cannot do without the salvific categories of Judaism to understand and express our religious identity, even as we cannot but recognize that Jesus, our savior, "was and always remained a Jew" (*Notes,* III, 20). In the proclamation of and reflection on the mystery of salvation great importance is given to the prophecies of Isaiah, especially the last part, called Deutero and Trito Isaiah, about the mission of the suffering servant and the universality of salvation, offered to all peoples. In traditional Jewish exegesis these expressions are applied to the people of Israel in its totality, while the Christian exegesis reads in these chapters the prophecy about the suffering and glorious Christ. These two exegeses are not contradictory. Saint Paul, in his meditation on Isaiah, will write to the Romans that God's saving plan does not change and Israel keeps its proper function: "God does not change his mind about whom he chooses and blesses" (Rom 11:20). Though in different ways, Christians and Jews know the vocation of a chosen people, but this does not mean that other peoples are rejected. We adore the endless mercifulness of the Almighty, Blessed be his Name, in his mysterious plan of salvation, designed for all humankind. In every human being we respect the image of the creator and we wait in faithful hope and adoration for the day that "all Israel will be saved" (Rom 11:26), "for he will come like a rushing stream, which the wind of the Lord drives. And he will come to Zion as redeemer" (Is 59:19–20).

The theological theme of salvation is not the only one that can be presented from two different sides, the Jewish and the Christian. There are other important and characteristic themes, such as messianism, the word of God, prayer, exegesis, and in particular the typos, *the covenant.* Entering together into these different issues in an attitude of humble openness to search for the will of God, Father and savior, we will each learn to know better the religious identity of the other in its characteristic traits, growing in mutual respect and esteem for those religious values which are common to both of us.

With the grace of God we will collaborate actively in this maturing process. We are therefore grateful to the authorities of the Pontifical University of St. Thomas Aquinas, to the Rev. Professors Fr. Charles Angell, S.A., Edward Kacynski and Bruce Williams, and the Rev. Gerald O'Collins, Dean of the Faculty of Theology of the Pontifical Gregorian University, for their sensitivity on this point. But also from the Jewish side we should not forget the corresponding precious initiative of the Anti-Defamation League of B'nai B'rith, in the persons of the Knight Commander Joseph Licthen, Mr. Theodore Freedman, Rabbi Ronald Sobel and all other personalities who have participated in this colloquium.

Furthermore we owe a special thanks to the Centro Pro Unione, of the Friars of the Atonement, and the Sisters of Sion of SIDIC for all their preparatory work carried out in collaboration with the Holy See's Commission for Religious Relations with the Jews. May God bless these efforts which are united in the service of his merciful will for peace and love for all persons, so that, as we pray in the Qaddish and in the Our Father: "Your kingdom may come soon and your name be hallowed."

V.

The Shoah—Auschwitz

The Impact of the Shoah
on Catholic-Jewish Relations*

It was with trepidation that I accepted the invitation of the Inter-faith Council on the Holocaust of Philadelphia to take part in this international conference on the theme "Captive and Free: Lessons of the Holocaust for Today and Tomorrow" to commemorate the forty-fifth anniversary of the liberation of the extermination camps. I said "with trepidation" because the theme of the holocaust is very sensitive, and it is difficult to understand its spiritual meaning for believers and for all the world. Certainly there is no consensus on this issue among Jews or among Christians. Indeed, I am ever more profoundly convinced that it is our common duty and responsibility to remember those moments of sorrow and of hope, to reflect about them, and to cooperate in the great commitment of making sure that such atrocities of genocide will never again be repeated in the world. As men of faith we have a particular responsibility for the future of mankind, for promoting freedom, justice and peace everywhere in the world, in accordance with the will of God, Creator, Father and Savior of all. "Have we not all one Father? Has not one God created us?" (Mal 2:10).

The experience of the liberation was recalled for us just a few minutes ago in a very moving and personal way by a protagonist in those events, and has made us understand how "those who have been captive know what it means to be free." This experience of liberation has been lived with great intensity this year in many regions of Central and Eastern Europe that have freed themselves of totalitarian regimes. And yet the fact of liberation by itself is not

* Talk delivered at the International Conference of the Interfaith Council on the Holocaust, November 18, 1990.

sufficient to ensure that the human person will effectively realize all the values to which he aspires, for all around us we see how easy it is for other fanaticisms and nationalisms to arise and to constitute new dangers to civil co-existence. Today we have to achieve another step: we have to pass beyond "freedom *from*" and move toward "freedom *for*," *to* and *toward* freedom, so that we may live all the dimensions of freedom and orientate it toward solidarity, co-responsibility and cooperation. On the other hand, too many other peoples, groups or persons are still enslaved, hungry, deprived of the basic liberties, deprived of their dignity and of human or religious rights, considered as objects of power rather than as persons, that is to say, as "images of God" and, as such, bearers of absolute values. Fully conscious of the past, of which we are harbingers and witnesses, how then can we act in the present to bring freedom *to* those others?

In the long series of twelve discussions and conferences already organized by your Council on the Holocaust since 1975, the present one has the distinctive feature of a special session for seminarians and theology students introduced for the very first time. This choice seems to reflect the conviction that the religious element plays a decisive part in the project of human liberation.[1] In the Bible, indeed, the message of salvation is presented to us as an experience of liberation from a servile state—the bondage of Egypt —for a free gesture of love: "Let my people go, that they may serve me in the wilderness" (Ex 7:16). And the psalmist sings the experience of liberation from the Babylonian exile in the following words:

> When God brought back Zion's captives
> we lived in a dream;
> then our mouths filled with laughter
> and our lips with song.
>
> Then the nations kept saying "What great deeds
> God has done for them!"
> Yes, God did great deeds for us,
> and we were overjoyed.
>
> Bring back, God, our people from captivity,
> like torrents in the Negeb.

Those who sow in tears
sing as they reap.

He went off, went off weeping,
carrying the seed.
He comes back, comes back singing,
bringing in his sheaves (Ps 126).

At the same time, history shows us that in certain circumstances the religious element proved to be a factor that—either by itself or together with causes of a different nature—exerted an influence on social discriminations, and thus had a relationship also with modern antisemitism and the persecution of the Jews in Europe that culminated in the shoah. And therefore, together with you, I should now like to face up to this theme of "The Shoah and its Impact on Christian-Jewish Relations."

If I personally prefer the term shoah and use it rather than holocaust, this is essentially for a religious reason. In common acceptance, certainly, holocaust may well have lost some of the religious connotations that lie at the root of this term; but in the Bible this word indicates a "sacrifice to God of an offering wholly consumed by fire." Under no circumstances can the extermination of the Jews in Europe between 1939 and 1945 be considered as "a sacrifice to God" offered by the persecutors. Moreover, even if we cannot know the hearts of the victims, from a Christian perspective, it is possible during persecutions to remain in a spiritual freedom based on faith and the love of God, and even to attain the possibility of offering suffering in martyrdom for a better humanity. Other Hebrew terms have been suggested, among them "khurban" ("destruction" or *shoah*, "catastrophe"). Fully aware that words cannot but remain wholly inadequate to describe the horrors and the sufferings lived by the Jewish people in those years, I shall nevertheless try to consider the shoah in the religious perspective in the first part of my talk. In the second part I then propose to examine some possible relationships between the shoah and the evolution of the dialogue and the cooperation between Jews and Christians in the last forty-five years, and this with particular reference to Vatican Council II and its declaration *Nostra aetate* about the church and other religions, and especially the Jewish people.

Lastly, we shall try to see whether and what lessons for the future we can draw therefrom.

I. THE SHOAH IN THE RELIGIOUS PERSPECTIVE

The memory of each and every victim, his face and his heart offended by hate, causes us to commence this reflection with immense respect, profound humility, and silent sorrow. But voices of witness have nevertheless reached us from that dark night of infinite suffering and desperate solitude in which it seemed as if we had touched the abyss of "God's silence."

In her diary written before she disappeared in the extermination camp Etty Hillesum expressed her hope in the following words: "If all this suffering will not produce a more profound humanity . . . it will all have been in vain."

And Elie Wiesel, commenting these words, adds: "This question must remain an open one, for if we say that this suffering was not in vain, it almost seems as if we were justifying it . . . And yet, if we say that it was in vain, would that not be equally terrible?"[2]

All the same, as Wiesel himself tells us, we have to seek the message and the promise contained in this excruciating pain: "Who could, who would have been able to reawaken all this suffering, make us sensitive to it, if it were to be lost; if no poem were to spring from it, no message to be handed on, if no promise were to be bound up with it, that would indeed be terrible, an irreparable loss twice over."[3]

Itzhak Katzenelson, who—together with his son—died at Auschwitz on May 3, 1944, wrote a poem in Yiddish, where he sings of the massacre of the Jewish people as follows:[4]

End of winter nineteen hundred and forty-two. I was there in that
    orphanage,
I saw them, all those children crowded in the street.
I saw the little girl, barely two years old, so gaunt and so pale,
With eyes of infinite sadness. I kept my eyes on her for long.
She seemed a woman a hundred years of age.
A hundred years was the age of that child, a hundred years of endless
    pain. . . .
Tears rolled from my eyes, but then I said to myself: Do not weep, the

traces of these sufferings will disappear, what really matters is
what shall remain.
It is like a Bible for the world, a prophecy, a holy writ. . . .

Here we seem to hear once more the lamentations of
Jeremiah:

> Arise, cry out in the night . . .
> Lift your hands to him
> for the lives of your children,
> Who faint for hunger
> at the head of every street. . . .
> Should women eat their offspring,
> the children of their tender care? . . .
> I am the man who has seen affliction
> under the rod of his wrath;
> He has driven and brought me
> into darkness without any light (Lam 2:19–20; 3:2).

And yet, just as the Lord freed his people in Babylon through
the hands of Cyrus, his anointed (Is 45:1), so also did the merciful
judgment of God, through other human hands, put an end to the
extermination of his people in our own days. I dare not, I cannot,
indeed, I do not know how to answer the anguished question: Why?
Why didst thou permit such sorrow? But one thing I know beyond
all doubt: it cannot have been to castigate the sins of Israel. The
faithfulness of the Lord endures forever (Ps 117), and the doors of
hope seem to open once more in the prophecy of Isaiah: "As one
whom his mother comforts, so will I comfort you; you shall be
comforted in Jerusalem. You shall see, and your heart shall rejoice . . ." (Is 66:13–14). According to the Bible, the human response to God is linked with eternal life: "Love is strong as death,
passion fierce as the grave. . . . Many waters cannot quench love,
neither can floods drown it" (Song 8:6–7).

To continue my reflections, it seems to me opportune at this
point to touch—albeit only briefly—upon the topic of modern
antisemitism that I mentioned a moment or two ago. Together
with the Nazi ideology of an altogether pagan character, it was a
powerful weapon for the abominable crime perpetrated against

millions of Jews—children, old people, men and women—all over Europe.

Already in 1985, I set myself the question: Is Christianity anti-semitic?[5] and then, in 1988, expressed some thoughts on "The Church Facing Antisemitism."[6] As soon as the first antisemitic episodes occurred, the church condemned them very forcefully and clearly, for Pope Pius X, in a letter to the Polish bishops—then under the dominion of the czars—dated December 3, 1905, expressed himself in the following terms about the pogroms that had occurred in those regions: ". . . these were public massacres committed against the Jews that the law of the gospel, which requires us to love all without distinction, detests and condemns."[7]

My conclusion, which reflects the exegetic and philosophical analyses made by Augustin Bea in 1920 and the subsequent declarations, condemnations and considerations of the holy office (1928), Pope Pius XI (1938), Jacques Maritain (1942) and such Jewish scholars as Aaron Steinberg (1939) and Abraham Heschel (1966),[8] was that antisemitism is simply anti-Christian. Nevertheless, I had to recognize that "some very nasty forms of antisemitism are part of the defects of Christianity."[9] As regards the shoah, in particular, we have to note—both before and after the shoah, and notwithstanding the specific condemnation of racial antisemitism by the Catholic hierarchy—the gap or void in Catholic culture that retarded the development of an analysis of the non-religious components of antisemitism. Such an analysis could have led to a severe condemnation of this phenomenon on the rational level. As regards the religious level, as also the religious components of antisemitism, it has to be borne in mind that the anti-Jewish prejudices deriving from the so called "teaching of contempt"[10] also had their effects on the overall atmosphere in Europe.

Before the shoah, moreover, Catholic theology failed to elaborate any systematic and positive teaching concerning the contemporary Jewish people in relation to the mystery of salvation. Allow me, however, to mention the firm and convinced position of the Dutch bishops with regard to the persecution of the Jews during World War II and the Nazi occupation of my country. This was a unanimous and convinced opposition of the episcopate, expressed also in pastoral letters. Its intention and goal was to support strongly the moral resistance of the people.

As I have already said, the antisemitic theories merged with the Nazi ideology of "Blut und Boden," blood and soil, founded wholly on pagan principles and myths. It became a kind of anti-religion, opposed to the God of the Bible and the Jewish people—as the chosen people—and the church. To put it in the words of Cardinal Jean-Marie Lustiger: "The center of this ideology was the persecution of the chosen people, the Jewish people, as the messianic people. . . . The aim of Nazism was more than Promethean, satanic. Its hostility to Christianity was fundamental. It could not afford a frontal attack, because the church represented a power that the Nazis had to live with. But the Jews, indeed, soon came to feel the full whip of persecution."[11] Jacques Maritain, writing in 1941, likewise said that the persecution of Israel by the Nazis was a persecution of the body of Christ.[12] This altogether diabolical ideology, established in a powerful totalitarian state, in actual fact became a form of idolatry, capable of producing the worst forms of bondage at all levels of society. The attempt was made to destroy God and his image in the human person, especially in the Jew, who was represented as the antagonist of the ideal human being. The result was the edification of an inhuman and dehumanizing society that found its expression in the extermination camps, which remained active right through to the last moment of the war.

The whole of Europe was reduced to an immense concentration camp, where innumerable people of all nations found their death, though the nadir, the ultimate flow of degradation and extermination, was undoubtedly the fate reserved to the Gypsies and, especially, the Jews. By completely extirpating the Jews from Europe, there were also being laid the implicit premises for extirpating the church from the society envisaged by the Nazis, because "spiritual ties link the people of the new covenant to the stock of Abraham" (*Nostra aetate,* No. 4).

The unspeakable horror of the events that then followed in the years of the war seem to defy description: the very words (genocide, holocaust, extermination, shoah, khurban) seem to lose sense. Are we then to remain silent because during that oppression the cries of the innocent victims encountered nothing but the inhuman silence of their persecutors? the silence of the world? of many Christians? of European culture? the silence of God? Yes, I think that we may remain silent, but only if our silence expresses and accompanies an action of resistance, of solidarity in sorrow, of confident expectation. Such a silence is indicative of human, of spiritual activity. As against this, I see the risk of remaining in mute, complete desperation, a seemingly tacit acceptance of the diabolical sense of the shoah. But this second form of silence, so it seems to me, is not the heredity left us by the millions of victims, as testified to us by David Rubinowicz, Anne Frank, Etty Hillesum, Benjamin Fondane, Janusz Korczak, Vladimir Jankelevitch and many, many others. Even in the gas chambers there remained an inextinguishable light of supernatural hope: we know that the feasts were celebrated, that liturgical hymns were sung and that the Shema was intoned to the very last breath, just as happened when Rabbi Akiba met his martyrdom in the year 135 (Berakhoth 61b). In these expressions of faith we can recognize an act of supreme interior freedom of the prisoners, so that their persecutors—rather—seemed to be the real slaves of an anti-human hatred. In this form of resistance, interior and exterior, the Bible with its message of consolation, liberation and redemption was a great source of hope for all the prisoners.

Unfortunately, the liberation of the camps was completed only as the Nazis' absurd war was coming to an end: the Allies, i.e. the forces of the western democracies and the Red army from the east, at long last entered the camps and saw the horrors that had been committed there by people against one another. The liberation was, first and foremost, a physical, exterior experience; but the interior drama lived by the victims had also lacerated their inferiority. The simple fact of exterior liberation could not be sufficient. We know of many who were liberated at that time and, even today, think of themselves as "survivors."[13] But in our eyes they rather appear as bearers of the image of the suffering God, just as in the action of the men who restored them to freedom and to life there appears a sign of God the liberator, who always intervenes to stay the hand of the angel of death, to arouse anew to hope his people whom he loves so dearly.

II. IMPACT OF THE SHOAH ON CHRISTIAN-JEWISH RELATIONS (1945–1990)

I hope these considerations will have prepared us for facing up to the second part of our reflections tonight, namely the relationships between the shoah and the evolution of the Christian-Jewish dialogue during the last forty-five years. To this end, let me first indicate very succinctly the principal stages on the road of Christian-Jewish dialogue, cooperation and friendship at the international and world level.

- 1946: Creation of the International Council of Christians and Jews, an organism that proved very active and also most attentive to the ecumenical implications of Jewish-Christian relations. The Council today has a membership of twenty-three national associations.
- 1965: The Catholic Church, assembled in the Second Vatican Council, promulgated the Declaration *Nostra aetate* about the relationships between the church and the non-Christian religions, especially the Jewish people.[14] This declaration has been described as a "milestone" in the relations with the Jews.[15]
- 1966: Creation of the Vatican Office for Catholic-Jewish Relations.
- 1970: The leading Jewish international organizations founded the International Jewish Committee on Interreligious Consultations (IJCIC) in New York. The IJCIC, together with the Vatican Office for Catholic-Jewish Relations, then set up a Liaison Committee.
- 1974: The holy see set up a Commission for Religious Relations with the Jews, which took the place of the Vatican Office of 1966, and published two important documents in 1974 and 1985.[16]
- 1986: Pope John Paul II, by his visit to the Rome synagogue, intended to set the seal upon a first period of post-conciliar dialogue with the Jews and, at one and the same time, with a gesture of fraternal reconciliation, to open another in a spirit of mutual knowledge, esteem, solidarity, and love.
- Between 1970 and 1990 the International Catholic-Jewish Liaison Committee held thirteen meetings, the last at Prague on September 3–6 of last year. The reports of all the previous meetings were published by the Vatican in 1988.[17]
- Between 1986 and 1990, following the visit to the Rome synagogue, the holy father has greatly intensified his activity and we

can count as many as thirty important public interventions in which he referred to Jews and their relations with Christians.

Face to face with such an enormous development, which has no precedents in twenty centuries of relations between church and synagogue and which manifests a firm and irrevocable commitment of the Catholic Church in a direction different from the past, there spontaneously arises the question: Just how great an influence did the shoah have in bringing about this turn of history?[18]

Obviously, we should try to avoid overhasty and simplistic theories of the type post hoc, ergo propter hoc. Vatican Council II was very extensively prepared by a renewal and a movement in the biblical, ecumenical, liturgical and patristic field that had its beginnings in the previous century. In particular, the evolution of friendly relations between Christians and Jews saw an important turning point as early as 1870, at the very beginning of modern antisemitism, when a motion about the Jews was submitted to Vatican Council I.[19] This positive evolution in thought about the contemporary Jewish people as the "people of God" and permanent "mystery" within the plan of salvation had commenced in an organic and systematic manner due to the work of Catholic theologians in the early years of the nineteenth century.[20] These concepts, very familiar in some environments (though not spread sufficiently at the popular level), inspired the Catholic initiatives during the Nazi persecutions in defense of children, women and men "qui ont l'honneur d'appartenir a la race de Jesus Christ."[21]

Apart from these considerations about what we might call the pre-history of the Catholic-Jewish dialogue, there is a second observation of a general character that should here be made. Vatican Council II was characterized by a global attitude of aperture to the world and the human, social, political and religious realities, and the particular meditation about the relationship with the Jews must be seen against this general background. In the conclusions of the Pastoral Constitution *Gaudium et spes* (No. 92), the mission of the church assumes the form of dialogue and inter-religious collaboration to construct peace: "Therefore, if we have been summoned to the same destiny, which is both human and divine, we can and should work together without violence and deceit in order to build up the world in genuine peace." Sincere dialogue thus came to be understood as a particularly appropriate instrument to this end: "For our part, the desire for such dialogue, which can lead to truth through love alone, excludes no one, though an appropriate measure of prudence must undoubtedly be exercised" (*ibid.*).

Following these necessary preliminary observations, which situate the evolution of the Catholic attitude within the context of the theological reflection and the pastoral concerns of the church, we can now pass on to some more specific considerations concerning our theme.

Cardinal Bea, who was the patient architect of the declaration *Nostra aetate,* used the following words to underscore the relationship between that document and the persecution of the Jews: "The relation of the church with the Jewish people is a two thousand year old problem, as old as Christianity itself. It became much more acute, particularly in view of the ruthless policy of extermination inflicted upon millions of Jews by the Nazi regime in Germany. And so it has attracted the attention of the Second Vatican Council."[22]

Here is another fact that tells us something about the relationship between the Council's reflection and antisemitism: as early as April 24, 1960, the Pontifical Biblical Institute, asked by the holy see to prepare a preliminary document for the council, had consigned a text bearing the title *De antisemitismo vitando,* in the drafting of which Father Stanislas Lyonnet, S.J. had played a very considerable part. It is in any case well known that Edith Stein, writing to Pope Pius XI, had invoked an encyclical on antisemitism already in 1933, in response to which the pope—in 1938—had caused a 125-page text to be prepared under the title *De unitate generis humani* (On the unity of humanity). The concept of the unity of humankind appeared again in the encyclical *Humani generis* promulgated by Pope Pius XII in 1950, and then also in No. 1 of *Nostra aetate* in 1965. The fact that Catholic biblical scholars like Lyonnet and Bea were among the protagonists of this long approach march both before and after the shoah seems to suggest once more that there did indeed occur an interchange between exegetical and theological reflection and contemporary historical events and that it was particularly fecund in terms of stimuli and results.

In the endeavor of gaining further insight into our theme, we could also ask ourselves whether—and, if so, when—the shoah became an event about which Catholic thought began to seriously question itself. Among the official documents of the church, the aforementioned *Notes* of June 1985 contained the following recommendation: "Catechesis should on the other hand help in understanding the meaning for the Jews of the extermination during the years 1939-1945, and its consequences."[23] That same year, in October, among the conclusions of the program outlined by the twelfth meeting of the International Liaison Committee, there appeared the following passage: "To undertake a joint study of the historical events and theological implications of the extermination of the Jews of Europe during World War II (frequently called the 'holocaust' or, in Hebrew, shoah)."[24]

Notwithstanding the difficulties of the last few years, these studies were continued and the final document of the thirteenth meeting of the International Liaison Committee, held in Prague in September, states as follows: "In a special meeting of the holy see's Commission and IJCIC in Rome in 1987, it was foreseen that the next meeting would seek to lay the basis of the presentation of a Catholic document on the shoah, the historical background of antisemitism, and its contemporary manifestations." During the Prague meeting this year, both the Catholic and the Jewish delegates recognized that *Nostra aetate* created a new spirit between us: a spirit of mutual knowledge, appreciation, respect, love, cooperation. This spirit presupposes repentance as expressed by Archbishop Edward Cassidy, president of the holy see's Commission for Religious Relations with the Jews, when he said in his opening statement that "antisemitism has found a place in Christian thought and practice, and this calls for an act of *teshuvah* (repentance) and of reconciliation on our part."

Finally, as the third—and last—aspect of this second part, let us now consider the developments and the results acquired by what has commonly become known as "theology (or theologies) of the holocaust."[25]

For an overall evaluation of these endeavors, I would refer you to the book by Clemens Thomas,[26] since this is hardly the place to attempt such a full summary. But some of the concepts there outlined will recur in the conclusions that I should now like to put before you.

III. CONCLUSIONS

1. After the shoah, and in line with the reflections I outlined in the first part of my talk, we have to make every effort of cleansing Catholic thought of any residue of religious anti-Judaism or anti-semitism, because we have seen the abyss of horror into which hatred for the Jewish people exploded in our midst in Europe. This task has to be assumed by education, theology, catechesis, social action, the legal field, and many more. A recent document by the Pontifical Commission on Justice and Peace (Church and Racism 1988) dedicates many pages to this topic.

2. In its positive form, the spiritual commitment to continue the liberation of the victims of the shoah has to be continued in its moral form and in a perspective of solidarity with the whole of the Jewish people, and in its religious, ethnic, and cultural dimensions. As liberation of positive energies within the church, this task assumes the form of a positive theological elaboration concerning the present-day Jewish people as "people of God" in the mystery of universal salvation pre-ordained by God for all nations (cf. Rom 11:25–26).

3. Apart from these dimensions of the shoah, there is also the dimension that we could call universal or even cosmic. To use the words of Pope John Paul II: "I think that today the nation of Israel, perhaps more than ever before, finds itself at the center of the attention of the nations of the world, above all because of this terrible experience, through which you have become a loud warning voice for all humanity, for all nations, all the powers of this world, all systems and every person. More than anyone else, it is precisely you who have become this saving warning. I think that in this sense you continue your particular vocation, showing yourselves to be still the heirs of that election to which God is faithful. This is your mission in the contemporary world before the peoples, the nations, all humanity, the church. And in this church all peoples and all nations feel united to you in this mission. Certainly

they give great prominence to your nation and its sufferings, its holocaust, when they wish to speak a warning to individuals and to nations" (Address to the Jewish Community in Warsaw, June 14, 1987).

4. On the premises of a solid theology concerning the Jewish people, a theology that in some respects has not yet been elaborated with sufficient maturity and organization, one can understand both the sense and the limits of Catholic solidarity with the Jews in the state of Israel that was set up after the shoah. Let me quote the pope's words once more: "After the tragic extermination of the shoah, the Jewish people began a new period in their history. They have a right to a homeland, as does any civil nation, according to international law. . . . For the Jewish people who live in the state of Israel and who preserve in that land such precious testimonies to their history and their faith, we must ask for the desired security and the due tranquility that is the prerogative of every nation and condition of life and of progress for every society" (Apostolic Letter *Redemptionis anno,* April 20, 1984). And this was also what the pope said in his speech at Miami on September 11, 1987, but then, moved by the same reasons of solidarity and universal liberation, he went on: "What has been said about the right to a homeland also applies to the Palestinian people, so many of whom remain homeless and refugees," and he called for a common initiative in this sense by Muslims, Jews and Christians to ensure complete peace in the region.

5. Special veneration is due to the land and the places in which the crime of frightful genocide was perpetrated against the Jewish people, dragged to the gas chambers "solely because they were sons of this people." All this was done on Polish soil, "perhaps to cover it with infamy. But a land cannot be covered with infamy by the death of innocent victims. By that death it becomes a sacred relic" (John Paul II, September 26, 1990). Théo Klein, an authoritative French Jewish leader, commented on these words of the pope by saying that this way of expression peculiar to the Catholic faith merits as much respect as the different expressions of Jewish religiousness. In keeping with these principles, the holy see, as I declared on September 18 last year, supports the construction of the Center and the new Carmel of the Sisters of Auschwitz/Oswiecim outside the perimeter of the extermination camp that was the sub-

ject of such painful polemics, mercifully now subsided. The work of constructing the new Carmel, begun on February 16 this year, has made rapid progress in the last nine months, thanks also to the generous gifts of many dioceses. But more help will be welcomed by the Cracow foundation responsible for the project.

6. After the shoah, above all, we cannot and must not keep silent or remain inert when we come face to face with violence, be it open or occult, physical or spiritual, against persons, groups, nations, for reasons of race, religion, or nationality. Quite the contrary, we must react with all the instruments that culture, the right of nations and religious thought put at our disposal, trying to eliminate every prejudice or religious fanaticism in the endeavor of constructing a civilization of love and solidarity.

7. It seems to me that the theologies of liberation and of the holocaust, today more than ever before, are called upon to confront themselves seriously with the *theologia crucis*. For us Christians, indeed, the supreme liberation is that from sin, from hate, from violence, a liberation that implies mercy, conversion, forgiveness, and is expressed and accomplished by Jesus, the crucified messiah, Son of God and of man, Jew. This intuition, which Marc Chagall expressed artistically in his famous picture of the crucifixion and the sufferings of the Jewish people, is to be found also in the words of the Jew Jules Isaac with which I want to conclude: "The glow of the Auschwitz crematorium is the beacon that lights, that guides all my thoughts. Oh, my Jewish brothers, and you as well, my Christian brothers, do you not think that it mingles with another glow, that of the cross?"[27]

Jews and Christians
at Auschwitz*

The Second Vatican Council marked a fundamental stage on the church's journey in the twentieth century and in its mission to the world at the dawn of the third millennium since the incarnation of Christ. Consolidating the inheritance of Pope John XXIII, during the pontificate of Paul VI, of John Paul I and the first decade of the present pontificate, the church's relations with the Jews, founded on the common "spiritual bond" with the stock of Abraham (cf. *Nostra aetate* 4; *Lumen gentium* 16; *Dei verbum* 3), have also been conducted with particular conformity to conciliar principles. In this context antisemitism in its various forms has been condemned. In 1970 the International Liaison Committee between Catholics and Jews was set up and has since held twelve plenary sessions. In 1974 the holy see's Commission for Religious Relations with the Jews was created. This commission has produced two important documents, one in 1974 and the other in 1985. John Paul II has personally made every effort toward reconciliation and fraternal dialogue through his gestures, his discourses, and various historic meetings and initiatives. Among these was his visit to the great synagogue of the Jewish community in Rome in 1986.

In spite of this work of some twenty-five years, ancient distrust, misunderstandings, and, in some cases, cultural, religious and even anti-religious prejudices persist and on occasion contribute to fueling polemics and divisions which cause bitterness almost to the extent of seeming to demonstrate that Jews and Christians are not brothers in their faith in the one Father and creator God and in their common fundamental precepts of love of God and neighbor.

* Vatican City, 1989; see Bibliography, n. 23.

Recently we have experienced the painful controversy concerning the initiative of contemplative prayer by Carmelite Sisters in the old building which the Nazis used for storing the extermination gas. We hope the matter has now been clarified and will no longer give rise to feelings of bitterness. One might have received the impression that, on the one hand, there was the intention to move the sisters with offensive pressure, with no respect for their liberty and dignity and for the religious values, both human and Christian, which they represent. The concept and the very word "relocation" may indeed evoke, especially in Poland and at Auschwitz, immense national pain. On the other hand, it appeared that a building situated beside a place symbolic of the shoah, this dark abyss of extermination which swallowed up the Jews of Europe, was being in some way deprived of its characteristic dimension linked to the historical and religious memory of the Jewish people. In reality, however, no religious spirit—be it Christian or Jewish—opposes prayer, including the prayer of Catholics at Auschwitz. The supreme value and necessity of prayer are well known to us and constitute an essential part of our common patrimony of faith.

Nevertheless, in spite of good intentions, an imperfect awareness of the feelings of others ran the risk of obscuring the broader horizons and the profound spiritual, religious and moral values which had been repeatedly and solemnly expressed on the part of Jewish and Catholic authorities, particularly in Geneva in 1986 and 1987. Those lofty declarations of intent which involved also reciprocal commitments and their own agenda seemed reduced to the level of accords or contracts diminishing the importance of the religious climate of mutual esteem in which they had matured. One came almost to overlook, to the detriment of mutual trust, the real progress made and the grave difficulties already overcome in part, by recalling deadlines and broken promises.

But, in reality, trust and dialogue did not diminish in anyone who, animated only by faith and good will, intended to underline, on the one hand, the solemn memory of the shoah or, on the other, the sacredness of the carmel. One was ever anxious to remain faithful to the undertaking given in spite of the obstacles and hesitations, the delays and unworthy polemics. This was confirmed by the important succession of declarations—perhaps not well known to everyone—particularly that of the sisters, that of Cardinal Ma-

charski and that of the Polish Episcopal Conference headed by
Cardinal Glemp in January and March of this year in harmony
with the desire expressed by the holy father on June 24, 1988. Msgr.
Henry Muszyński, president of the Polish Episcopal Commission
for Dialogue with Judaism, made authoritative interventions on
several occasion and more recently, with great firmness, to reiterate
that the principal object of the Geneva Declaration was the expressed intention to proceed to the setting up of a center for information, meetings, dialogue and prayer whose primary objective is
that of promoting reflection on the shoah and also on the martyrdom of the Polish people and other European peoples in the years
1939–1945.

The initiative of the Auschwitz carmel, which was to be in a
certain sense the heart of such a center, thus acquired a new value
and deeper significance. At the same time it was equally clear that,
given the immensity of Jewish suffering evoked by that storehouse
of lethal gas and of the cherished remains of so many victims, it was
especially necessary from the Christian standpoint, to recognize
and respect Jewish sensitivities regarding the choice of the carmel's
location.

The holy see, through the competent Commission for Religious Relations with the Jews, wishes in its turn to express satisfaction, gratitude and concrete solidarity with all those—Jews and
Christians—who seek to promote religious values and Christian-
Jewish dialogue. In particular it wishes to express solidarity with
this planned project in Poland for which the prayer and sacrifice of
the Carmelite Sisters will be especially precious and will express in
the most effective manner both the sentiment of the Polish people
and respect for Jewish remembrance.

To continue working in the spirit of respectful dialogue, it is
more important than ever to see attentively to the speedy realization of this Religious and Cultural Center while hoping also for the
successful outcome of other initiatives which the competent Episcopal Commission has already in view, such as the publication of
texts and guidelines concerning dialogue between Catholics and
Jews in Poland, colloquia, and conferences like the international
one held in Krakow-Tyniec in 1988 or the seminar held in Chicago
in July and August this year. Equally necessary will be a cessation
of any polemical demands, the dutiful preference of patience over

intemperance, of pardon over offense, of love's generosity over mistrust. This is particularly necessary in those places which Jewish remembrance surrounds with contemplative and grief-stricken silence, and which Christian devotion surrounds with prayer and worship.

"Eli, Eli, lema sabachthani?" "My God, my God, why have you abandoned me?" This is the cry of anguish which, according to Jewish tradition, introduces Psalm 22 to the melody "The Hind of Dawn," evoking the lament of Israel like a hind or dove oppressed and suffering. In Christian tradition, this is the same final anguished cry of Christ in final agony on the cross. Before Auschwitz and the horror of the sufferings endured by millions of people— Jews, Christians, people of different races and religious convictions —this cry of infinite depth reverberates almost endlessly in us: the dark abyss of the shoah, the black night prior to the dawn of resurrection, the absolute loss of the sense of human existence. Yet the psalmist dares to raise once more a cry of prophetic hope: "Lord, be not far from me!" Shall he not respond to this cry with a dawn of redemption? And here we find ourselves once more, fifty years after, at the gates of Auschwitz: Jews, Christians, Muslims, Gypsies, non-believers. Why? Not to find ourselves once again divided, set almost one against the other, but because of an irresistible though perhaps unconscious aspiration to a path of love and brotherhood in memory of those who suffered and in respect for their dignity before God. May this augur serenely at the start of the Jewish New Year, introducing the expiatory mood of the day of Kippur. We wish that our Jewish brothers taste that day of compassion and shalom, open and directed toward the fullness of redemption.

Statement on the Auschwitz Controversy*

The holy see's Commission for Religious Relations with Judaism noted with satisfaction the communiqué published September 6 by His Excellency Monsignor Henry Muszynski, president of the Polish Episcopal Commission for Dialogue with Judaism.

The intention expressed to proceed to the establishment of an information center, a center of meeting, dialogue and prayer, as foreseen in the Geneva agreement of February 1987, is positively received, because the holy see is convinced that such a center would contribute in an important way to the development of good relations between Christians and Jews.

The holy father, in effect, in his speech to the Jewish community in Vienna, on June 24, 1988, expressed the hope that "this center will produce fruitful results and serve as a model for other nations."

The prayer and the sacred life of the Carmelites, whose monastery will be in a certain sense the heart of the center, will contribute in a decisive way to its success.

Toward the realization of this important but expensive project, the holy see is disposed to offer its financial support.

* Vatican City, September 18, 1989; see Bibliography, n. 22.

VI.

Various Addresses

The Place of SIDIC as a Center for Study and Dialogue*

I am very happy to have the opportunity of inaugurating this Center and to say a word of greeting to all those who, by coming here, have shown that they understand and, let us add, share its important ends, thereby giving a sign of recognition to the undertaking, full of courage and the spirit of sacrifice, and to those who took the initiative and who bear and will continue to bear its burden, day by day, and for many years to come.

Trying to give some illustration of the significance and importance of this initiative, there came to my mind a parallel that, albeit with all its obvious limitations, seems to me to be truly illuminating. A few days ago there was presented to the press the second part of the Ecumenical Directory, which is wholly dedicated to a single theme: ecumenism in higher education. This document has been prepared by the Secretariat for Christian Unity in cooperation with the episcopal conferences and the dicasteries of the church's central government that are particularly interested in this subject. The purpose of the document is to stimulate and order the practical application of the Catholic principles of ecumenism in the vast field of university-level education. Now this center, even though it constitutes a private initiative, also sets out to stimulate and promote, above all in circles that in one way or another dedicate themselves to study, the practice of the dispositions that the council outlined in its Declaration *Nostra aetate* about the attitude of the church to the non-Christian religions, in the part relating to the dialogue with the Jewish people. In this document the church clearly and solemnly affirmed the fundamental importance of this dialogue, together with her firm will that it should be commenced

* Talk at the inauguration of the SIDIC Center, Rome, May 21, 1990.

and developed by all her sons and daughters at all levels. This solemn declaration appears all the more important when one bears in mind the concrete circumstances in which it was made, when one remembers the difficulties that had to be overcome in order to bring home this short but extremely significant document. It is well known that the president of the Secretariat for Christian Unity, who had so greatly and so personally taken this cause to heart, used the following words when it was all over: "Had I foreseen how many difficulties and obstacles we were to encounter, I don't know whether I would have had the courage to come to grips with this problem."

Today, too, there exists in the church the same firm will about the dialogue, even though today, more often than not, the church finds herself in the same situation in which our secretariat found itself on more than one occasion during the council. Indeed, the painful conflict in the Middle East makes it even more delicate and difficult today to make clear and get people to understand the purely religious reasons that move the church in asking and promoting the dialogue with the Jewish people. It therefore seems important to me to underscore this clear and firm will once more on this occasion, though not without drawing attention to the objective difficulties that stand in the way of this will and with which it has to struggle.

What I have so far said already brings out the importance of the Center we are inaugurating today. In fact, it proposes to create important conditions for this dialogue and—what is ultimately the decisive factor—to be at the service of all who will shoulder the responsibility for this dialogue. In this sense, therefore, the church is truly grateful to the Congregation of the Sisters of Our Lady of Zion for what they have so far done in this difficult field and for the enlargement of their radius of action that they are now trying to achieve.

May I be permitted to underscore some aspects of the new orientation of this Congregation and underlying the origin of SIDIC. Even before the council approved and promulgated *Nostra aetate,* the general chapter of the Congregation had sought to reexamine the Congregation's position and task in the church both in the light of the orientations that were coming to the fore in the council and in that of the Congregation's own charisma as transmitted to it by its founder. The chapter had therefore asked Cardinal Bea, who had been given the task of preparing the council document about the attitude toward the Jewish people—for such was the name of the "schema" at the time—to come and address the general chapter about these council orientations and to outline a program by means of which the Congregation could translate these orientations into practice in its life and apostolic activity, always, of course, in the light of its original charisma. That was on January 15, 1964, a memorable day. Studying the suggestions made by Cardinal Bea and their concrete applications, the chapter laid down the main features of a new orientation that were subsequently further elaborated by other chapters and partial assemblies of the Congregation. It was from this fertile soil that there sprang the SIDIC initiative, the idea of the Documentation and Information Center with its staff of appropriately trained people, which today is coming down to the city center from its erstwhile quarters in Via Garibaldi on the Janiculum, so that henceforth it may be more readily accessible and at the disposal of the greatest possible number of students or scholars who in one way or another are now involved, or will in the future become involved, in the religious dialogue with the Jewish people.

It is hardly necessary for me to underscore the importance of this transfer to the center of the city, Rome, as a center of tourism and of ancient and modern culture and, what is more, as the home of the oldest Jewish community in the western world; there were some very great advantages for an undertaking of this kind, but only on the absolutely essential condition that the Center should be easily accessible. Today this condition has been satisfied. As from today, indeed, the Center is within reach of the large numbers of Christians, Catholics or otherwise, who come to the eternal city each year. Even more important seems to me the fact that the Center is now within easy reach of the many students, especially ecclesiastic students, who converge on Rome from every part of the world to complete their studies at the Roman universities. No matter whether they study theology (which is the history of salvation) or the concrete life of the church in the world, they will necessarily and in various ways encounter the chosen people of the Old Testament in both its past and its present life. And here, at this Center, they will find information, unique of its kind, for both one purpose and the other. To this one must add that presence in the heart of the city makes it possible for the Center to collaborate with the pontifical universities. The specialized information obtained from this Center can henceforth complete what is taught at the universities or, vice versa, be itself completed thereby.

Everything I have just sketched in a few words is also reason for congratulating the Congregation of the Sisters of Our Lady of Zion, and particularly the sisters charged with the activities of SIDIC, on account of their provident initiative in moving to the city center, thereby making sure that henceforth it will be practically impossible to be unaware of their presence in Rome and, at the same time, placing their Center within reach and at the disposal of all. And, hand in hand with these congratulations, there goes my heartfelt wish—and prayer to the Lord—that the Center, in this new home, may perform an activity, be it even silent and not by any means readily observable, but not for that reason any the less fertile and effective, of gradually forming the men who will carry forward and develop a dialogue that is essential for the life of the church, because it touches her very roots, as is pointed out in the Declaration on the Relation of the Church to Non-Christian religions: "The church acknowledges that in God's plan of salvation the beginning of her faith and election is to be found in the patriarchs, Moses and the prophets" (No. 4). My good wishes for fecund work also comprise the hope that the Center may find numerous and willing helpers of all kinds: in the intellectual and scientific field, in the field of spiritual support by prayer and—let us add—also in that of material support. Indeed, it is not difficult to understand just how many everyday sacrifices had to be shouldered by those who took this initiative and that the work in this new home will imply new and not by any means easy sacrifices. With the help of the Lord, therefore, may the Center flourish, develop and find—in the church and in various ways—every possible support, because the dialogue with the Jewish people, wanted by the council, is a duty that, in one way or another, concerns all the members of the church.

Declaration after the UN Resolution on Zionism and Racism*

On November 10 the United Nations passed a resolution on Zionism. I am amazed that it treats of such complex phenomena as Zionism and racism without defining precisely the way in which these terms are to be understood. In *Le Monde* of November 12 I found three linguistic-conceptual definitions of Zionism and three others of racism, the constitutive elements of which did not agree. What then can be the meaning of a statement which does not define the terms it uses nor clarify the sense in which it means these terms to be understood? In my opinion this procedure can serve neither justice nor the peace which we all desire for the Middle East.

* Vatican City, November 16, 1975; see Bibliography, n. 2.

One God, One Hope:
The Heritage of Cornelius Rijk*

Holy Scripture was at the center of the life and teaching of Father Adriaan Cornelius Rijk, and his whole heart was in it. The Bible inspired his meditation on the vocation of Israel, his priestly vocation and mission. In the light of the word of God, we may understand his permanent heritage to us. Professor Rijk understood the relationship between Christians and Jews under two aspects: searching into the mystery of the church, whose beginnings rise from Abraham's faith, from the covenant of Mount Sinai; then going on to affirm that, for all men, salvation comes through the people of Israel (cf. Jn 4:22). In this sense, the Christ of the covenant brings us the true freedom and vocation of the people of Israel, which are the root of the bond between Christians and Jews, because we are grafted onto the good olive tree to bring forth fruits of salvation. This was the thought and inspiration of Professor Rijk; he carried this work forward wholeheartedly and with all his strength.

Indeed, Professor Rijk discovered in his priestly vocation this specific mission and wanted to dedicate himself to it with all his strength and his gifts which were numerous. And all this he had wanted to put at the service of the church. In this way his work in the Secretariat for Promoting Christian Unity developed, as collaborator of Cardinal Bea, precisely because, in the context of this secretariat, he could and should busy himself with the Jewish people, though with a different plan and orientation than the one con-

* Rome, 1979; see Bibliography, n. 4.

cerning relationships between Christians. When he left the secretariat, he did so in order to develop his work more freely, to give every latitude to his spiritual qualities by creating spiritual, human and social contacts between Christians and Jews in the organized and firm structure of SIDIC.

HIS HERITAGE

Thus Professor Rijk has left us a heritage: the work he began must continue in the future, with the same zeal, inspiration and perseverance; we need, in fact, patience and spiritual strength that will overcome the obstacles of our time.

In this effort, he was sustained by the consciousness of the wider background of Jewish-Christian relationships: one God, one hope without which there will be no true peace on earth. If all men should recognize each other as sons of God, how much more so should Jews and Christians. In this, too, Professor Rijk mapped out for us a road. Called to the heavenly church, his work goes on and he is still most certainly fulfilling his vocation. His death may seem premature, but in reality it is like the "grain of wheat that bears fruit only if it dies" (cf. Jn 12:23). Hence, we should entrust our friend to divine providence and continue the witness of his word, his work and his life, to bring about full reconciliation between the two peoples, Jews and Christians, so that, like the grain of wheat, it may bear much fruit.

Mary of Nazareth,
Daughter of Zion*

We are gathered around the altar of the Lord to commemorate once more the appearance of the Holy Virgin to Alphonse de Ratisbonne—which happened in this very place—and his answer of faith, which was immediate and total.

Alphonse de Ratisbonne was a Jew, and therefore a man who belonged to the great tradition of the chosen people, far closer to our faith than we are wont to imagine. Indeed, our Christian faith and the very mystery of the church rest on the foundation of Judaism, as the branches of the olive tree rest on its root, as the apostle Paul already affirmed in his letter to the Romans (11:16).

Alphonse may not have known just how close he was to the faith of the apostles and the prophets, and therefore to the faith in the Son of God and son of Mary, Jesus, the Christ, come into the world to unite Jew and Gentile (cf. Eph 2:14–18).

It was Mary, mother of the Lord, who revealed it to him.

This, too, is a sign, and—together with you—I should like to linger for a moment to reflect about it.

There are many occasions when our Lady intervened on the road of men and women who sought the Lord, often even without knowing it. She may well have intervened also in our personal history.

In the case of Alphonse de Ratisbonne, however, this intervention was altogether special and became, as I have already said, a sign. Mary of Nazareth was herself a Jewess. Not only that, but in her we have Judaism and the Israel of the Bible in their purest and

* Homily for the feast of the apparition of the Virgin Mary to Alphonse de Ratisbonne, Rome, January 20, 1984.

186

most sublime form. In her, indeed, the Jewish people attain a culmination point along the road that leads to God, the God who had chosen them.

Let us turn our minds for a moment to the scene of the covenant on Mount Sinai (cf. Ex 24). God appeared on the mountain and called Moses, the great patriarch, to climb up to him, to stipulate the covenant with the people camped at the foot of the mountain, to give them the law, the ten commandments, which are our very own law.

Through Moses, God proclaimed the statute of the covenant to the people, the commandments that the community must observe in its relations with God and with other men. And the people answered: "All the words which the Lord has spoken we will do." And again, after the ceremony of the covenant: "All that the Lord has spoken we will do, and we shall be obedient." "To harken and to do"—rather, if we were to translate the Hebrew text of the book of Exodus quite literally, we shall find that it says: "we shall do and listen." The first thing, therefore, is to do, to put into practice, and then to harken, that is, to obey. Doing is already obeying the will of the Lord. The whole of the spirituality of the Jewish people is centered on these words: to do and to obey.

And now let us take a look at the scene of the annunciation, the event that brought the new covenant into being. Mary was there to harken to the words of the angel, who represents and personifies God, and heard the ineffable announcement. As soon as it is made clear how her motherhood is to come about, she replies with the words that we all know by heart: "Behold, I am the handmaid of the Lord; let it be done to me according to your word" (Lk 1:38).

And in her, we have all Israel responding, as never before; in her, wholly bent on "doing" the will of the Lord—rather, on allowing the will of the Lord to be fulfilled within her, his humble handmaid. The Jewish spirituality of "doing" and obeying that I have just put before you here attains its very vertex.

And it is Mary the Jewess, transfigured in the heavenly glory of the Son, who turns to the Jew Alphonse de Ratisbonne to tell him to do the will of the Lord and to come to Jesus.

And there we have the sign. Between Mary and Alphonse there exists a vital and intimate relationship, a relationship that is different from the one between her and others to whom she has appeared in the same form. Here we have, as it were, a family relationship based on a common heritage, a common reference to a spirituality that, even though it was no longer practiced by Alphonse, had remained at the bottom of his heart. In the appearance of which we celebrate the anniversary today it was the "daughter of Zion," Mary of Nazareth, who spoke to a "son of Zion" to turn him into a Christian.

This predilection of Mary for Alphonse, based also on their common origin, forms part of the mysterious plans of God. This man, in fact, just like his brother Theodore, was called upon to play a part in the relations between the Catholic Church and Judaism. First, because in a period of deplorable antisemitism he underscored the love and the respect for which we, as Christians, are debtors of our Jewish brothers. Furthermore, with the Congregations of the Sisters and the Fathers of Our Lady of Zion, he has left in the church a precious instrument to facilitate relations between Jews and Christians, to open and educate Christians to these relations, and to ensure that Jews would have a different image of the church and of Christianity.

The facts are there to demonstrate the validity of this message, today perhaps more topical than ever before.

The Second Vatican Council, in No. 4 of its Declaration *Nostra aetate,* wished to underscore the "spiritual bond" between the Catholic Church and Judaism and exhorted the faithful to find a way of carrying forward a dialogue of esteem and respect with our Jewish brothers.

Father Alphonse de Ratisbonne, faithful to his encounter with our Lady, was a precursor of these ideas.

The Holy Virgin asked him, just as she is asking of us at this moment, to "obey" the Lord.

In the gospel passage of the marriage at Cana that has just been read we hear how she turned to the servants to say: "Do whatever he tells you" (Jn 2:5).

Here, once again, the "doing," the "putting into practice," the "obeying" becomes the very center of Mary's message. And obedience had its reward: the water transformed into wine, the good wine of the mystery of Jesus.

Just like Father Alphonse, let us be ready to do everything that Jesus may tell us. In that way, in our personal life—and each one of us knows how—the water will become good wine. And in our relationships with Jews and Judaism, indifference or even—unfortunately—diffidence, if not actually enmity, will become the good wine of Christian love for brothers, members of our own spiritual family and members of the same people to which Jesus and Mary belonged.

The bust that we inaugurate today, here in this Church of Sant'Andrea delle Fratte, is intended both as a testimony of all this and as an admonishment for all those who, in ever greater numbers, come to pray before this altar of the apparition.

The figure of Father Alphonse de Ratisbonne by the side of this altar bears witness to the relationship that exists between him and our Lady, but also between our Lady and the Jewish people, between the Jewish people and the Christian people, the members of the church.

And it is there to exhort us to "do" always "what the Lord wants," to do it in every moment of our life and especially in our relations with the people from which Mary and Alphonse have sprung: the Jewish people.

The Specific Religious Dimensions of Christian-Jewish Relations*

Thank you for inviting me to visit you today, a visit which is taking place in such an open atmosphere. May that spirit of peace, which is a special gift from God during this Passover time, give impetus to our words and actions as we move toward more open dialogue and fruitful relations. Passover was, and continues to be, a time of freedom and liberation from slavery. But God gives us this freedom in order to serve him. The Lord commanded Moses to say to Pharaoh, "Let my son go that he may serve me" (Ex 4:23).

The most profound dimension of freedom includes faithful obedience to and service of God, and consequently love of our neighbor, made in the image of God, in a spirit of respect and love, justice and peace. The ancient Jewish prayer, "Shema Israel," "Hear O Israel: the Lord our God is one Lord; and you shall love the Lord your God . . ." (Deut 6:4–5), is complemented by the command, "You shall love your neighbor as yourself" (Lev 19:18).

As you know, we Christians, like you, have received and venerate the commandments of the Torah. But in your case this veneration is confirmed by our faith in Jesus Christ, who affirmed, "Think not that I have come to abolish the Torah and the Nevi'im; I have come not to abolish them but to fulfil them" (Mt 5:17). This is confirmed by Paul when he wrote, "Do we then overthrow the Torah by this faith? By no means! On the contrary, we uphold the Torah" (Rom 3:31).

This is why the Catholic Church, at the Second Vatican Council, emphasized the importance of her relations with the Jewish

---

* New York, 1989; see Bibliography, n. 20.

people. This was underlined in the Dogmatic Constitutions *Lumen gentium* (nn. 9, 16) and *Dei verbum* (nn. 4, 14–16), and in the Declaration *Nostra aetate* (n. 4). These documents assert that there are two principal theological foundations of our relationship. Our relations are based first of all on the unity of all humanity created in God's image, as revealed in the book of Genesis ("Bereshit," the first book of the Torah). And secondly, the specifically religious dimension of our relationship flows from God's wonderful plan of redemption as revealed in a series of covenants: with Abraham, Isaac, Jacob, and David, and culminating, according to our Christian faith, in Jesus Christ.

We understand and respect, however, your fundamental reservation regarding the mystery of the person of Jesus, because for you the absolute uniqueness of God makes it impossible that Jesus could be the universal redeemer, the Go'el. Moreover, we deeply admire your fidelity to the one God, and we believe that we share with you a common responsibility toward the world, based not only on the Noahide precepts, but also on the universal ethical and prophetic message of the Torah and the Nevi'im (the prophets). We have a common commitment to fulfill God's will within human-divine history, as described in the writings (Ketuvim). In this sense we greet you, in the words of Pope John Paul II, as "our beloved brothers in the faith of Abraham, Isaac, and Jacob."

This complex, and primarily religious, set of relationships between us has many implications at every level of human activity. Pope John Paul II referred to this in his encyclical *Sollicitudo rei socialis* (VII: 47), when he wrote, "Every individual is called to play his or her part in this peaceful campaign, a campaign to be conducted by peaceful means, in order to secure development in peace, in order to safeguard nature itself and the world about us." Another example is found in a recent document ("The Church and Racism") of the pontifical commission "Iustitia et Pax" which commits the Catholic Church to oppose every form of racism such as discriminatory legislation, and bio-engineering manipulation, including antisemitism, even when it is hidden in the guise of anti-Zionism.

Since the Second Vatican Council, the Catholic Church has been engaged in an effort to promote these principles among all Christians, and has endeavored to inculcate positive attitudes of love, esteem, and openness toward the Jews. We believe this is also necessary for a better understanding of our own identity as members of a church established in a tradition closely connected with your history of faith. Consequently, the holy see's Commission for Religious Relations with the Jews has published two important documents: *Guidelines and Suggestions for Implementing the Conciliar Declaration Nostra Aetate (no. 4)* in 1974, and *Notes on the Correct Way To Present the Jews and Judaism in Preaching and Catechesis in the Catholic Church* in 1985.

The Catholic Church is, therefore, deeply committed to fostering dialogue and cooperation with the Jews. Given the reality of misunderstandings between us in the past, it may be expected that there will be occasional tensions in this relationship. But it is essential that we work together in order to reduce these tensions, and to search for solutions in the same spirit of sincerity and confidence which characterized the beginning of this new era of fraternal relations during and immediately following the Vatican Council.

Even today we are facing together the tension arising from the presence of a Carmelite convent in the so-called "Old-Theatre" at Auschwitz. Its presence there is a result of the genuine piety of Roman Catholics in Poland. I want to express my full confidence in Cardinal Macharski, archbishop of Cracow, in both his words and his actions. In a spirit of mutual trust, an agreement was reached on this matter in Geneva in 1987. The subsequent delay in the building of a new educational and spiritual center and convent results from unforeseen difficulties which we hope will soon be overcome. But the greatest difficulty would arise from a loss of mutual confidence.

For many years I have worked to build up better knowledge of the Jews among Catholics, and to foster a new relationship with the Jews on the basis of the Declaration *Nostra aetate.* Many of you appreciate how important and significant a conciliar declaration of this type is for our church. We must reaffirm our commitment to promote and improve our relationship. The International Liaison Committee remains the most important instrument for the building up of this relationship, and its activity must continue without interruption.

In the Jewish Mishnah it is written, "The day is short and the task is great and the laborers are idle and the wage is abundant and

the master of the house is urgent. . . . It is not your part to finish the task, yet you are not free to desist from it" (Mishnah Avot 2, 15–16). And in the gospel of Matthew we read, "The harvest is plentiful, but the laborers are few; pray therefore the Lord of the harvest to send out laborers into his harvest" (Mt 9:37).
Therefore, let us pray:

"Let the favor of the Lord our God be upon us, and establish thou the work of our hands upon us, yea, the work of our hands establish thou it" (Ps 90:17).

Jewish Religious and Cultural Contribution to European Civilization*

When one speaks of Europe in the perspective of a "common home" and a "new evangelization," one cannot pass over the relationship with the Jewish people in silence, whether this relationship be historical, cultural, or religious. There are various reasons—theological and historical, but ultimately convergent—which induce us to speak about this: the *spiritual affinity* which binds us together (cf. *Nostra aetate,* n. 4) and the two thousand-year-long experience of our relationship which often has not been easy. All this makes it urgent for Christians and Jews to share the responsibility, the challenges, and the needs of today's world.

Our common spiritual patrimony is found essentially in the faith of the patriarchs and great women of Israel, in the messianic hope, in love for God and neighbor. Such are the gifts which characterize the unique people of God to which God revealed himself in history as creator, Father, and merciful redeemer. This mystery of salvation is announced in the Hebrew scriptures, received and venerated by the church as coming from the tradition of Israel. On this "holy root" (Rom 11:16) of the good olive tree developed the holy foliage of the church, united in its trinitarian and christological faith. But other holy branches, that is, the religious family of the Jewish people, have continued to grow, united around the sacred Torah—studied with love (*Tal-*

* Text submitted to the meeting of the Council of European Bishops Conference—Conference of European Churches, November 16, 1992, Santiago de Compostela.

194

mud), and put into practice (*Halakha*)—in the midst of the synagogue prayer, family traditions, and the messianic desire to arrive in the "land of holiness."

The patrimony of European civilization received a fundamental contribution from both the Christians and the Jews. The history of the Jews in Europe, while being marked at certain times by dramatic events—exiles, inquisition, ghettos—and not exempt from religious prejudices and misunderstandings, constantly witnesses to the positive and rich influences which Jewish culture contributed—at different periods and places of Europe —to the European people in the midst of which a Jewish diaspora lived.

The Jewish people gave the people of Europe the Septuagint, which is a translation of the Bible into a European language. The narrative of the genesis of the Greek Bible, originating with the Jews of Alexandria, was taken up by the Talmud, the Samaritans, and the fathers of the church. The Jewish tradition recognized in the Greek Bible—even though this story is legendary—a holiness coming from the Hebrew text and transmitted in a foreign, European language. The Alexandrian Greek text was used as the official text in the Greek-speaking Christian world. Here I am considering its cultural value: Greek culture was a major element in the genesis and evolution of European culture. Thanks to the Greek translation of the Bible, this Greek root of our culture is not only of a profane nature. The Septuagint is a contribution of the Jewish people to the formation of European culture.

Contributions such as these have been constant throughout the centuries. During the middle ages one finds the exegetical work of Rashi of Troyes which was a source of inspiration for Christian exegesis of his time. There is also the philosophical reflection of Moses Maimonides, taken up by St. Thomas Aquinas. In the same period, marked by the crusades, Saint Bernard made his appeal: Leave the Jews in peace because those who offend them touch the very apple of God's eye. The renaissance interest in the *Qabbala* and the *Talmud* was unfortunately suffocated in the atmosphere of the western schism. It is also necessary to mention the spiritual affinity of two movements which greatly influenced Europe: *Franciscanism* and *Hassidism*.

And, since we are in Spain, it would be impossible not to mention the very positive influence in religion, science, and literature made by the Jewish Sephardic culture. It is also our duty to call to mind—precisely in order to deplore it—that with the 1492 expulsion, this rich experience of dialogue was unfortunately broken off.

More recently, and especially after the French revolution, the Jews distinguished themselves in their civil and social role, and in the various arts. There are also more recent examples: the work of Marc Chagall in the figurative arts, that of Emmanuel Levinas in religious philosophy, and that of Henry Bernard Lévy in his biblically-inspired call to civil resistance. This is why it is so tragic that our times and our Europe experienced the attempt to annihilate the Jewish people during the dark night of the shoah. This wound, which is still open, calls for reflection on antisemitism and the anti-Jewish stereotypes which are still so common, as well as a desire for conversion and reconciliation.

In response to the urgent needs not only of Europe but of the entire world, I would like to point out here some possible areas of cooperation between Jews and Christians. Certainly these thoughts presuppose mutual trust and dialogue in truth and love, as well as the institution, at various levels, of places where the two communities of faith can meet one another. The European Jewish Congress has already had contacts with high-level church officials in relation to the Synod for Europe, and an international Jewish organization exists (International Jewish Committee on Interreligious Consultations) which has an ongoing relationship with the holy see. Let me suggest some examples of possible cooperation.

1. Together we could promote reflection and witness, inspired by the religious and ethical principles of *biblical revelation,* on the autonomy of the various cultures and their positive value, as well as on the principle of religious freedom existing today in our pluralist society.

2. More concretely, we can work together in certain social areas (cf. *Sollicitudo rei socialis,* 47; *Centesimus annus,* 60) for justice, peace, and the integrity of creation, possibly taking in the faithful of Islam and other religions. Here one could also include the struggle against racism, discrimination, and antisemitism as a "sin against God and humanity" (John Paul II).

3. Based on these presuppositions, many other possibilities

for cooperation can be found: in the area of religious education, the mass media, assistance for persons or groups in difficulty. The special bond of the Jewish people with the land of Israel could evoke an historic and geographical European responsibility and vocation toward the Mediterranean area and, through North Africa, toward the southern part of the planet. The yearning to make the Mediterranean a "sea of peace," to use the prophet's image, around the "holy mountain" of Jerusalem (Is 11:9), could unite us in truly ecumenical and universal service.

Appendices

I. Official Catholic Texts on Jews and Judaism from Vatican Council II (1963–1965)

Dogmatic Constitution
Lumen gentium, no. 16

Finally, those who have not yet received the gospel are related in various ways to the people of God. In the first place there is the people to whom the covenants and the promises were given and from whom Christ was born according to the flesh (cf. Rom 9:4–5). On account of their fathers, this people remains most dear to God, for God does not repent of the gifts he makes nor of the calls he issues (cf. Rom 11:28–29).

[. . .]

Rome, November 21, 1964

Declaration
Nostra aetate

1. In our times, when every day men are being drawn closer together and the ties between various peoples are being multiplied, the church is giving deeper study to her relationship with non-Christian religions. In her task of fostering unity and love among men, and even among nations, she gives primary consideration in this document to what human beings have in common and to what promotes fellowship among them.

For all peoples comprise a single community, and have a single origin, since God made the whole race of men dwell over the entire face of the earth (cf. Acts 17:26). One also is their final goal: God. His providence, his manifestation of goodness, and his saving designs extend to all men (cf. Wis 8:1; Acts 14:17; Rom 2:6–7; 1 Tim 2:4) against the day when the elect will be united in that holy city ablaze with the splendor of God, where the nations will walk in his light (cf. Rev 21:23f).

Men look to the various religions for answers to those profound mysteries of the human condition which, today even as in olden times, deeply stir the human heart: What is a man? What is the meaning and the purpose of our life? What is goodness and what is sin? What gives us rise to our sorrows and to what intent? Where lies the path to true happiness? What is the truth about death, judgment, and retribution beyond the grave? What, finally, is that ultimate and unutterable mystery which engulfs our being, and whence we take our rise, and whither our journey leads us?

2. From ancient times down to the present, there has existed among diverse peoples a certain perception of that hidden power which hovers over the course of things and over the events of hu-

man life; at times, indeed, recognition can be found of a supreme divinity and of a supreme Father too. Such a perception and such a recognition instill the lives of these peoples with profound religious sense. Religions bound up with cultural advancement have struggled to reply to these same questions with more refined concepts and in more highly developed language.

Thus in Hinduism men contemplate the divine mystery and express it through an unspent fruitfulness of myths and through searching philosophical inquiry. They seek release from the anguish of our condition through ascetical practices or deep meditation or a loving, trusting flight toward God.

Buddhism in its multiple forms acknowledges the radical insufficiency of this shifting world. It teaches a path by which men, in a devout and confident spirit, can either reach a state of absolute freedom or attain supreme enlightenment by their own efforts or by higher assistance.

Likewise, other religions to be found everywhere strive variously to answer the restless searching of the human heart by proposing "ways," which consist of teachings, rules of life, and sacred ceremonies.

The Catholic Church rejects nothing which is true and holy in these religions. She looks with sincere respect upon those ways of conduct and of life, those rules and teachings which, though differing in many particulars from what she holds and sets forth, nevertheless often reflect a ray of that truth which enlightens all men. Indeed, she proclaims and must ever proclaim Christ, "the way, the truth, and the life" (Jn 14:6), in whom men find the fullness of religious life, and in whom God has reconciled all things to himself (cf. 2 Cor 5:18–19).

The church therefore has this exhortation for her sons: prudently and lovingly, through dialogue and collaboration with the followers of other religions, and in witness of Christian faith and life, acknowledge, preserve, and promote the spiritual and moral goods found among these men, as well as the values in their society and culture.

3. Upon the Moslems, too, the church looks with esteem. They adore one God, living and enduring, merciful and all-powerful, maker of heaven and earth and speaker to men. They strive to submit wholeheartedly even to his inscrutable decrees, just as did

Abraham, with whom the Islamic faith is pleased to associate itself. Though they do not acknowledge Jesus as God, they revere him as a prophet. They also honor Mary, his virgin mother; at times they call on her, too, with devotion. In addition they await the day of judgment when God will give each man his due after raising him up. Consequently, they prize the moral life, and give worship to God especially through prayer, almsgiving, and fasting.

Although in the course of the centuries many quarrels and hostilities have arisen between Christian and Moslems, this most sacred synod urges all to forget the past and to strive sincerely for mutual understanding. On behalf of all mankind, let them make common cause of safeguarding and fostering social justice, moral values, peace, and freedom.

4. As this sacred synod searches into the mystery of the church, it recalls the spiritual bond linking the people of the new covenant with Abraham's stock.

For the church of Christ acknowledges that, according to the mystery of God's saving design, the beginnings of her faith and her election are already found among the patriarchs, Moses, and the prophets. She professes that all who believe in Christ, Abraham's sons according to faith (cf. Gal 3:7), are included in the same patriarch's call, and likewise that the salvation of the church was mystically foreshadowed by the chosen people's exodus from the land of bondage.

The church, therefore, cannot forget that she received the revelation of the Old Testament through the people with whom God in his inexpressible mercy deigned to establish the ancient covenant. Nor can she forget that she draws sustenance from the root of that good olive tree onto which have been grafted the wild olive branches of the Gentiles (cf. Rom 11:17–24). Indeed, the church believes that by his cross Christ, our peace, reconciled Jew and Gentile, making them both one in himself (cf. Eph 2:14–16).

Also, the church ever keeps in mind the words of the apostle about his kinsmen, "who have the adoption as sons, and the glory and the covenant and the legislation and the worship and the promises; who have the fathers, and from whom is Christ according to the flesh" (Rom 9:4–5), the son of the Virgin Mary. The church recalls too that from the Jewish people sprang the apostles, her foundation stones and pillars, as well as most of the early disciples who proclaimed Christ to the world.

As holy scripture testifies, Jerusalem did not recognize the time of her visitation (cf. Lk 19:44), nor did the Jews in large number accept the gospel; indeed, not a few opposed the spreading of it (cf. Rom 11:28). Nevertheless, according to the apostle, the Jews still remain most dear to God because of their fathers, for he does not repent of the gifts he makes nor of the calls he issues (cf. Rom 11:28–29). In company with the prophets and the same apostle, the church awaits that day, known to God alone, on which all peoples will address the Lord in a single voice and "serve him with one accord" (Zeph 3:9; cf. Is 66:23; Ps 65:4; Rom 11:11–32).

Since the spiritual patrimony common to Christians and Jews is thus so great, this sacred synod wishes to foster and recommend that mutual understanding and respect which is the fruit above all of biblical and theological studies, and of brotherly dialogues.

True, authorities of the Jews and those who followed their lead pressed for the death of Christ (cf. Jn 19:6); still, what happened in his passion cannot be blamed upon all the Jews then living, without distinction, nor upon the Jews of today. Although the church is the new people of God, the Jews should not be presented as repudiated or cursed by God, as if such views followed from the holy scriptures. All should take pains, then, lest in catechetical instruction and in the preaching of God's word they teach anything out of harmony with the truth of the gospel and the Spirit of Christ.

The church repudiates all persecutions against any man. Moreover, mindful of her common patrimony with the Jews, and motivated by the gospel's spiritual love and by no political considerations, she deplores the hatred, persecutions and displays of antisemitism directed against the Jews at any time and from any source.

Besides, as the church has always held and continues to hold, Christ in his boundless love freely underwent his passion and death because of the sins of all men, so that all might attain salvation. It is, therefore, the duty of the church's preaching to proclaim the cross of Christ as the sign of God's all-embracing love and as the fountain from which every grace flows.

5. We cannot in truthfulness call upon that God who is the

Father of all if we refuse to act in a brotherly way toward certain men, created though they be to God's image. A man's relationship with God the Father and his relationship with his fellow men are so linked together that scripture says: "He who does not love does not know God" (1 Jn 4:8).

The ground is therefore removed from every theory or practice which leads to a distinction between men or peoples in the matter of human dignity and the rights which flow from it.

As a consequence, the church rejects, as foreign to the mind of Christ, any discrimination against men or harassment of them because of their race, color, condition of life, or religion. Accordingly, following in the footsteps of the holy apostles Peter and Paul, this sacred synod ardently implores the Christian faithful to "maintain good fellowship among the nations" (1 Pet 2:12), and, if possible, as far as in them lies, to keep peace with all men (cf. Rom 12:18), so that they may truly be sons of the Father who is in heaven (cf. Mt 5:45).

Each and every one of the things set forth in this Declaration has won the consent of the fathers of this most sacred council. We too, by the apostolic authority conferred on us by Christ, join with the venerable fathers in approving, decreeing, and establishing these things in the Holy Spirit, and we direct that what has thus been enacted in synod be published to God's glory.

Rome, October 28, 1965

Dogmatic Constitution
Dei Verbum, nn. 14–16

14. In carefully planning and preparing the salvation of the human race, the God of supreme love, by a special dispensation, chose for himself a people to whom he might entrust his promises. First he entered into a covenant with Abraham (cf. Gen 15:18) and, through Moses, with the people of Israel (cf. Ex 24:8). To this people which he had acquired for himself, he so manifested himself through words and deeds as the one true and living God that Israel came to know by experience the ways of God with men, and with God himself speaking to them through the mouth of the prophets, Israel daily gained a deeper and clearer understanding of his ways and made them more widely known among the nations (cf. Ps 21:28–29; 95:1–3; Is 2:1–4; Jer 3:17). The plan of salvation, foretold by the sacred authors, recounted and explained by them, is found as the true word of God in the books of the Old Testament; these books, therefore, written under divine inspiration, remain permanently valuable. "For whatever things have been written have been written for our instruction, that through the patience and the consolation afforded by the scriptures we may have hope" (Rom 15:4).

15. The principal purpose to which the plan of the old covenant was directed was to prepare for the coming both of Christ, the universal redeemer, and of the messianic kingdom, to announce this coming by prophecy (cf. Lk 24:44; Jn 5:39; 1 Pet 1:10), and to indicate its meaning through various types (cf. 1 Cor 10:11). Now the books of the Old Testament, in accordance with the state of mankind before the time of salvation established by Christ, reveal to all men the knowledge of God and of man and the ways in which

God, just and merciful, deals with men. These books, though they also contain some things which are incomplete and temporary, nevertheless show us true divine pedagogy. These same books, then, give expression to a lively sense of God, contain a store of sublime teachings about God, sound wisdom about human life, and a wonderful treasury of prayers, and in them the mystery of our salvation is present in a hidden way. Christians should receive them with reverence.

16. God, the inspirer and author of both Testaments, wisely arranged that the New Testament be hidden in the Old and the Old be made manifest in the New. For, though Christ established the new covenant in his blood (cf. Lk 22:20; 1 Cor 11:25), still the books of the Old Testament with all their parts, caught up into the proclamation of the gospel, acquire and show forth their full meaning in the New Testament (cf. Mt 5:17; Lk 24:27; Rom 16:25–26; 2 Cor 3:14–16) and in turn shed light on it and explain it.

Rome, November 18, 1965

II.

The Commission for Religious Relations with the Jews

Guidelines and Suggestions for Implementing the Conciliar Declaration *Nostra aetate* (n. 4) (1974)

INTRODUCTORY NOTE

The document is published over the signature of Cardinal Wille-brands, in his capacity as president of the new Commission for the Catholic Church's Religious Relations with the Jews, instituted by Paul VI on October 22, 1974. It comes out a short time after the ninth anniversary of the promulgation of *Nostra aetate,* the Second Vatican Council's Declaration on the Relationship of the Church to Non-Christian Religions.

The *Guidelines and Suggestions,* which refer to no. 4 of the Declaration, are notable for their almost exclusively practical nature and for their sobriety.

This deliberately practical nature of the text is justified by the fact that it concerns a pragmatic document. It does not propose a Christian theology of Judaism. Such a theology certainly has an interest for specialist research and reflection, but it still needs considerable study. The new Commission for Religious Relations with the Jews should be able to play a part in the gradual fruition of this endeavor.

The first part of the document recalls the principal teachings of the council on the condemnation of antisemitism and of all discrimination, and the obligation of reciprocal understanding and of renewed mutual esteem. It also hopes for a better knowledge on the part of Christians of the essence of the religious tradition of Judaism and of the manner in which Jews identify themselves.

The text then proposes a series of concrete suggestions. The section dedicated to dialogue calls for fraternal dialogue and the establishment of deep doctrinal research. Prayer in common is also proposed as a means of encounter.

With regard to the liturgy, mention is made of the links between the Christian liturgy and the Jewish liturgy and of the caution which is needed in dealing with commentaries on biblical texts and with liturgical explanations and translations.

The part concerning teaching and education allows the relations of the two to be explored, and stress is laid on the note of expectation which characterizes both the Jewish and the Christian religion. Specialists are invited to conduct serious research, and the establishment of chairs of Hebrew studies is encouraged where it is possible, as well as collaboration with Jewish scholars.

The final section deals with the possibilities of common social action in the context of a search for social justice and for peace.

The conclusion touches on, among other things, the ecumenical aspect of the problem of relations with Judaism, the initiatives of local churches in the area, and the essential lines of the mission of the new Commission instituted by the holy see. The great sobriety of the text is noted also in the concrete suggestions which it puts forward. But it would certainly be wrong to interpret such sobriety as being indicative of a limiting program of activities. The document does propose limited suggestions for some key sectors, but it is a document meant for the universal church, and as such it cannot take account of all the individual situations. The suggestions put forward are intended to give ideas to those who were asking themselves how to start on a local level that dialogue which the text invites them to begin and to develop. These suggestions are mentioned because of their value as examples. They are made because it seems that they could find ample application and that their proposal at the same time constitutes an apt program for aiding local churches to organize their own activities, in order to harmonize with the general movement of the universal church in dialogue with Judaism.

The document can be considered from a certain point of view as the Commission's first step for the realization of religious relations with Judaism. It will devolve on the new Commission to prepare and put forward, when necessary, the further developments which may seem necessary in order that the initiative of the Second Vatican Council in this important area may continue to bear fruit on a local and on a worldwide level, for the benefit and peace of heart and harmony of spirit of all who work under the protection of the one Almighty God.

The document, which gives the invitation to an effort of mutual understanding and collaboration, coincides with the opening of the Holy Year, which is consecrated to the theme of reconciliation. It is impossible not to perceive in such a coincidence an invitation to study and to apply in concrete terms throughout the whole world the suggestions which the document proposes. Likewise one cannot fail to hope that our Jewish brothers too may find in it useful indications for their participation in a commitment which is common.

PREAMBLE

The Declaration *Nostra aetate,* issued by the Second Vatican Council on October 28, 1965, "on the relationship of the church to non-Christian religions" (no. 4), marks an important milestone in the history of Jewish-Christian relations. Moreover, the step taken by the council finds its historical setting in circumstances deeply affected by the memory of the persecution and massacre of Jews which took place in Europe just before and during the Second World War.

Although Christianity sprang from Judaism, taking from it certain essential elements of its faith and divine cult, the gap dividing them was deepened more and more, to such an extent that Christians and Jews hardly knew each other.

After two thousand years, too often marked by mutual ignorance and frequent confrontation, the Declaration *Nostra aetate* provides an opportunity to open or to continue a dialogue with a view to better mutual understanding. Over the past nine years, many steps in this direction have been taken in various countries. As a result, it is easier to distinguish the condition under which a new relationship between Jews and Christians may be worked out and developed. This seems the right moment to propose, following the guidelines of the council, some concrete suggestions born of experience, hoping they will help to bring into actual existence in the life of the church the intentions expressed in the conciliar document.

While referring the reader back to this document, we may simply restate here that the spiritual bonds and historical links binding the church to Judaism condemn (as opposed to the very spirit of Christianity) all forms of antisemitism and discrimination, which in any case the dignity of the human person alone would suffice to condemn. Further still, these links and relationships render obligatory a better mutual understanding and renewed mutual esteem. On the practical level in particular, Christians must therefore strive to acquire a better knowledge of the basic components of the religious tradition of Judaism; they must strive to learn by what essential traits the Jews define themselves in the light of their own religious experience.

With due respect for such matters of principle, we simply propose some first practical applications in different essential areas of the church's life, with a view to launching or developing sound relations between Catholics and Jewish brothers.

I. DIALOGUE

To tell the truth, such relations as there have been between Jew and Christian have scarcely ever risen above the level of monologue. From now on, real dialogue must be established. Dialogue presupposes that each side wishes to know the other, and wishes to increase and deepen its knowledge of the other. It constitutes a particularly suitable means of favoring a better mutual knowledge and, especially in the case of dialogue between Jews and Christians, of probing the riches of one's own tradition. Dialogue demands respect for the other as he is—above all, respect for his faith and his religious convictions.

In virtue of her divine mission, and her very nature, the church must preach Jesus Christ to the world (*Ad gentes,* 2). Lest the witness of Catholics to Jesus Christ should give offense to Jews, they must take care to live and spread their Christian faith while maintaining the strictest respect for religious liberty in line with the teaching of the Second Vatican Council (Declaration *Dignitatis humanae*). They will likewise strive to understand the difficulties which arise for the Jewish soul—rightly imbued with an extremely high, pure notion of the divine transcendence—when faced with the mystery of the incarnate Word.

While it is true that a widespread air of suspicion, inspired by an unfortunate past, is still dominant in this particular area, Christians, for their part, will be able to see to what extent the responsibility is theirs and deduce practical conclusions for the future.

In addition to friendly talks, competent people will be encouraged to meet and to study together the many problems deriving from the fundamental convictions of Judaism and of Christianity. In order not to hurt (even involuntarily) those taking part, it will be vital to guarantee, not only tact, but a great openness of spirit and diffidence with respect to one's own prejudice.

In whatever circumstances as shall prove possible and mutually acceptable, one might encourage a common meeting in the presence of God, in prayer and silent meditation, a highly efficacious way of finding that humility, that openness of heart and mind, necessary prerequisites for a deep knowledge of oneself and of others. In particular, that will be done in connection with great causes such as the struggle for peace and justice.

II. LITURGY

The existing links between the Christian liturgy and the Jewish liturgy will be borne in mind. The idea of a living community in the service of God, and in the service of men for the love of God, such as it is realized in the liturgy, is just as characteristic of the Jewish liturgy as it is of the Christian one. To improve Jewish-Christian relations, it is important to take cognizance of those common elements of the liturgical life (formulas, feasts, rites, etc.) in which the Bible holds an essential place.

An effort will be made to acquire a better understanding of whatever in the Old Testament retains its own perpetual value (cf. *Dei verbum,* 14–15), since that has not been canceled by the later interpretation of the New Testament. Rather, the New Testament brings out the full meaning of the Old, while both Old and New illumine and explain each other (cf. ibid., 16). This is all the more important since liturgical reform is now bringing the text of the Old Testament ever more frequently to the attention of Christians.

When commenting on biblical texts, emphasis will be laid on

the continuity of our faith with that of the earlier covenant, in the perspective of the promises, without minimizing those elements of Christianity which are original. We believe that those promises were fulfilled with the first coming of Christ. But it is nonetheless true that we still await their perfect fulfillment in his glorious return at the end of time.

With respect to liturgical readings, care will be taken to see that homilies based on them will not distort their meaning, especially when it is a question of passages which seem to show the Jewish people as such in an unfavorable light. Efforts will be made so to instruct the Christian people that they will understand the true interpretation of all the texts and their meaning for the contemporary believer.

Commissions entrusted with the task of liturgical translation will pay particular attention to the way in which they express those phrases and passages which Christians, if not well informed, might misunderstand because of prejudice. Obviously, one cannot alter the text of the Bible. The point is that, with a version destined for liturgical use, there should be an overriding preoccupation to bring out explicitly the meaning of a text, while taking scriptural studies into account.

The preceding remarks also apply to introductions to biblical readings, to the Prayer of the Faithful, and to commentaries printed in missals used by the laity.

III. TEACHING AND EDUCATION

Although there is still a great deal of work to be done, a better understanding of Judaism itself and its relationship to Christianity has been achieved in recent years thanks to the teaching of the church, the study and research of scholars, as also to the beginning of dialogue.

In this respect, the following facts deserve to be recalled: It is the same God, "inspirer and author of the books of both Testaments" (*Dei verbum,* 16), who speaks both in the old and new covenants.

Judaism in the time of Christ and the apostles was a complex reality, embracing many different trends, many spiritual, religious, social and cultural values. The Old Testament and the Jewish tradition founded upon it must not be set against the New Testament in such a way that the former seems to constitute a religion of only justice, fear and legalism, with no appeal to the love of God and neighbor (cf. Dt 6:5; Lv 19:18; Mt 22:34–40).

Jesus was born of the Jewish people, as were his apostles and a large number of his first disciples. When he revealed himself as the messiah and Son of God (cf. Mt 16:16), the bearer of the new gospel message, he did so as the fulfillment and perfection of the earlier revelation. And, although his teaching had a profoundly new character, Christ nevertheless, in many instances, took his stand on the teaching of the Old Testament. The New Testament is profoundly marked by its relation to the Old. As the Second Vatican Council declared: "God, the inspirer and author of the books of both Testaments, wisely arranged that the New Testament be hidden in the Old and the Old be made manifest in the New" (*Dei verbum,* 16). Jesus also used teaching methods similar to those employed by the rabbis of his time. With regard to the trial and death of Jesus, the council recalled that "what happened in his passion cannot be blamed upon all the Jews then living, without distinction, nor upon the Jews of today" (*Nostra aetate,* 4).

The history of Judaism did not end with the destruction of Jerusalem, but rather went on to develop a religious tradition. And although we believe that the importance and meaning of that tradition were deeply affected by the coming of Christ, it is still nonetheless rich in religious values.

With the prophet and the apostle Paul, "the church awaits the day, known to God alone, on which all peoples will address the Lord in a single voice and 'serve him with one accord' (Zeph 3:9)" (*Nostra aetate,* 4).

Information concerning these questions is important at all levels of Christian instruction and education. Among sources of information, special attention should be paid to the following:

- catechisms and religious textbooks;
- history books;
- the mass-media (press, radio, cinema, television).

The effective use of these means presupposes the thorough formation of instructors and educators in training schools, seminaries and universities.

Research into the problems bearing on Judaism and Jewish-Christian relations will be encouraged among specialists, particularly in the fields of exegesis, theology, history and sociology. Higher institutions of Catholic research, in association if possible with other similar Christian institutions and experts, are invited to contribute to the solution of such problems. Wherever possible, chairs of Jewish studies will be created, and collaboration with Jewish scholars encouraged.

IV. JOINT SOCIAL ACTION

Jewish and Christian tradition, founded on the word of God, is aware of the value of the human person, the image of God. Love of the same God must show itself in effective action for the good of mankind. In the spirit of the prophets, Jews and Christians will work willingly together, seeking social justice and peace at every level—local, national and international. At the same time, such collaboration can do much to foster mutual understanding and esteem.

CONCLUSION

The Second Vatican Council has pointed out the path to follow in promoting deep fellowship between Jews and Christians. But there is still a long road ahead. The problem of Jewish-Christian relations concerns the church as such, since it is when "pondering her own mystery" that she encounters the mystery of Israel. Therefore, even in areas where no Jewish communities exist, this remains an important problem. There is also an ecumenical aspect of the question: the very return of Christians to the sources and origins of their faith, grafted onto the earlier covenant, helps the search for unity in Christ, the cornerstone.

In this field, the bishops will know what best to do on the pastoral level, within the general disciplinary framework of the church and in line with the common teaching of her magisterium. For example, they will create some suitable commissions or secretariats on a national or regional level, or appoint some competent person to promote the implementation of the conciliar directives and the suggestions made above.

On October 22, 1974, the holy father instituted for the universal church this Commission for Religious Relations with the Jews, joined to the Secretariat for Promoting Christian Unity. This special Commission, created to encourage and foster religious relations between Jews and Catholics—and to do so eventually in collaboration with other Christians—will be, within the limits of its competence, at the service of all interested organizations, providing information for them and helping them to pursue their task in conformity with the instructions of the holy see. The Commission wishes to develop this collaboration in order to implement, correctly and effectively, the express intentions of the council.

Given at Rome, December 1, 1974.

Johannes Cardinal Willebrands
President of the Commission

Pierre-Marie de Contenson, OP
Secretary

Presentation of the *Notes*
by Jorge Mejía

The document published here is the result of long and considered work by our Commission.

At the beginning of March 1982, delegates of episcopal conferences and other experts met in Rome to examine a first draft. It was in the course of preparations for this meeting that requests from various quarters came to the Commission, asking that a guide be prepared. Such a guide would be for the use of all those in the church who have the difficult task of presenting Jews and Judaism to the Catholic faithful in the light of new pastoral and doctrinal developments. These developments flow from the conciliar Declaration *Nostra aetate,* 4, published twenty years ago and also from the *Guidelines and Suggestions for Implementing the Conciliar Declaration "Nostra aetate" (no. 4),* published by our Commission at the end of 1974.

The idea was to be of help to those engaged in catechetical work, in teaching and also in preaching, and to put into practice the new directions just mentioned, which are not always easy to translate into teaching methods.

The preparatory work went on for three years. There were several consultations with our consultors in Rome and elsewhere, resulting in several subsequent drafts. Clearly, throughout these stages of the work, and above all in the final one, the drafters kept well in mind what the holy father has had to say on Jewish-Catholic relations. He has addressed this subject on various important occasions, from Paris to Mainz, from Brooklyn to Caracas and Madrid, and many times in Rome itself. Neither could the drafters forget the various documents published in recent years by several episcopal conferences. And, at the same time, the Commission along with these consultors and experts took into account the accumulated experience of many years of nearly daily contact with our Jewish partners. For all of that, the text is and remains a document of the Catholic Church. This means that its language, its structure, and the questions it intends to address belong to the teaching and pastoral practice of the Catholic Church.

As is normal procedure with any document published by a department of the holy see, other departments with competency in the subject matter were consulted. Their observations have been dutifully and carefully taken into account. It is both our duty and our pleasure to express our gratitude and appreciation publicly to them for their patient and fruitful collaboration with us.

The document, in this its final version, bears the title *Notes on the Correct Way To Present the Jews and Judaism in Preaching and Catechesis in the Roman Catholic Church.* The first word of the title (*Notes*) appropriately indicates the aim of the text. It is intended to provide a helpful frame of reference for those who are called upon in various ways in the course of their teaching assignments to speak about Jews and Judaism and who wish to do so in keeping with the current teaching of the church in this area. As everyone knows, this happens quite often. In fact, it is a practical impossibility to present Christianity while abstracting from the Jews and Judaism, unless one were to suppress the Old Testament, forget about the Jewishness of Jesus and the apostles, and dismiss the vital cultural and religious context of the primitive church. Neither is it an alternative to present one and the other in a prejudiced, unfavorable light. It is precisely this way of acting that the council wanted to put an end to. That was also the aim that the 1974 *Guidelines* addressed more or less on the level of general principles. It is exactly the same aim that the present *Notes* address on a more concrete level—one might almost say in handbook style, as long as one keeps in mind the limitations of a text that cannot and should not be too lengthy.

Hence, the structure of the document. It starts with a series of "Preliminary Considerations," which introduce the spirit and the rationale of the text, mostly with the help of quotations from the council, the holy fathers, or preceding documents. Thereupon follows a first section called "Religious Teaching and Judaism," in which the doctrinal and pastoral principles underlying such teaching are set forth. Of special note is paragraph no. 3, which speaks about Judaism as a present reality and not only as an "historical" (and thus superseded) reality.

Also to be noted is no. 5 on the complexity of both the historical and the religious relationships between the church and Judaism. In this same section there is an affirmation that is important for the Catholic Church concerning the centrality of Christ and his unique value in the economy of salvation (no. 7). Clearly this does not mean, however, that the Jews cannot and should not draw salvific gifts from their own traditions. Of course they can and should do so.

A second section is entitled "Relations Between the Old and New Testaments." This tries to help put into practice the directions of the Second Vatican Council that call for providing the Catholic faithful with access to a fuller and richer knowledge of holy scripture (cf. *Dei verbum,* 21–22 and *Sacrosanctum concilium,* 51). This especially included the Old Testament. It is not always an easy matter to present the relations between both Testaments in a way that fully respects the validity of the Old Testament and shows its permanent usefulness for the church. At this point, an effort is made to explain the meaning of what is called "typology," since on this a large part of our liturgical use of the Old Testament is grounded. In no way is "typological" usage a devaluation of the validity proper to the Old Testament. Rather to the contrary. One can see this from another angle, since it has always been taught in the Catholic tradition that there is also a "typological" use of the New Testament with respect to the "last things" or eschatological realities (cf. no. 16). The importance of the Old Testament for Judaism is underlined. So, too, is the importance of Jews and Christians hearing the Old Testament together, so that together, in the path opened by the prophetic tradition, we may become more deeply engaged as fellow partisans for humanity today (no. 18, 19). The significance of the continuity of the Jewish people in history is again mentioned toward the end of this document (cf. no. 33). It should also be noted that the limits of "typological" usage are acknowledged, and other possible ways of reading the Old Testament in relation to the New are not excluded (cf. no. 11).

The third section speaks about the "Jewish Roots of Christianity." Here we turn to the New Testament and try to show that the Jewishness of Jesus and the Judaism of his time are far from being something marginal or incidental. On the contrary, they are connected with the very dynamic of the incarnation. Thus, they have a specific value in the divine plan of salvation. The relationship of Jesus to the biblical law is carefully assessed (no. 21). So, too, are his relations to the Jewish religious institutions of his time, including the temple (no. 22). Also carefully assessed are his contacts with the Pharisees, who constituted a movement within the Judaism of his time with which, beyond doubt, he had very close relations and to which he was very near—notwithstanding appearances to the contrary, about which more is said in the subsequent section.

This fourth section is, in fact, given over to the problem of the way "The Jews in the New Testament" are presented. On the basis of an exceedingly superficial analysis, some (Jews and Christians) feel that the New Testament is "antisemitic." By contrast in this document the sound and proven results of recent scholarly exegesis are taken into account. Relying on this evidence, principles and criteria are offered to teachers for the presentation and explanation of texts that can create difficulty, whether these are found in the gospel of John or in other New Testament writings. There is no intention, however, of hiding the fact of the disbelief of Jews in Jesus, a fact which is here called "sad," just as it is in the well-known text of the letter to the Romans (9:2). In fact, it is from this point that the division and enmity between Christians and Jews originated, and it is also from this fact that the present urgent need for reconciliation derives, as is very carefully noted (cf. no. 29D). At the same time, with no less care, it is emphasized that no one can judge the conscience of another, neither of others in the past nor—still less—of others today (ibid., E, F). In this connection, the teaching of the Second Vatican Council on religious liberty must constantly be kept in mind, since this is "one of the bases on which rests the Jewish-Christian dialogue promoted by the council" (ibid., F). A special paragraph is dedicated to the "delicate question of responsibility for the death of Christ" (no. 30). No attempt is made, however, to enter into complex and difficult historical questions. Rather, in keeping with the viewpoint of the Catechism of the Council of Trent (here quoted explicitly), the text focuses on the theological significance of the death of Christ and our participation in it as sinners. From this perspective, the historical role of "those few Jews" and those few Romans in Jesus' passion becomes a very secondary matter. (The Creed of the Catholic Church has always mentioned Pontius Pilate in relation with the death of Christ, not the Jews).

In the fifth section, reference is made to the liturgy and to similarities and points of contact with Jewish worship. Specific mention is made of the source of our prayers, of the cycle of feasts, and of the very structure itself of our eucharistic prayers.

A sixth section contains material altogether new in this series of documents. It intends to offer some information on the common history of Judaism and Christianity down through the centuries, a history that unfortunately is largely unknown or poorly understood if not altogether distorted. In this section, the central elements are chiefly three. First, the permanence of Judaism and, as we say, its theological significance, "which allowed Israel to carry to the whole world a witness—often heroic—of its fidelity to the one God" (no. 33). Second, the "religious attachment of the Jews" to the "land of their forefathers," which Christians are encouraged to try to understand (ibid.). And third, the creation of the state of Israel. This is taken up with extreme precision. It is said that the "perspective" in which the state should be "envisaged" is not "in itself religious." It should be seen "in . . . reference to the common principles of international law" which govern the existence of the various states and their place in the community of nations (ibid.). It will surely be noted that for the first time in a document of this commission, in different but related paragraphs, reference is made to the land and the state. A brief sentence at the end of the paragraph refers to the "extermination" of the Jews (in Hebrew, the shoah, i.e., the catastrophe) during the dark years of the Nazi persecution. It calls upon Catholics to understand how decisive such a tragedy was for the Jews, a tragedy that is also obviously ours. Several teaching aids have been prepared, including those by Catholic offices for education, to help Catholics better comprehend the senseless dimensions of this tragedy and to grasp better its significance. Our Commission is gratified by these efforts and, with this brief emphasis, would like to indicate in them the path to be followed. Here again (cf. no. 34), as well as toward the beginning of the document (cf. no. 8), the text repeats its condemnation of antisemitism. This time, however, that condemnation is explicitly linked with the necessity of a "precise, objective, and rigorously accurate teaching on Judaism," which is the aim of these *Notes.* We are well aware that much has been done to dispel what has been called the "teaching of contempt" (the expression comes from the famous Jewish historian from France, Jules Isaac). But much still remains to be done, not least because new forces of racism and antisemitism remain ever ready to rise.

The aim of the *Notes* is, thus, a thoroughly positive one, as the "Conclusion" states. They seek to promote the formation of Catholics equipped "not only for objectivity, justice, and tolerance" (which would already mean a lot), but "also for understanding dialogue." Indeed, "our two traditions are so related that they cannot ignore each other (as is still frequently the case)." It remains a constant necessity that "mutual knowledge . . . be encouraged at every level."

It is our hope that the in-depth study of this text can be carried out by both parties in an atmosphere free of pre-conceptions and attentive to the meaning and often delicate nuances of many paragraphs. This will help us toward our highly desired goal, which is also the indispensable condition for our united truly efficacious action together in behalf of the ideals we hold dear and which we have inherited from our shared biblical tradition.

Notes on the Correct Way To Present the Jews and Judaism in Preaching and Catechesis in the Catholic Church (1985)

PRELIMINARY CONSIDERATIONS

On March 6, 1982, Pope John Paul II told delegates of episcopal conferences and other experts meeting in Rome to study relations between the Church and Judaism: ". . . you yourselves were concerned, during your sessions, with Catholic teaching and catechesis regarding Jews and Judaism. . . . We should aim, in this field, that Catholic teaching at its different levels, in catechesis to children and youth, presents Jews and Judaism, not only in an honest and objective manner, free from prejudices and without any offenses, but also with full awareness of the heritage common" to Jews and Christians.

In this passage, so charged with meaning, the holy father plainly drew inspiration from the council Declaration *Nostra aetate*, 4, which says:

> "All should take pains, then, lest in catechetical instruction and in the preaching of God's word they teach anything out of harmony with the truth of the gospel and the spirit of Christ," as also from these words: "Since the spiritual patrimony common to Christians and Jews is thus so great, this sacred synod wishes to foster and recommend mutual understanding and respect. . . ."

In the same way, the *Guidelines and Suggestions* for implementing the conciliar declaration *Nostra aetate* (no. 4) ends its chapter III, entitled "Teaching and Education," which lists a number of practical things to be done, with this recommendation: "Information concerning these questions is important at all levels of Christian instruction and education. Among sources of information, special attention should be paid to the following:

- catechisms and religious textbooks;
- history books;
- the mass media (press, radio, cinema, television).

The effective use of these means presupposes the thorough formation of instructors and educators in training schools, seminaries and universities" (AAS 77 [1975] 73). The paragraphs which follow are intended to serve this purpose.

I. RELIGIOUS TEACHING AND JUDAISM

1. In *Nostra aetate,* 4, the council speaks of the "spiritual bonds linking" Jews and Christians and of the "great spiritual patrimony" common to both, and it further asserts that "the church of Christ acknowledges that, according to the mystery of God's saving design, the beginning of her faith and her election are already found among the patriarchs, Moses and the prophets."

2. Because of the unique relations that exist between Christianity and Judaism—"linked together at the very level of their identity" (John Paul II, March 6, 1982)—relations "founded on the design of the God of the covenant" (ibid.), the Jews and Judaism should not occupy an occasional and marginal place in catechesis: their presence there is essential and should be organically integrated.

3. This concern for Judaism in Catholic teaching has not merely an historical or archeological foundation. As the holy father said in the speech already quoted, after he had again mentioned the "common patrimony" of the church and Judaism as "considerable": "To assess it carefully in itself, and with due awareness of the faith and religious life of the Jewish people as they are professed and practiced still today, can greatly help us to understand better cer-

tain aspects of the life of the church." It is a question then of
pastoral concern for a still living reality closely related to the remarkable theological formula, in his allocution to the Jewish community of West Germany at Mainz, on November 17, 1980:
". . . the people of God of the old covenant, which has never been
revoked. . . ."

4. Here we should recall the passage in which the *Guidelines
and Suggestions,* I, tried to define the fundamental condition of
dialogue: "respect for the other as he is," knowledge of the "basic
components of the religious tradition of Judaism," and again learning "by what essential traits the Jews define themselves in the light
of their own religious experience" (Introduction).

5. The singular character and the difficulty of Christian teaching about Jews and Judaism lies in this, that it needs to balance a
number of pairs of ideas which express the relation between the two
economies of the Old and New Testament:

- promise and fulfillment;
- continuity and newness;
- singularity and universality;
- uniqueness and exemplary nature.

This means that the theologian and the catechist who deal with the
subject need to show in their practice of teaching that:

- promise and fulfillment throw light on each other;
- newness lies in a metamorphosis of what was there before;
- the singularity of the people of the Old Testament is not exclusive
  and is open, in the divine vision, to a universal extension;
- the uniqueness of the Jewish people is meant to have the force of
  an example.

6. Finally, "work that is of poor quality and lacking in precision would be extremely detrimental" to Judeo-Christian dialogue
(John Paul II, speech of March 6, 1982). But it would be above all
detrimental—since we are talking of teaching and education—to
Christian identity (ibid.).

7. "In virtue of her divine mission, the church," which is to be
"the all-embracing means of salvation" in which alone "the full-

ness of the means of salvation can be obtained" (*Unitatis redinte-gratio,* 3), "must of her nature proclaim Jesus Christ to the world" (cf. *Guidelines and Suggestions,* I). Indeed we believe that it is through him that we go to the Father (cf. Jn 14:6), "and this is eternal life, that they know thee the only true God and Jesus Christ whom thou hast sent" (Jn 17:3).

Jesus affirms (Jn 10:16) that "there shall be one flock and one shepherd." Church and Judaism cannot then be seen as two parallel ways of salvation, and the church must witness to Christ as the redeemer for all, "while maintaining the strictest respect for religious liberty in line with the teaching of the Second Vatican Council (Declaration *Dignitatis humanae*)" (*Guidelines and Suggestions,* I).

8. The urgency and importance of precise, objective and rigorously accurate teaching on Judaism for our faithful follows too from the danger of antisemitism which is always ready to reappear under different guises. The question is not merely to uproot from among the faithful the remains of antisemitism still to be found here and there, but much rather to arouse in them, through educational work, an exact knowledge of the wholly unique "bond" (*Nostra aetate,* 4) which joins us as a church to the Jews and to Judaism. In this way, they would learn to appreciate and love the latter, who have been chosen by God to prepare the coming of Christ and have preserved everything that was progressively revealed and given in the course of that preparation, notwithstanding their difficulty in recognizing in him their messiah.

II. RELATIONS BETWEEN THE OLD AND NEW TESTAMENTS

9. Our aim should be to show the unity of biblical revelation (O.T. and N.T.) and of the divine plan, before speaking of each historical event, so as to stress that particular events have meaning when seen in history as a whole—from creation to fulfillment. This history concerns the whole human race and especially believers. Thus the definitive meaning of the election of Israel does not become clear except in the light of the complete fulfillment (Rom 9–11), and election in Jesus Christ is still better

understood with reference to the announcement and the promise (cf. Heb 4:1–11).

10. We are dealing with singular happenings which concern a singular nation but are destined, in the sight of God who reveals his purpose, to take on universal and exemplary significance. The aim is moreover to present the events of the Old Testament not as concerning only the Jews but also as touching us personally. Abraham is truly the father of our faith (cf. Rom 4:11–12; Roman Canon: *patriarchae nostri Abrahae*). And it is said (1 Cor 10:1): "Our fathers were all under the cloud, and all passed through the sea." The patriarchs, prophets and other personalities of the Old Testament have been venerated and always will be venerated as saints in the liturgical tradition of the oriental church as also of the Latin church.

11. From the unity of the divine plan derives the problem of the relation between the Old and New Testaments. The church already from apostolic times (cf. 1 Cor 10:11; Heb 10:1) and then constantly in tradition resolved this problem by means of typology, which emphasizes the primordial value that the Old Testament must have in the Christian view. Typology, however, makes many people uneasy and is perhaps the sign of a problem unresolved.

12. Hence, in using typology, the teaching and practice which we have received from the liturgy and from the fathers of the church, we should be careful to avoid any transition from the Old to the New Testament which might seem merely a rupture. The church, in the spontaneity of the Spirit which animates her, has vigorously condemned the attitude of Marcion and always opposed his dualism.

13. It should also be emphasized that typological interpretation consists in reading the Old Testament as preparation and, in certain aspects, outline and foreshadowing of the New (cf., e.g., Heb 5:5–10, etc.). Christ is henceforth the key and point of reference to the scriptures: "the rock was Christ" (1 Cor 10:4).

14. It is true then, and should be stressed, that the church and Christians read the Old Testament in the light of the event of the dead and risen Christ and that on these grounds there is a Christian reading of the Old Testament which does not necessarily coincide with the Jewish reading. Thus Christian identity and Jewish identity should be carefully distinguished in their respective reading of

the Bible. But this detracts nothing from the value of the Old Testament in the church and does nothing to hinder Christians from profiting discerningly from the traditions of Jewish reading.

15. Typological reading only manifests the unfathomable riches of the Old Testament, its inexhaustible content and the mystery of which it is full, and should not lead us to forget that it retains its own value as revelation that the New Testament often does no more than resume (cf. Mk 12:29–31). Moreover, the New Testament itself demands to be read in the light of the Old. Primitive Christian catechesis constantly had recourse to this (cf. e.g., 1 Cor 5:6–8; 10:1–11).

16. Typology further signifies reaching toward the accomplishment of the divine plan, when "God will be all in all" (1 Cor 15:28). This holds true also for the church which is realized already in Christ, yet awaits its definitive perfecting as the body of Christ. The fact that the body of Christ is still tending toward its full stature (cf. Eph 4:12–19) takes nothing from the value of being a Christian. So also the calling of the patriarchs and the exodus from Egypt do not lose their importance and value in God's design from being at the same time intermediate stages (cf., e.g., *Nostra aetate,* 4).

17. The exodus, for example, represents an experience of salvation and liberation that is not complete in itself, but has in it, over and above its own meaning, the capacity to be developed further. Salvation and liberation are already accomplished in Christ and gradually realized by the sacraments in the church. This makes way for the fulfillment of God's design, which awaits its final consummation with the return of Jesus as messiah, for which we pray each day. The kingdom, for the coming of which we also pray each day, will be finally established. With salvation and liberation the elect and the whole of creation will be transformed in Christ (Rom 8:19–23).

18. Furthermore, in underlining the eschatological dimension of Christianity we shall reach a great awareness that the people of God of the Old and New Testaments are tending toward a like end in the future: the coming or return of the Messiah—even if they start from two different points of view. It is more clearly understood that the person of the messiah is not only a point of division for the people of God but also a point of convergence (cf. *Sussidi*

per l'ecumenismo nella diocesi di Roma, n. 140). Thus it can be said that Jews and Christians meet in a comparable hope, founded on the same promise made to Abraham (cf. Gn 12:1–3; Heb 6:13–18).

19. Attentive to the same God who has spoken, on the same word, we have to witness to one same memory and one common hope in him who is the master of history. We must also accept our responsibility to prepare the world for the coming of the messiah by working together for social justice, respect for the rights of persons and nations, and social and international reconciliation. To this we are driven, Jews and Christians, by the command to love our neighbor, by a common hope for the kingdom of God and by the great heritage of the prophets. Transmitted soon enough by catechesis, such a conception would teach young Christians in a practical way to cooperate with Jews, going beyond simple dialogue (cf. *Guidelines,* IV).

III. JEWISH ROOTS OF CHRISTIANITY

20. Jesus was and always remained a Jew; his ministry was deliberately limited "to the lost sheep of the house of Israel" (Mt 15:24). Jesus was fully a man of his time, and of his environment —the Jewish Palestinian one of the first century, the anxieties and hopes of which he shared. This cannot but underline both the reality of the incarnation and the very meaning of the history of salvation, as it has been revealed in the Bible (cf. Rom 1:3–4; Gal 4:4–5).

21. Jesus' relations with biblical law and its more or less traditional interpretations are undoubtedly complex, and he showed great liberty toward it (cf. the "antitheses" of the sermon on the mount: Mt 5:21–48, bearing in mind the exegetical difficulties; his attitude to rigorous observance of the sabbath: Mk 3:1–6, etc.).

But there is no doubt that he wished to submit himself to the law (cf. Gal 4:4), that he was circumcised and presented in the temple like any Jew of his time (cf. Lk 2:21–24), that he was trained in the law's observance. He extolled respect for it (cf. Mt 5:17–20) and invited obedience to it (cf. Mt 8:4). The rhythm of his life was marked by observance of pilgrimages on great feasts, even from his infancy (cf. Lk 2:41–50; Jn 2:13; 7:10, etc.). The importance of the cycle of the Jewish feasts has been frequently underlined in the gospel of John (cf. 2:13; 5:1; 7:2, 10, 37; 10:22; 12:1; 13:1; 18:28; 19:42, etc.).

22. It should be noted also that Jesus often taught in the synagogues (cf. Mt 4:23; 9:35; Lk 4:15–18; Jn 18:20, etc.) and in the temple (cf. Jn 18:20, etc.), which he frequented as did the disciples even after the resurrection (cf., e.g., Acts 2:46; 3:1; 21:26, etc.). He wished to put in the context of synagogue worship the proclamation of his messiahship (cf. Lk 4:16–21). But above all he wished to achieve the supreme act of the gift of himself in the setting of the domestic liturgy of the Passover, or at least of the paschal festivity (cf. Mk 14:1, 12 and parallels; Jn 18:28). This also allows of a better understanding of the "memorial" character of the eucharist.

23. Thus the Son of God is incarnate in a people and a human family (cf. Gal 4:4; Rom 9:5). This takes away nothing, quite the contrary, from the fact that he was born for all men (Jewish shepherds and pagan wise men are found at his crib: Lk 2:8–20; Mt 2:1–12) and died for all men (at the foot of the cross there were Jews, among them Mary and John: Jn 19:25–27, and pagans like the centurion: Mk 15:39 and parallels). Thus he made two peoples one in his flesh (cf. Eph 2:14–17). This explains why with the *ecclesia ex gentibus* we have, in Palestine and elsewhere, an *ecclesia ex circumcisione,* of which Eusebius for example speaks (H.E., IV, 5).

24. His relations with the Pharisees were not always or wholly polemical. Of this there are many proofs: It is Pharisees who warn Jesus of the risks he is running (Lk 13:31); some Pharisees are praised—e.g., "the scribe" of Mark 12:34; Jesus eats with Pharisees (Lk 7:36; 14:1).

25. Jesus shares, with the majority of Palestinian Jews of that time, some Pharisaic doctrines: the resurrection of the body; forms of piety, like almsgiving, prayer, fasting (cf. Mt 6:1–18) and the liturgical practice of addressing God as Father; the priority of the commandment to love God and our neighbor (cf. Mk 12:28–34). This is also true of Paul (cf. Acts 23:8), who always considered his membership in the Pharisees as a title of honor (cf. Acts 23:6; 26:5; Phil 3:5).

26. Paul also, like Jesus himself, used methods of reading and

interpreting scripture and of teaching his disciples which were common to the Pharisees of their time. This applies to the use of parables in Jesus' ministry, as also to the method of Jesus and Paul of supporting a conclusion with a quotation from scripture.

27. It is noteworthy too that the Pharisees are not mentioned in accounts of the passion. Gamaliel (Acts 5:34–39) defends the apostles in a meeting of the sanhedrin. An exclusively negative picture of the Pharisees is likely to be inaccurate and unjust (cf. *Guidelines,* Note 1; *AAS* 77, p. 76). If in the gospels and elsewhere in the New Testament there are all sorts of unfavorable references to the Pharisees, they should be seen against the background of a complex and diversified movement. Criticisms of various types of Pharisees are moreover not lacking in rabbinical sources (cf. the Babylonian Talmud, the Sotah treatise 22b, etc.). "Phariseeism" in the pejorative sense can be rife in any religion. It may also be stressed that, if Jesus shows himself severe toward the Pharisees, it is because he is closer to them than to other contemporary Jewish groups (cf. supra no. 25).

28. All this should help us to understand better what St. Paul says (Rom 11:16ff) about the "root" and the "branches." The church and Christianity, for all their novelty, find their origin in the Jewish milieu of the first century of our era, and more deeply still in the "design of God" (*Nostra aetate,* 4), realized in the patriarchs, Moses and the prophets (ibid.), down to its consummation in Christ Jesus.

IV. THE JEW IN THE NEW TESTAMENT

29. The *Guidelines* already say (note 1) that "the formula 'the Jews' sometimes, according to the context, means 'the leaders of the Jews' or 'the adversaries of Jesus,' terms which express better the thought of the evangelist and avoid appearing to arraign the Jewish people as such."

An objective presentation of the role of the Jewish people in the New Testament should take account of these various facts:

A. The gospels are the outcome of long and complicated editorial work. The Dogmatic Constitution *Dei verbum,* following the Pontifical Biblical Commission's Instruction *Sancta Mater Ecclesia,* distinguished three stages: "The sacred authors wrote the four gospels, selecting some things from the many which had been handed on by word of mouth or in writing, reducing some of them to a synthesis, explicating some things in view of the situation of their churches, and preserving the form of proclamation, but always in such fashion that they told us the honest truth about Jesus" (no. 19).

Hence it cannot be ruled out that some references hostile or less than favorable to the Jews have their historical context in conflicts between the nascent church and the Jewish community. Certain controversies reflect Christian-Jewish relations long after the time of Jesus.

To establish this is of capital importance if we wish to bring out the meaning of certain gospel texts for the Christians today. All this should be taken into account when preparing catechesis and homilies for the last weeks of Lent and Holy Week (cf. already *Guidelines* II, and now also *Sussidi per l'ecumenismo nella diocesi di Roma,* 1982, 144 b).

B. It is clear on the other hand that there were conflicts between Jesus and certain categories of Jews of his time, among them Pharisees, from the beginning of his ministry (cf. Mk 2:1-11, 24; 3:6, etc.).

C. There is moreover the sad fact that the majority of the Jewish people and its authorities did not believe in Jesus—a fact not merely of history but of theological bearing, of which St. Paul tries hard to plumb the meaning (Rom 9-11).

D. This fact, accentuated as the Christian mission developed, especially among the pagans, led inevitably to a rupture between Judaism and the young church, now irreducibly separated and divergent in faith, and this stage of affairs is reflected in the texts of the New Testament and particularly in the gospels. There is no question of playing down or glossing over this rupture; that could only prejudice the identity of either side. Nevertheless it certainly does not cancel the spiritual "bond" of which the council speaks (*Nostra aetate,* 4) and which we propose to dwell on here.

E. Reflecting on this in the light of scripture, notably of the chapters cited from the epistle to the Romans, Christians should never forget that the faith is a free gift of God (cf. Rom 9:12) and that we should never judge the consciences of others. St. Paul's exhortation to "not boast" in your attitude to "the root" (Rom 11:18) has its full point here.

F. There is no putting the Jews who knew Jesus and did not believe in him, or those who opposed the preaching of the apostles, on the same plane with Jews who came after or those of today. If the responsibility of the former remains a mystery hidden with God (cf. Rom 11:25), the latter are in an entirely different situation. Vatican II in the Declaration on Religious Freedom teaches that "all men are to be immune from coercion . . . in such wise that in matters religious no one is to be forced to act in a manner contrary to his own beliefs, nor . . . restrained from acting in accordance with his own beliefs" (no. 2). This is one of the bases—proclaimed by the council—on which Judeo-Christian dialogue rests.

30. The delicate question of responsibility for the death of Christ must be looked at from the standpoint of the conciliar Declaration *Nostra aetate,* 4 and of *Guidelines and Suggestions* (III): "What happened in [Christ's] passion cannot be blamed upon all the Jews then living without distinction nor upon the Jews of today," especially since "authorities of the Jews and those who followed their lead pressed for the death of Christ." Again, further on: "Christ in his boundless love freely underwent his passion and death because of the sins of all men, so that all might attain salvation" (*Nostra aetate,* 4). The Catechism of the Council of Trent teaches that Christian sinners are more to blame for the death of Christ than those few Jews who brought it about—they indeed "knew not what they did" (cf. Lk 23:34), and we know it only too well (Pars I, caput V, Quaest. XI). In the same way and for the same reason, "the Jews should not be presented as repudiated or cursed by God, as if such views followed from the holy scriptures" (*Nostra aetate,* 4) even though it is true that "the church is the new people of God" (ibid.).

V. THE LITURGY

31. Jews and Christians find in the Bible the very substance of their liturgy: for the proclamation of God's word, response to it, prayer of praise and intercession for the living and the dead, and recourse to the divine mercy. The liturgy of the word in its own structure originates in Judaism. The Liturgy of the Hours and other

liturgical texts and formularies have their parallels in Judaism as do the very formulas of our most venerable prayers, among them the Our Father. The eucharistic prayers also draw inspiration from models in the Jewish tradition. As John Paul II said (Allocution of March 6, 1982): ". . . the faith and religious life of the Jewish people, as they are professed and practiced still today, can greatly help us to understand better certain aspects of the life of the church. Such is the case of liturgy. . . ."

32. This is particularly evident in the great feasts of the liturgical year, like the Passover. Christians and Jews celebrate the Passover: the Jews, the historic Passover looking toward the future; the Christians, the Passover accomplished in the death and resurrection of Christ, although still in expectation of the final consummation (cf. supra n. 17). It is still the "memorial" which comes to us from the Jewish tradition, with a specific content different in each case. On either side, however, there is a like dynamism: for Christians it gives meaning to the eucharistic celebration (cf. the antiphon *O sacrum convivium*), a paschal celebration and as such a making present of the past, but experienced in the expectation of what is to come.

VI. JUDAISM AND CHRISTIANITY IN HISTORY

33. The history of Israel did not end in 70 A.D. (cf. *Guidelines,* II). It continued, especially in a numerous diaspora which allowed Israel to carry to the whole world a witness—often heroic —of its fidelity to the one God and to "exalt him in the presence of all the living" (Tob 13:4), while preserving the memory of the land of their forefathers at the heart of their hope (Passover Seder).

Christians are invited to understand this religious attachment which finds its roots in biblical tradition, without however making their own any particular religious interpretation of this relationship (cf. Declaration of the U.S. Conference of Catholic Bishops, November 20, 1975).

The existence of the state of Israel and its political options should be envisaged not in a perspective which is in itself religious, but in their reference to the common principles of international law.

The permanence of Israel (while so many ancient peoples

have disappeared without trace) is an historic fact and a sign to be interpreted within God's design. We must in any case rid ourselves of the traditional idea of a people punished, preserved as a living argument for Christian apologetic. It remains a chosen people, "the pure olive on which were grafted the branches of the wild olive which are the Gentiles" (John Paul II, March 6, 1982, alluding to Rom 11:17–24). We must remember how much the balance of relations between Jews and Christians over two thousand years has been negative. We must remind ourselves how the permanence of Israel is accompanied by a continuous spiritual fecundity, in the rabbinical period, in the middle ages and in modern times, taking its start from a patrimony which we long shared, so much so that "the faith and religious life of the Jewish people, as they are professed and practiced still today, can greatly help us to understand better certain aspects of the life of the church" (John Paul II, March 6, 1982). Catechesis should on the other hand help in understanding the meaning for the Jews of the extermination during the years 1939–1945, and its consequences.

34. Education and catechesis should concern themselves with the problem of racism, still active in different forms of antisemitism. The council presented it thus: "Moreover, [the church], mindful of her common patrimony with the Jews and motivated by the gospel's spiritual love and by no political considerations, deplores the hatred, persecutions and displays of antisemitism directed against the Jews at any time and from any source" (*Nostra aetate*, 4). The *Guidelines* comment: "The spiritual bonds and historical links binding the church to Judaism condemn (as opposed to the very spirit of Christianity) all forms of antisemitism and discrimination, which in any case the dignity of the human person alone would suffice to condemn" (*Guidelines*, Preamble).

CONCLUSION

35. Religious teaching, catechesis and preaching should be a preparation not only for objectivity, justice, tolerance but also for understanding and dialogue. Our two traditions are so related that they cannot ignore each other. Mutual knowledge must be encouraged at every level. There is evident in particular a painful igno-

rance of the history and traditions of Judaism, of which only negative aspects and often caricature seem to form part of the stock ideas of many Christians.

That is what these notes aim to remedy. This would mean that the council text and *Guidelines and Suggestions* would be more easily and faithfully put into practice.

Johannes Cardinal Willebrands
President of the Commission

Pierre Duprey
Vice President

Jorge Mejía
Secretary

III.

Pope John Paul II

Address on the 25th Anniversary of *Nostra aetate**

YOUR EMINENCES,
YOUR EXCELLENCIES,
DISTINGUISHED VISITORS,

As Delegates of the International Jewish Committee on Interreligious Consultations and Members of the Commission for Religious Relations with the Jews, you have come together to commemorate the Twenty-fifth Anniversary of the Second Vatican Council's Declaration *Nostra aetate.* In effect, what you are celebrating is nothing other than the divine mercy which is guiding Christians and Jews to mutual awareness, respect, cooperation and solidarity. Conscious of our sharing in the same hope and promises made to Abraham and to his descendants, I am indeed pleased to welcome you in this house! "Baruch ha-bah be-Shem Adonai!" "Blessed is he who comes in the name of the Lord!" (Ps 119:26).

The brief but significant document *Nostra aetate* occupied an important place in the work of the council. After a quarter of a century it has lost none of its vigor. The strength of the document and its abiding interest derive from the fact that it speaks to all peoples and about all peoples from a religious perspective, a perspective which is the deepest and most mysterious of the many dimensions of the human person, the image of the creator (cf. Gn 1:26).

The universal openness of *Nostra aetate,* however, is anchored in and takes its orientation from a high sense of the absolute singularity of God's choice of a particular people, "his own" people, Israel according to the flesh, already called God's church (*Lumen*

* Rome, December 6, 1990.

gentium, 9; cf. Nm 20:4; Dt 23:1ff; Neh 13:1). Thus the church's reflection on her mission and on her very nature is intrinsically linked with her reflection on the stock of Abraham and on the nature of the Jewish people (cf. *Nostra aetate,* 4). The church is fully aware that sacred scripture bears witness that the Jewish people, this community of faith and custodian of a tradition thousands of years old, is an intimate part of the "mystery" of revelation and of salvation. In our own times many Catholic writers have spoken of that "mystery" which is the Jewish people: among them Geremia Bonomelli, Jacques Maritain and Thomas Merton.

The church therefore, particularly through her biblical scholars and theologians, but also through the work of other writers, artists and catechists, continues to reflect upon and express more thoroughly her own thinking on the mystery of this people. I am happy that the Commission for Religious Relations with the Jews is intensely promoting study on this theme in a theological and exegetical context.

When we consider Jewish tradition we see how profoundly you venerate sacred scripture, the Miqrā, and in particular the Torah. You live in a special relationship with the Torah, the living teaching of the living God. You study it with love in the Talmud Torah, so as to put it into practice with joy. Its teaching on love, on justice and on the law is reiterated in the prophets—Nevi'im, and in the Ketuvim. God, his holy Torah, the synagogal liturgy and family traditions, the land of holiness, are surely what characterize your people from the religious point of view. And these are things that constitute the foundation of our dialogue and of our cooperation.

At the center of the holy land, almost as its hallowed heart, lies Jerusalem. It is a city holy to three great religions, to Jews, Christians and Muslims. Its very name evokes peace. I should like you to join in praying daily for peace, justice and respect for the fundamental human and religious rights of the three peoples, the three communities of faith who inhabit that beloved land.

No dialogue between Christians and Jews can overlook the painful and terrible experience of the shoah. During the meeting at Prague in September of this year, the Jewish-Catholic International Liaison Committee considered at length the problems of the shoah and of antisemitism, and came to conclusions that are of great importance for the continuation of our dialogue and cooperation. It is my hope that these may be widely recognized and that the recommendations then formulated will be implemented wherever human and religious rights are violated.

May God grant that the commemoration of the Twenty-fifth Anniversary of *Nostra aetate* will bring fresh results of spiritual and moral renewal for us and for the world. May it bring above all the fruit of cooperation in promoting justice and peace. In the Babylonian Talmud we read: "The world stands upon the single column that is the just man" (Hagigha, 12 b). In the gospel, Jesus Christ tells us that blessed are the peacemakers (cf. Mt 5:9). May justice and peace fill our hearts and guide our steps toward the fullness of redemption for all peoples and for the whole universe. May God hear our prayers!

IV.

International Catholic-Jewish Liaison Committee

Joint Statement on the Shoah and Antisemitism (Prague, 1990)

Representatives of the International Jewish Committee on Interreligious Consultations (IJCIC) and the holy see's Commission for Religious Relations with the Jews met in Prague from September 3 through September 6. This was the thirteenth meeting of the International Catholic-Jewish Liaison Committee. Before the deliberations began, the Catholic and Jewish delegations made a visit of homage to Theresienstadt, one of the Nazi death camps.

The last meeting of this Committee took place in Rome in 1985. Difficulties which arose led to a delay of a further meeting until now. However, during these years the Steering Committee continued to meet on a regular basis to enable its work to proceed. In a special meeting of the holy see's Commission and IJCIC in Rome in 1987, it was foreseen that the next meeting would seek to lay the basis for the presentation of a Catholic document on the shoah, the historical background of antisemitism, and its contemporary manifestations. The intention to prepare such a document was confirmed by the holy see's Commission.

In this connection, the meeting in Prague discussed the religious as well as the secular basis of antisemitism over the past 1,900 years and its relationship to the shoah. This discussion led to the recognition that certain traditions of Catholic thought, teaching, preaching, and practice in the patristic period and in the middle ages contributed to the creation of antisemitism in western society. In modern times, many Catholics were not vigilant enough to react against manifestations of antisemitism. The Catholic delegates condemned antisemitism as well as all forms of racism as a sin against God and humanity, and affirmed that one cannot be authentically Christian and engage in antisemitism.

At the conference, Jewish and Catholic witnesses to the shoah spoke of their experiences. They offered testimony that many Christians failed themselves as well as Jews and other victims by too weak a response to Nazi and Fascist ideologies. Witness was also given to the many courageous Christian church leaders and members who acted to save Jews, thereby risking their own lives during the Nazi terror. Nor was it forgotten that people other than Jews also perished.

The conference acknowledged the monumental role of the Declaration of the Second Vatican Council *Nostra aetate,* as well as later efforts by the popes and church officials, to bring about a substantive improvement in Catholic-Jewish relations.

Nostra aetate created a new spirit in these relationships. Pope John Paul II expressed that new spirit in an audience with Jewish leaders on February 15, 1985, when he said: "The relationship between Jews and Christians has radically improved in these years. Where there was ignorance and therefore prejudice and stereotype, there is now growing mutual knowledge, appreciation and respect. There is, above all, love between us—that kind of love I mean, which is for both of us a fundamental injunction of our religious traditions and which the New Testament has received from the Old."

While echoing the pope's recognition that a new spirit is in the making, the delegates called for a deepening of this spirit in Catholic-Jewish relations, a spirit which emphasizes cooperation, mutual understanding and reconciliation, good-will and common goals to replace the past spirit of suspicion, resentment and distrust.

This spirit presupposes repentance as expressed by Archbishop Edward Idris Cassidy, president of the holy see's Commission for Religious Relations with the Jews, when he said in his opening statement: "That antisemitism has found a place in Christian thought and practice calls for an act of Teshuvah (repentance) and of reconciliation on our part as we gather here in this city which is a testimony to our failure to be authentic witnesses to our faith at times in the past."

This new spirit would also manifest itself in the work that the two faith communities could do together to respond to the needs of today's world. This need is for the establishment of human rights, freedom, and dignity where they are lacking or imperiled, and for responsible stewardship of the environment. A new image and a new attitude in Jewish-Catholic relations are required to spread universally the trail-blazing work that has been done in a number of communities in various parts of the world. For example, in the United States an ongoing structure engaging in Catholic-Jewish dialogue recently issued a joint document on the teaching of moral values in public education. Furthermore, the Catholic Church there is effectively working to teach Judaism in its seminaries, school texts and educational materials in a positive and objective manner, scrupulously eliminating anything that would go against the spirit of Second Vatican Council.

Likewise, the Jewish community in the United States in a growing atmosphere of confidence and trust has conducted its own self-study of its texts in terms of what Jewish schools teach about Christians and Christianity. Many similar examples of such Catholic and Jewish initiatives in other countries could be cited.

Over and above the study of the history of antisemitism, the meeting devoted special attention to recent manifestations of antisemitism, particularly in Eastern and Central Europe. It stressed the need to disseminate the achievements of *Nostra aetate* and past Catholic-Jewish dialogues in those countries where new political developments have created the possibility for cooperative work.

Recognizing the importance of widening the circulation of the teachings of *Nostra aetate,* the meeting noted with satisfaction the establishment of joint Jewish-Christian Liaison Committees in Czechoslovakia and Hungary and the diffusion by the Polish church authorities of official documents concerning Catholic-Jewish relations in their own language.

It was stressed that systematic efforts must be made to uproot sources of religious antisemitism wherever they appear through the publication of texts, priestly training, liturgy, and the use of Catholic media.

The Liaison Committee hopes that the new Catechism for the

Universal Church now in preparation can serve as an effective instrument to this end.

With regard to the special problems of antisemitism in Eastern and Central Europe, the Committee recommended the following:

(1) Translation into the vernacular languages and broad dissemination of all relevant church documents on relations with Judaism (notably the Declaration on the Relationship of the Church to Non-Christian religions, *Nostra aetate,* N. 4, October 28, 1965; the *Guidelines and Suggestions for Implementing the Conciliar Declaration Nostra Aetate N. 4,* December 1, 1974, and the *Notes on the Correct Way To Present the Jews and Judaism in Preaching and Catechesis in the Catholic Church,* June 24, 1985).

(2) The inclusion of the teaching of these documents in the curricula of theological seminaries, in order to eliminate all remnants of the teaching of contempt, and the setting up of special courses on the same subject in the seminaries for priests who have not yet received such theological instruction.

(3) The monitoring of all trends and events which threaten an upsurge of antisemitism with a view to countering promptly such developments.

(4) Ongoing actions aimed at guaranteeing freedom of worship and religious education for all citizens (Christians, Jews and others).

(5) Active support of general legislation against discrimination on grounds of race or religion including antisemitism, and against incitement to religious or racial hatred; promotion of legislative action curtailing freedom of association to racist organizations.

(6) Support of general educational programs which would foresee:

(a) Inclusion in school curricula of knowledge and respect for different civilizations, cultures and religions, in particular of peoples and denominations inhabiting the national territory concerned;

(b) Special attention to be paid in education to the problem of racial, national and religious prejudice and hatred. This should include the teaching of the history of the disasters brought about by such prejudice or hatred;

(c) Elimination from the textbooks of all racially or religiously prejudiced content and of material conducive to creating inter-group strife.

It was recommended that a special joint commission be es-tablished by the competent authorities of the respective commu-nities in each of the countries of Eastern and Central Europe to facilitate and promote these goals. The holy see's Commission for Religious Relations with the Jews and the International Jew-ish Committee for Interreligious Consultations are ready to as-sist such efforts.

We continue to see the need, already envisaged, for closer and more rapid cooperation and exchange of information between IJCIC and the holy see's Commission, in order to avoid future misunderstanding and face together trends and concerns within the two communities.

With regard to the Carmelite Convent at Auschwitz, we note with satisfaction the declaration of the holy see's Commission for Religious Relations with the Jews made by Cardinal Johannes Wil-lebrands in September 1989, confirming the intention to establish in another location "a Center of Meeting, Dialogue and Prayer, as foreseen in the Geneva agreement of February 1987, which would contribute in an important way to the development of good rela-tions between Christians and Jews."

We look to the early completion of the new edifice in which the Carmelite Monastery will find its natural setting and hope that all difficulties will be overcome. The Jewish delegation ex-pressed its commitment to the state of Israel and stressed the need for Catholic understanding of the special place Israel has in Jewish consciousness. It manifested its concern with the lack of full diplomatic relations between the holy see and the state of Israel.

Furthermore, the Jewish delegation expressed the hope that Vatican archival material would be made accessible for better un-derstanding of the darkest period in Jewish history. After two mil-lennia of estrangement and hostility, we have a sacred duty as Catholics and Jews to strive to create a genuine culture of mutual esteem and reciprocal caring.

Catholic-Jewish dialogue can become a sign of hope and

inspiration to other religions, races, and ethnic groups to turn away from contempt and toward realizing authentic human fraternity. This new spirit of friendship and caring for one another may be the most important symbol that we have to offer to our troubled world.

Prague, September 6, 1990

Notes to Articles

"CARDINAL BEA'S ATTITUDE TO RELATIONS WITH THE JEWS"

1. In the papers left by the cardinal the proofs are labeled R 1962/29.

2. It is obvious that the author, in speaking of the divine-human *nature* of Christ, means to refer to the divine-human *reality* of Christ.

3. Allocution given on Radio Catholique Belge; cf. *La Libre Belgique* of Sept. 14, 1938, quoted in *La Documentation Catholique,* 1938, pp. 1459–60.

4. *Stimmen der Zeit* 88 (1961–1962), Vol. I, pp. 16–25.

5. For the English translation of the *relatio,* see Augustin Cardinal Bea, *The Church and the Jewish People,* London 1966, pp. 154–159.

6. The Italian original was translated into French, English, Dutch, Spanish and German.

"UNITY BETWEEN OLD AND NEW COVENANT"

1. Text originally published in German and Italian (see Bibliography, p. 267). Lecture delivered at Munich University, July 9, 1987.

2. M. Wyschogrod, "La Torah en tant que Loi dans le Judaïsme," in *SIDIC,* 19, 3 (1986), pp. 10–16.

3. Cf. the Jewish morning prayer: "Lord of the universe, we do not rely on our virtues . . . but on your mercy."

4. Ed. Parish Sanders, *Paul and Palestinian Judaism,* 1984²; Jacob Neusner, "Scripture and Tradition in Judaism—With Spe-

cial Reference to the Mishnah," in *Enoch* II (1980), 285–306; "Giudaismo e Scrittura. Il caso del Levitico Rabbah," in *Enoch* VII (1985), 45–66.

5. Jacob Neusner, "Scripture and tradition in Judaism," *art. cit.*

6. Saint John Damascene, *La foi orthodoxe, suivi de Defense des Icônes,* Paris 1966, p. 12.

7. Cf. *Istituzione cristiana* IV, XVII, 22.

8. Thus the recent collection *Le siècle des Lumières et la Bible,* Beauchesne 1987.

9. Cf. a synthesis of this present-day evolution in Louis Boyer. *Le Fils Eternel,* Paris 1974.

"THE CHURCH AND MODERN ANTISEMITISM"

1. This lecture was delivered at the Malcolm Hay Memorial, Aberdeen University on October 17, 1988 and in London at the Royal Aeronautical Society, under the auspices of the Institute of Jewish Affairs on October 18, 1988.

2. Gerhart M. Riegner, "Von der Pogromnacht zur Endlösung. Erlebnisse und Lehren," lecture delivered at the Humboldt University, Berlin (DDR), April 25, 1988. See *Christian Jewish Relations,* vol. 21, no. 3, 5.

3. Stjepan Schmidt, *Agostino Bea, il Cardinale dell'Unità,* Roma, Città Nuova Editrice, 1987, 571.

4. The word "condemns" was not employed here, nor in any of the conciliar documents, in accordance with the intention of the council to avoid any "damnatio." This was consistent with the pastoral perspective of the council.

5. *Ibid.,* 353–54.

6. *Ibid.,* 356.

7. In *L'Osservatore Romano,* June 25, 1988, 6; for further reflection see *ibid.,* Franz Cardinal Koenig, "Solidarietà fraterna e responsabilità personale."

8. J. Willebrands, "Is Christianity antisemitic?" *Christian Jewish Relations,* vol. 18, no. 2, 1985, 8–20.

9. François Delpech, *Sur les Juifs,* Presses Universitaires de Lyon, 1983, 62–63.

10. *Ibid.,* 136.

11. Bernard Lazare, "Les causes de l'antisémitisme moderne

sont nationales, religieuses, politiques et économiques," in *L'antisémitisme, son histoire et ses causes,* 1894; Nouv. éd. Paris. Editions de la Différence, 1982, 190.

12. Malcolm Hay, *The Roots of Christian Antisemitism.* Anti-Defamation League of B'nai B'rith and Alice Ivy Hay, New York 1981, 211.

13. *Ibid.,* 213.

14. Tommaso Federici, *Monologo e dialogo. Incontri e non incontri con Israele,* A.V.E., Roma 1965.

15. M. Hay, *The Roots of Christian Antisemitism,* 207.

16. *Ibid.,* 211.

17. Geremia Bonomelli, *Tre mesi al di là delle Alps,* Milano, Cogliati, 1909, 413 26. On this particular point of the responsibility for the condemnation of Jesus, the most recent and clear statement was made by John Paul II on September 28, 1988, during the general audience; see *L'Osservatore Romano,* September 29, 1988, 4.

18. Augustin Bea, SJ, "Antisemitismus, Rassentheorie und Altes Testament," in *Stimmen der Zeit,* 100, 3 (1920), 171–83.

19. AAS, XX (1928): 103–04; *La Civiltà Cattolica,* 1928, II, 171.

20. Renzo Fabris, "Il cammino da Seelisberg alla *Nostra Aetate* e oltre," in *Vita monastica* XL, 166–67, n. 29. Concerning the positive attitude of Cardinal Merry del Val toward the Jews we can remember its influence on the Holy See's answer to Theodore Herzl in 1904: "If the Jews believe they might greatly ease their lot by being admitted to the land of their ancestors, then we would regard that as a humanitarian question. We shall never forget that without Judaism, we would have been nothing." Cited by Eugene Fisher, "Zionism and Catholic-Jewish Relations," in *Jewish Frontier,* July/August, 1988: 13.

21. "Il pericolo giudaico e gli 'Amici d'Israele,' " in *La Civiltà Cattolica* 79, II (1928), 335–44.

22. Gerhart M. Riegner, "Verpasste Chancen zu einem Christlich Jüdischen Dialog vor der Shoah," lecture delivered at the "Evangelischer Kirchentag," 1987 Berlin (DDR). "Arbeitsgruppe Judentum und Christentum," in *Theologische Literatur Zeitung,* February 1989, 82.

23. J.H. Nota, SJ, "Edith Stein und der Entwurd für eine Enzy-

258   CHURCH AND JEWISH PEOPLE

klika gegen Rassismus und Antisemitismus," in *Freiburger Rundbrief* XXVI (1974), 36.

24. Henri de Lubac, *Résistance chrétienne à lantisémitisme, souvenirs 1940–1944,* Fayard, Paris 1988, 30.

25. Aaron Steinberg, *History as Experience: Selected Essays and Studies,* Ktav, New York 1983, 390.

26. *Ibid.,* 391.

27. *Ibid.,* 386.

28. *Ibid.,* 405.

29. Richard von Weizsaecker, cited in the Declaration "After 50 years, how can we talk about guilt, suffering and reconciliation?" Zentralkommittee der Deutschen Katholiken, June 1988, 15.

30. Marcel J. Dubois, "The challenge of the Holocaust and the history of salvation," in *Judaism and Christianity under the Impact of National Socialism.* The Historical Society of Israel and the Zalman Shazar Center for Jewish History, Jerusalem 1987, 512.

31. Basil Cardinal Hume, speech to the Holocaust conference "Remembering for the Future," Westminster Central Hall, July 15, 1988.

32. See in particular Jean Dujardin. "The Shoah: What should it teach?" Preliminary Papers, Supplementary Volume, Pergamon Press, 1988, 80–89.

33. Pinchas Lapide, *Rom und die Juden.* Freiburg, Basel, Wien 1967.

34. Joseph L. Lichten, *A Question of Judgement: Pius XII and the Jews,* 1963; It. ed. *Pio XII e gli ebrei: Un contributo per la storia,* preface by Jorge Mejia, Centro Editoriale Dehoniano, Bologna 1988.

35. Raul Hilberg. *La Destruction des Juifs d'Europe,* Fayard, Paris, 1988.

36. Carlo Maria Martini, "Christianity and Judaism," paper delivered at the "Workshop on Anti-Semitism," Princeton Theological Seminary, Philadelphia, May 1–2, 1987, soon to be published.

37. Jean Marie Lustiger, *Le Choix de Dieu,* de Fallois, Paris 1987, 126.

38. See International Catholic Jewish Liaison Committee. *Fifteen Years of Catholic-Jewish Dialogue, 1970–1985. Selected Papers,* Libreria Editrice Vaticana, Libreria Editrice Lateranense, Città del Vaticano–Roma, 1988, xv.

39. *Ibid.,* 300.
40. *Ibid.,* 293.
41. *Ibid.,* 34.
42. *Ibid.,* xix.
43. Very helpful for this synthesis is the short booklet *John Paul II on the Holocaust,* selected and introduced by Eugene J. Fisher, National Conference of Catholic Bishops, Washington, DC, 1988.
44. John Paul II, "Homily at the beatification of Edith Stein," May 11, 1987 in "Information Service" 64 (1987) 73; Address to Jewish Leaders (Miami, September 11, 1987) in "Information Service" 65 (1987), 117.

"THE IMPACT OF THE SHOAH ON CATHOLIC-JEWISH RELATIONS"

1. Cf. Congregation for the Doctrine of the Faith, Instruction *Libertatis conscientiae* on Christian freedom and liberation, March 22, 1986, No. 73.
2. *Le mal et l'éxil,* Paris 1988, pp. 83ff: "Cette question-là doit rester ouverte, car si nous disons que cette souffrance n'a pas été vaine, c'est, à la limite, comme si nous la justifions. . . . Mais en même temps, si nous disions que cette souffrance fut vaine, ne serait-ce pas également terrible?"
3. *Ibid.,* p. 117: "Toute cette souffrance qui pourrait, qui aurait pu reveiller, sensibiliser, si elle se perd, si aucun poème n'en sort, si aucun message n'en vient, si aucune promesse n'y est liée, c'est terrible, c'est un perte deux fois irréparable."
4. Cf. L. Sestieri, *La spiritualità ebraica,* Rome 1987, pp. 296–97.
5. J. Willebrands, *Is Christianity Antisemitic?* (Oxford 1985), in "Christian-Jewish Relations" 18, 2 (1985):8–20.
6. Idem, *The Church Facing Modern Antisemitism* (Aberdeen and London, 1988), in "Christian-Jewish Relations" 22, 1 (1988):5–17.
7. ". . . publicae fuerunt iudaeorum caedes, quas quidem Evangelii lex, quae omnes promiscue diligendos iubet, detestatur ac reprobat," in *Pii X Pontificis Maximi acta,* Vol. II, Rome 1907, p. 199.
8. A. Bea, *Antisemitismus, Rassentheory und AT,* in "Stimmen

der Zeit" (1920): 171–183; AAS XX (1928):103–104; Pius XI, Allocution of 6 September 1938; J. Maritain, Preface to J. Oesterreicher, *Racisme-Antisémitisme, Antichristianisme,* 1942; A. Steinberg, *History as Experience* (New York 1983); A. Heschel, *No Religion is an Island,* 1966. See also *Het mysterie van Israel,* Utrecht-Antwerp 1957.

9. J. Willebrands, *The Church* . . . , *op. cit.,* p. 7.

10. Cf. J. Isaac, *L'enseignement du mépris,* Paris 1962.

11. J.-M. Lustiger, *Le choix de Dieu,* Paris, p. 126: "Le centre de cette idéologie, c'était la persécution du peuple élu, du peuple juif, parce que peuple messianique . . . la visée du nazisme était plus que prométhéenne, satanique. Son hostilité au christianisme était fondamentale. Il ne pouvait pas s'y attaquer de front, car l'Eglise représentait une puissance que les nazis étaient obligés de ménager. Mais les juifs, eux, tombaient de plein fouet sous la persécution."

12. J. Maritain, *Racisme* . . . , *op. cit.,* p. 19: "Persécuter la maison d'Israël c'est aussi persécuter le Christ . . . dans sa souche charnel." Thoughts similar to those of Lustiger and Maritain recur also in the writings of Edith Stein.

13. Cf. E. Wiesel, *Un ebreo oggi,* Brescia 1985: "We were all absent, dead and survivors."

14. Cf. A. Bea, *The Church and the Jewish People,* 1966.

15. *Ibid.,* p. 7.

16. *Guidelines and Suggestions for Implementing the Conciliar Declaration "Nostra aetate" (No. 4),* December 1, 1974. *Notes on the correct way to present the Jews and Judaism in preaching and catechesis in the Catholic Church,* June 24, 1985.

17. International Catholic-Jewish Liaison Committee, *Fifteen Years of Dialogue (1970–1985). Selected Papers,* Rome-Vatican City, 1988.

18. Cf. J. B. Metz, *Im Angesichte der Juden. Christliche Theologie nach Auschwitz,* "Concilium" 20 (1984):382–389.

19. J. Willebrands, *The Church Facing* . . . , *op. cit.,* p. 8: "In 1870 the French brothers Joseph and Augustin Lémann . . . prepared a project concerning the preeminent position of the Jews in the Church . . . the project received the support of 510 conciliar fathers out of 1087." See also *"La cause des restes d'Israël"* introduite au Concile Oecuménique du Vatican sous la bénédiction de

S.S. le Pape Pie IX—Entreprise et récit des deux frères Joseph et Augustin Lémann, Lyon-Paris, 1912.

20. Cf. G. Bonomelli, *Tre mesi al di là delle Alpi,* Milan 1909, pp. 413–426; the germs of a positive conception of the "mystère d'Israël," to use an expression dear to Jacques Maritain, can already be found in Léon Bloy, who dedicated his "Le salut par les Juifs" to Raissa Maritain.

21. J. Maritaine, *Racisme . . . , op. cit.,* p. 14.

22. A. Bea, *The Church . . . , op. cit.,* p. 7.

23. *Fifteen Years . . . , op. cit.,* p. 314; see also p. 238 in this volume.

24. *Ibid.,* p. xix.

25. Among the more recent studies, cf. Friedrich-Wilhelm Marquardt, *Von Elend und Heimsuchung der Theologie,* 1988, pp. 118–47.

26. Clemens Thoma, *Christliche Theologie des Judentums,* 1978, III, II, 186–201.

27. Jules Isaac, *Jesus and Israel,* 1971, p. 400.

General Bibliography
and Abbreviations

AAS   *Acta Apostolica Sedis*

Documents   *The Documents of Vatican II,* with commentaries and notes, edited by Walter M. Abbott, S.J. Geoffrey Chapman (London) and America Press (New York), 1966.

EV   *Enchiridion Vaticanum* (official documents of the Holy See, original texts and Italian translation), Centro Editoriale Dehoniano (Bologna), 1985–1990, vols. 1–10.

ILC   International Catholic-Jewish Liaison Committee, *Fifteen Years of Dialogue, 1970–1985, Selected Papers,* Libreria Editrice Vaticana–Pontificia Università Lateranense (Vatican City–Rome), 1988.

Dokumente   *Die Kirchen und das Judentum, Dokumente von 1945 bis 1985,* herausgegeben von Rolf Rentdorff und Hans Hermann Henrix, Bonifatius-Kaiser (Paderborn-Munich), 1989².

Żydzi   *Żydzi i Judaizm w dokumentach Kościoła i nauczaniu Jana Pawła II, 1965–1989* (Jews and Judaism in the Church's Documents and in the Teaching of John Paul II), edited by W. Chrostowski and R. Rubinkiewicz, Akademia Teologii Katolickej (Warsaw), 1990.

IS *Information Service,* official quarterly review of the Secretariat for Promoting Christian Unity, 1–68 (1967–1988); also The Pontifical Council for Promoting Christian Unity, 69 (1989)–73 (1990).

Sidic *Sidic*—Service international de documentation judéo-chrétienne, I–XXI (1968–1988).

OR *L'Osservatore romano* (Italian daily edition)

OR engl *L'Osservatore romano* (English weekly edition)

OR fr *L'Osservatore romano* (French weekly edition)

OR pol *L'Osservatore romano* (Polish monthly edition)

Actes et documents du Saint Siège relatifs à la seconde guerre mondiale, edited by P. Blet, R.A. Graham, A. Martini, B. Schneider, Libreria Editrice Vaticana (Vatican City), 1970 (revised and enlarged 1981), vols. 1–11.

Gerusalemme nei documenti pontifici, edited by E. Farhat, Libreria Editrice Vaticana (Vatican City), 1987 (Studi Giuridici, XIII).

Vatican Diplomacy and the Jews During the Holocaust, 1939–1943, John F. Morley, Ktav Publishing House (New York), 1980.

The Papacy and the Middle East, The Role of the Holy See in the Arab-Israeli Conflict, 1962–1984, George Emile Irani, University of Notre Dame Press (Notre Dame), 1986.

Christliche Theologie des Judentums, Clemens Thoma, Pattloch (Aschaffenburg) 1978; published in English as *A Christian Theology of Judaism,* Paulist Press (Mahwah, N.J.), 1980.

The Theology of the Churches and the Jewish People, Statements by the World Council of Churches and its member churches, with commentary by Allan Brockway, Paul Van Buren, Rolf Rentdorff, Simon Schoon, WCC Publications (Geneva), 1988.

Pope John Paul II on Jews and Judaism, 1976–1986, with introduction and commentary by Eugene J. Fisher and Leon Klenicki, United States Catholic Conference (Washington, D.C.), 1987.

Selected Bibliography
Johannes Cardinal Willebrands
On Christian-Jewish Relations
(1975–1990)

1. "Dieci anni di Nostra aetate," address at a gathering to celebrate the tenth anniversary of the Council Declaration, at the Sidic center, Rome, Nov. 12, 1975 published in *Sidic* VIII, 3 (1975): 33–35; also published as "Tenth Anniversary of Nostra aetate" in *IS* 28 (1975): 17–19.

2. "Statement about UN Resolution on Zionism" published in *OR,* Nov. 16, 1975: 1; in *IS* 28 (1975): 35; in *Sidic* VIII, 3 (1975): 19.

3. "Catechesis and Judaism," intervention to the Synod of Bishops, Vatican, Oct. 18, 1977 published in *IS* 36 (1978): 3–4; in *Sidic* XI, 1 (1978): 21–22; also published as "Catechèse et Judaïsme" in *Documentation Catholique* 1731, Dec. 4, 1977: 1022–1023; as "Intervention . . ." in *Dokumente:* 170–173.

4. "One God, One Hope," homily in memory of Cornelis Adriaan Rijk, Rome, Oct. 15, 1979 (excerpts), published in *Sidic* XIII, 1 (1980): 35.

5. "Fifteenth Anniversary of Nostra aetate," address in Sidic Centre, Rome, Oct. 25, 1980 published in *Sidic* XIV, 1 (1981): 28–30.

6. "Champion of Christian Unity and of a New Relationship with the Jews," talk delivered at the Katholische Akademie, Freiburg i.Br., May 9, 1981, published in *Christian-Jewish Relations* 14, 4 (1981): 3–17.

7. "Il cardinale Agostino Bea: il suo contributo al movimento ecumenico, alla libertà religiosa e all'instaurazione di nuove relazioni con il popolo ebraico," contribution to *Atti del Simposio Card. Agostino Bea,* Rome, Dec. 16–19, 1981 at the Pontifical Lateran University, published in *Communio,* N.S. 14: 1–23.

8. "Cardinal Bea's Attitude to Relations with the Jews—Unpublished Details," in *Atti del Simposio Card. Agostino Bea:* 79–83.

9. "Vatican II and the Jews: Twenty Years Later," published in *Christian-Jewish Relations* 18, 1 (1985): 16–30; also published as "Nostra aetate: The Fundamental Starting Point for Jewish-Christian Relations" in *ILC:* 270–275.

10. "Is Christianity Antisemitic?" talk delivered to the Oxford Union Society, March 13, 1985, published in *Christian-Jewish Relations* 18, 2 (1985): 8–20.

11. "Nostra aetate: A Catholic Retrospective," address at the Anniversary Colloquium of *Nostra aetate,* Rome, April 17, 1985, published in *Face to Face* XII (1985): 10–12.

12. "Christians and Jews: A New Vision" in *Vatican II by Those Who Were There,* ed. by Alberic Stracpoole, London, Geoffrey Chapman, 1986: 220–236.

13. Closing remarks at the Second International Catholic-Jewish Theological Colloquium, Rome, Nov. 5, 1986, published in *IS* 63 (1987): 15–16.

14. "Je Nový Zákon antisemitský?," talk delivered at the Amicizia Ebraico-Christiana, Rome, Nov. 24, 1986 (Czech translation

from the original Italian), published in *Studie* II–III (1987): 85–100.

15. "Die Einheit zwischen Altem und Neuem Bund," talk delivered at Munich University, July 9, 1987, published in *Münchener Theologisch Zeitschrift* 38, 4 (1987): 295–310; also published as "L'unità fra Antica e Nuova Alleanza" in *Fist informazione* (Federazione Interreligiosa per gli Studi Teologici, Torino) 9, V, 1 (1989–90): 69–81.

16. The Preface for the volume: *ILC* [VII].

17. "Giovanni Paolo II e gli Ebrei: il cammino della riconciliazione" published in *OR,* Nov. 11, 1988: 4.

18. "Quindici anni di dialogo tra la Chiesa a l'Ebraismo," address at the occasion of the publication of *Fifteen Years of Dialogue,* Rome, March 22, 1988, published in *OR,* March 24, 1988: 6; also published as "Relations between the Church and Judaism: History, Themes, Perspectives" in *IS* 68 (1988): 165–168.

19. "The Church Facing Modern Antisemitism," talk delivered at Aberdeen University and at the Royal Aeronautical Society in London, Oct. 17–18, 1988, published in *Christian-Jewish Relations* 22 1 (1989): 5–17.

20. Address at the reception of the International Jewish Committee on Interreligious Consultations, New York, May 16, 1989, published in *IS* 70 (1989): 76–78.

21. Address at the occasion of the Patriarch Abraham Prize, São Paulo, June 11, 1989, published in *IS* 70 (1989) 75–76.

22. "Déclaration sur la controverse d'Auschwitz," Sept. 18, 1989, published in *OR,* Sept. 20, 1989: 1; also published as "Statement on Auschwitz Controversy" in *IS* 70 (1989): 78; published in Polish translation in *OR pol,* 10–11 (1989): 13.

23. "Ébrei e cristiani ad Auschwitz: l'umile cammino della riconciliazione" published in *OR,* Sept. 30, 1989: 6; also published as "Jews and Christians at Auschwitz, The Humble Path of Reconciliation" in *IS* 70 (1989) 78–79; as "Juifs et crétiens à Auschwitz: l'humble chemin de la réconciliation" in *OR fr* 42, Oct. 17, 1989: 3; as "Pokorna Droga do pojednania, Żydzi i chrzescijanie w Oswiecimiu" in *Tygodnik Poszechny* 46, Nov. 12, 1989; 1, and in *OR pol* 10–11 (1989): 13.

24. "Religious Pluralism within and beyond the Catholic Church," address at the 12th National Workshop on Christian-Jewish Relations, Chicago, Nov. 5, 1990 published in *Catholic International,* 1–14 February 1991: 140–145.

25. Foreword to *No Religion Is an Island: Abraham Joshua Heschel and Interreligious Dialogue,* edited by Harold Kasimow and Byron L. Sherwin, Maryknoll, N.Y., Orbis Books, 1991, pp. xi–xii.

Index of Names

Abraham, 8, 136–38, 139, 140
Acta Apostolicae Sedis, 17
Action Française, 128
Adversus Haereses (Irenaeus), 103
Akiba, Rabbi, 164
Aleppo Codex, 106
'Al Farabi, 107
'Al-Ghazzali, 107
Alliance Israelite Universelle, 126
Ambrose, St., 95, 104, 105, 113
American Jewish Committee, 22
"Amici Israel," 128, 129
Angelicum, 22
Angell, Charles, 154
Anti-Defamation League of B'nai B'rith, 22
Antiochene school, 97, 104
Augustine, St., 95, 103, 109, 142
Averroes, 98
Avicenna, 98, 107

Barth, Karl, 97, 111, 130
Bea, Augustin, Cardinal, 7, 15, 22–23, 39–41, 46, 57–61, 115–16, 123, 128, 139, 148, 162, 167, 181, 182, 184
Ben Asher, 106
Benedict XIV, Pope, 93
Bentzen, Aaage, 110
Bernard, St., 93, 195
Bible Societies, 146
Billerbeck, Paul, 100
Bodelschwingh, Friedrich, 130–31
Body of Faith, The (Wyschogrod), 97
Bonhoeffer, Dietrich, 98, 130
Bonomelli, Geremia, 127, 244
Bousset, Wilhelm, 100
Buber, Martin, 96
Bullinger, 112–13
Bultmann, Rudolf Karl, 95, 100, 111

Calvin, John, 109
Carmelites, 170–71, 174, 176, 192, 253
Cassidy, Edward Idris, Archbishop, 168, 250
Centers of Judeo-Christian Studies, 121
Central Committee of German Catholics, 113

Biblical Index